LEAVING THE 20TH CENTURY

THE INCOMPLETE WORK OF THE SITUATIONIST INTERNATIONAL

Translated and edited by
Christopher Gray

Rebel Press, 1998

While contemporary impotence rambles on about the belated project of 'getting into the 20th century', we think it is time to put an end to the dead time which has dominated this century, and to finish the Christian era with the same stroke. The road of excess leads to the palace of wisdom. Ours is the best effort so far towards leaving the 20th century.

'Now the SI', IS no. 9, 1964

First published by
Free Fall Publications, 1974

This edition published by
Rebel Press, 1998
84b Whitechapel High Street, London E1

Printed by
Aldgate Press in Great Britain

ALSO PUBLISHED BY REBEL PRESS

Enragés & Situationists in the Occupation Movement, France, May '68, René Viénet, Co-published with Autonomedia, £5.95.

The Revolution of Everyday Life, Raoul Vaneigem, Translated by Donald Nicholson-Smith, Co-published with Left Bank Books, £7.95

The Society of the Spectacle, Guy Debord, Translated by Fredy Perlman, Black & Red edition, £5

Society of the Spectacle & other Films, Guy Debord, £5.50

Cover photograph by Dave O'Neill

CONTENTS

PREFACE

Leaving the 20th Century has assumed almost mythical status since its disappearance from circulation some twenty years ago.

However, its position as one of the seminal texts of situationist ideas is peculiar to English readers, as only 4,000 copies were ever produced and its distribution was mainly limited to the *cognoscenti* of the urban centres of Britain. There is no doubt that its scarcity increased its value.

Chris Gray's compilation still resonates as a component of my youthful Arcadia. I recall my delight on capturing the book, my elation in soaking up texts that were a fusion of lyricism and dialectics.

I managed to obtain a last, dog-eared copy from a battered box found in a dusty corner of Compendium Bookshop, north London, in the winter of '79.

Devouring the book within twenty-four hours, the energy of the text almost physically warmed me – such was its transparent passion and searing critique. I was to experience the same feeling in more magnified form on reading Vaneigem's magnificent *Revolution of Everyday Life.* Two true love affairs.

Leaving the 20th Century contains most of the important texts from the SI's journal, *Internationale Situationniste*, and arguably the best chapters of Vaneigem's *Traité* and Debord's *Société du Spectacle*. Subtitled 'The Incomplete Work of the SI', it never pretended to be more than a basic but powerful and, above all, accessible, introduction to situationist ideas.

There is no doubt in my mind that the book's popularity lay in the way it so easily engaged the reader. Bound in a lurid green cover with an unusual format, printed on strange, satin-sheened paper and liberally illustrated with press cuttings, photos from May '68 in Paris, quotes and cartoon strips, it had a playful, poetic quality that translated the anarchic spirit of smashing the state, while keeping a smile on the lips and a song in the heart.

Gray was assisted in the layout and graphics by members of Suburban Press, a group based in Croydon, just south of London, who had links with a north-London-based group of situationist squatters. One of the first graphics in the book was supplied by Jamie Reid and later illustrated the picture sleeve of the Sex Pistols' fourth single, 'Holidays in the Sun', released in 1978.

Chris Gray's occasionally idiosyncratic, but undogmatic commentary exhibited an honesty that was endearing, although the source of much criticism – as were his translations. Certainly they were a little free, but the sense came through strongly enough, even where they may not have been sufficiently accurate for some. In some ways it is almost refreshing to reread the 'bad' old translations, given the current, almost scholastic, approach to situationist texts. They are now 'authorised', revised and soon, no doubt, to be the subject of textual analysis and deconstruction in learned academic theses.

Ken Knabb derisively dismisses *Leaving the 20th Century* as a "confusionist hodgepodge". His *Situationist International Anthology*, published in 1981, is exemplary, and his translations to be praised for their accuracy of style and lexicography. But his was clearly a very different project and he forgets that for several years *Leaving the 20th Century* was the only good source of situationist texts in the UK. Indeed, the *Anthology* reproduces all but four of the twenty SI texts compiled by Chris Gray, showing that the latter was not entirely injudicious in his selection. And Knabb makes no concessions to the uninitiated. He does not attempt to seduce the new reader, simply proclaiming, "Here are the texts. Now read!"

Furthermore, to understand the significance of *Leaving the 20th Century*, it has to be placed in its historical context.

The first situationist book published in England, it appeared at a time when the class struggle was still much more alive in England than it was perhaps in France or North America, where the heyday had been the Sixties. In 1974, the year of its publication, the second miners' strike effectively brought down the Tory government. The early Seventies were marked by mass and wildcat strikes, street fighting and terrorism in Ireland, and political protest in England from mass-demonstrations to attacks by the Angry Brigade.

While the movement in England was still dominated by the trade unions and the Labour Party, it showed increasing signs of getting out of control, as evidenced by the growth of direct action and the increasing numbers of wildcat strikes. This was a development also opposed by the various (mostly Leninist) leftist parties, who sought to bring the movement under party control and whose obsolescence had been clearly demonstrated, yet again, in France in 1968.

Situationist ideas and texts had only been poorly disseminated in England and North America before 1974, although not without consequence. In England the Angry Brigade began a series of attacks on various manifestations of the 'spectacle', from cabinet ministers to trendy boutiques, and their communiqués were littered with situationist references. But their methods were not emulated and clearly failed to ignite the proletariat.

It was into this melting pot that Chris Gray threw *Leaving the 20th Century*, an astringent to burn away the tired old dogmas of the left, as well as the pretensions of modernism.

In 1974, the SI had been defunct for two years, and had done little but wrangle internally since 1970. The last edition of *Internationale Situationniste*, no. 12, came off the press in a print run of 10,000 in September 1969. And from there it was all downhill. Future texts – *The Real Splits in the International*, *On Terrorism*, and Vaneigem's *Book of Pleasures* – did not carry the weight of the earlier classics. A spate of resignations decimated the French and Italian sections in 1970, and by the end of 1971 only Debord and Sanguinetti were left.

The two members of the US section were excluded in January 1970, and the other two split off in December. The English section had already been terminated by the exclusions of Chris Gray and two others as far back as December 1967. It's not surprising, therefore, that most of the translations from the original French were carried out by various American radicals from Detroit, Seattle, Berkeley and New York, before being imported into the UK.

At the time *Leaving the 20th Century* was published there was little in the way of situationist literature circulating in the UK. *Society of the Spectacle* was available as an import from Detroit, where it had been published by Black and Red in 1970 in a much-criticised translation by Fredy Perlman.

On the Poverty of Student Life was reprinted by the same group in 1973. Samizdat versions of Viénet's *Enragés and Situationists in May '68*, parts of Vaneigem's *Traité* and the whole of his *Banalités de Base* (translated by Chris Gray in 1966) were in limited circulation. Anything other than these had to be obtained from the USA.

All this further explains why, for those of us who were able to scrounge, thieve or even buy a copy before they all disappeared, this book was a revelation, a work of empowerment, a text that was sorely needed, and which required emulation and improvement.

Chris Gray took the title from one of the key early texts, 'Now, the SI!' which appeared in the 1964 edition of the IS magazine:

We think it is high time to put an end to the dead time that has dominated this century and to finish the Christian Era with the same stroke. Here as elsewhere the road of excess leads to the palace of wisdom. Ours is the best effort so far towards leaving the twentieth century.

This claim may have sounded precocious in 1964, two years before the Strasbourg scandal, three before the publication of *Society of the Spectacle* and *The Revolution of Everyday Life*, and almost four before the revolutionary upsurge of May '68. But it was prescient.

As a point of departure that year for their revolutionary critique of existing conditions, the SI redefined themselves in this article as having superseded their former 'artistic' incarnation and as being in opposition to all forms of modernist recuperation. It is therefore all the more surprising that Chris Gray failed to include this text, for it perfectly articulates the division between the two halves of his book.

The 1964 article perhaps assumes more relevance with hindsight, for in the last decade of the twentieth century there have been increasing attempts to portray and recuperate the SI as an essentially artistic movement located firmly within the cultural fold of modern art. The post-'64 theoretical development of the SI as a profoundly *political* movement aiming at the overthrow of capitalist social relations has been largely glossed over or treated as an aberration. This has been the theme and result of the exhibitions mounted at the Pompidou Centre in Paris and the Institute of Contemporary Art in London.

The response to those who would portray the SI in such a fashion is best contained in the opening statement from the original 1964 text. It deals neatly with any second-rate plagiarists who champion the primacy of the artistic faction (the 'Nashists', excluded in 1962) over the situationist project of the SI's 'heroic' years:

The SI's element of failure is what is commonly considered success – the artistic value that is beginning to be appreciated in us; the fact that certain of our theses have come to be sociologically or urbanistically fashionable; or simply the personal success that is virtually guaranteed any situationist as soon as he is excluded. Our element of success, which is more profound, is the fact that we have not clung to our original pilot program but have proved that its main avant-garde character, in spite of some more apparent ones, lay in the fact that it had to lead further, and the fact that we have thus far been refused any recognition within the established framework of the present order.

The original 1952 project to search for the supersession of art had moved too far ten years later for the SI to look back. Those who wished to remain artists *tout simple* were quite rightly abandoned.

Debord characterised the SI as an extremist group that did most to bring back revolutionary contestation to modern society, imposing its victory on the terrain of critical theory. The difficulty now is to uphold that victory. The texts gathered here are a testament to the first ideas in the period of reappearance of the modern revolutionary movement, the last of which has hopefully not yet been heard.

As we leave the twentieth century this book is presented to the reader both as historical tribute and as revolutionary inspiration for the present.

Richard Parry, May 1998

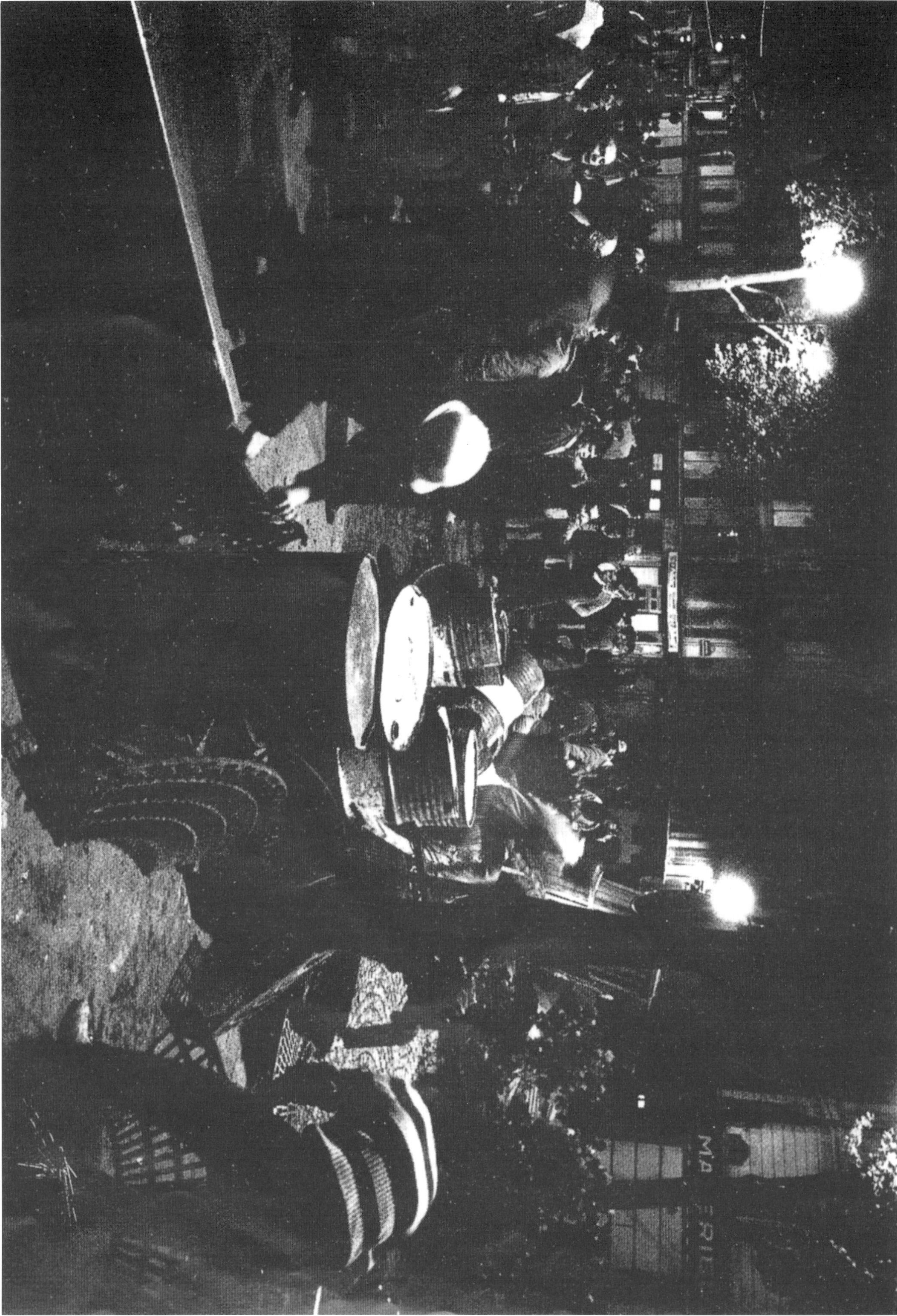

"EVERYONE WILL LIVE IN HIS OWN CATHEDRAL": THE SITUATIONISTS, 1958-1964

by Christopher Gray

YOUNG GUYS, YOUNG GIRLS
Talent wanted for getting out of this and playing
No special qualifications
Whether you're beautiful or you're bright
History could be on your side
WITH THE SITUATIONISTS
No telephone. Write or turn up:
32 rue de la Montagne-Geneviève, Paris 5e.

Internationale Situationniste no. 1, 1958

Summer of 1958: number one of a new, unusually glossy, avant-garde magazine, *Internationale Situationniste,* began to appear around the Latin Quarter of Paris. Its contents were quite as terrifying as its name. Surrealism, the cinema, automation, town planning, politics, games theory, the beat generation and the freedom of the press were all, in rapid succession, dismissed as being beneath contempt. Western culture and civilisation in their entirety were, so it seemed, totally bankrupt. Yet, there was something in which these 'situationists' believed – only its nature was from clear. What were the 'transcendence of art', 'the construction of situations', 'drifting', 'psychogeography', 'unitary urbanism' and 'revolutionary play'? Why choose pinups of girls in raincoats, on beaches, or supine on the backs of horses to illustrate these concepts? Why the maps of Utopian countryside, the photos and detailed diagrams of modern cities? Why the line drawings of an apparatus for generating Gaussian distribution? And how could you feel such disgust with everything?

Intellectual terrorism has never been anything particularly surprising on the Left Bank. What was unusual was that *Internationale Situationniste* seemed to have financial and organisational backing on a par with its megalomania. It wasn't just a 'magazine'. The articles presented a coherent and interwoven attack on the whole of the contemporary social life and culture. Half were written collectively and left unsigned. Editors and contributors were French, Dutch, Belgian, German, Scandinavian, Italian and Arab – all apparently belonging to the same international organisation. Physically the magazine was well co-ordinated. The layout was eminently sober, the paper the highest gloss and the covers glowing gold metal-board. These, which must have been ludicrously expensive, were apparently to stop the thing getting wet in the rain. And it was dead cheap. And there was no copyright.

Basically, the first number revolved around an attack on art. The situationists' central thesis was that art, in all its traditional forms, was completely played out. Dada had marked the end of western culture; no major self-regeneration was possible. At the same time, western civilisation had reached the point where mechanisation and automation had, potentially at least, eliminated the need for almost all traditional forms of labour, opening up perspectives of unprecedented leisure. The situationists suggested that this leisure could only be filled *by a new type of creativity* – a creativity that started where 'art' left off. Imagination should only be applied directly to the transformation of reality itself, not to its symbols in the form of philosophy, literature, painting and so on. Equally, this transformation should not be in the hands of a small body of specialists but should be made by everyone. It was normal, everyday life that should be made passionate and rational and dramatic, not its reflection in a separated 'world of art'. *The modern artist does not paint, but creates directly... Life and art make One* (Tristan Tzara).

The situationists however, were not just art theorists. The cultural crisis was a symptom of a far greater breakdown. *A new form of mental illness has swept the planet: banalisation. Everyone is hypnotised by work and by comfort: by the garbage disposal unit, by the lift, by the bathroom, by the washing machine. This state of affairs, born of a rebellion against the harshness of nature, has far overshot its goal – the liberation of man from material cares – and become a life-destroying obsession. Young people everywhere have been allowed to choose between love and a garbage disposal unit. Everywhere they have chosen the garbage disposal unit. A totally different spiritual attitude has become essential – and it can only be brought into being by making our unconscious desires conscious, and by creating entirely new ones. And by a massive propaganda campaign to publicise these desires* (Gilles Ivain, 'Formula for a new city', IS no. 1, 1958).

The situationists' programme was based on what they called 'the construction of situations'. In the first place this meant the bringing together and fusion of various separated art forms in the creation of a single, unified environment. Nor was this process restricted to a new focusing of contemporary artistic activity. All the great artistic visions and masterpieces of the past should be pillaged and their contents made *real*: 'subverted', as the situationists called it, as part of a real script. All scientific knowledge and technical skill could be brought into play in the same way. For the first time, art and technology could become one: put on the same practical footing with reality. Working out the widest possible unified field of such 'situations' would reveal the true dynamic and shape of the city. Most utopian visionaries since Fourier paled before the situationists: *Everyone will live in their own cathedral. There will be rooms awakening more vivid fantasies than any drug. There will be houses where it will be impossible not to fall in love. Other houses will prove irresistibly attractive to the benighted traveller...* ('Formula for a new city').

The point was not just the creation of an exterior environment, however vast or however lovely. *What we should be aiming at is a sort of situationist-oriented psychoanalysis. Those concerned having to discover within themselves desires for particular environments in order to make them real – the diametrically opposed attitude to that taken by the various neo-Freudian groups. Everyone must search for what they love, for what attracts them* ('The construction of situations: An introduction', IS no. 1, 1958). The point was the conjuring up and the mastery of immediate subjective experience. *Art need no longer be an account of past sensations. It can become the direct organisation of more highly-evolved sensations. It is a question of producing ourselves, not things that enslave us* (from an article by Guy Debord in the same issue). Thus, the situationist project, as originally outlined, was the liberation of desire in the building of a new world – a world with which we will be permanently in love.

This put them in much the same position as the *first* surrealists – and beyond Surrealism in the same position as a liberated psychoanalysis. Or, more simply, in exactly the same position as children. For their underlying philosophy was one of experiment and *play* – but play equipped with the whole of twentieth-century technology. Ultimately, all that was involved was the simplest thing in the world: wanting to make your dreams come true. And its enemies were equally simple: sterile, subjective fantasy on the one hand and, on the other, its objective counterpart: the world of art.

Rediscovery of the complete cultural turning point reached by a number of small, avant-garde groups during 1910 to 1925 – above all by the dadaists and the surrealists – was the main achievement of the Lettrist movement. The lettrists, another movement almost totally unknown in this country, evolved in Paris during the years immediately after the second world war. Starting from Dada, from the complete dissolution of the artistic form, they developed in a number of different directions. One group was concerned with Dada-type cultural sabotage, another with inventing a new activity to replace art; another, crystallising around Isadore Isou, concerned with aesthetics and art in itself.

Perhaps the most famous stunt pulled off by the first two groups was their sabotage of the Easter high mass at Notre-Dame in 1950. Just before the high mass, a small group of lettrists, including one who had previously intended to be ordained, slipped unobserved into the back of the cathedral. In a side-room they caught, gagged, stripped and bound one of the priests. The ex-Catholic lettrist put on the priest's vestments and, just before the service was about to begin, gravely ascended the steps to the main pulpit. A moment's respectful silence. "*Frères, Dieu est mort*", he said; and began benignly to discuss the implications of this conclusion. Several minutes passed before the congregation actually registered what was happening. He managed to escape out of the back of the cathedral, but the congregation caught up with him on the *quais*, where they proceeded to try and lynch him. The lettrist, alas, was forced to surrender to the police in order to save his neck.

Their taste for this kind of contribution to culture led to a complete break between the anti- and post-artistic factions and Isadore Isou and his followers. The left wing of the lettrists had, after a hectic summer in 1952, just wrecked Chaplin's press conference for 'Limelight' at the Ritz Hotel and left for Brussels, when they heard that Isou had denounced them to the newspapers. They promptly denounced him back, called themselves '*l'Internationale Lettriste*' and set up their own magazine, *Potlach*. If, until this time, Isou had been the dominant personality in the lettrist movement, *l'International Lettriste* saw the rising of the star of Guy Debord.

Debord, born in 1931, was at this time producing some brilliantly nihilistic anti-art. 'Mémoires', his first essay in 'subversion',

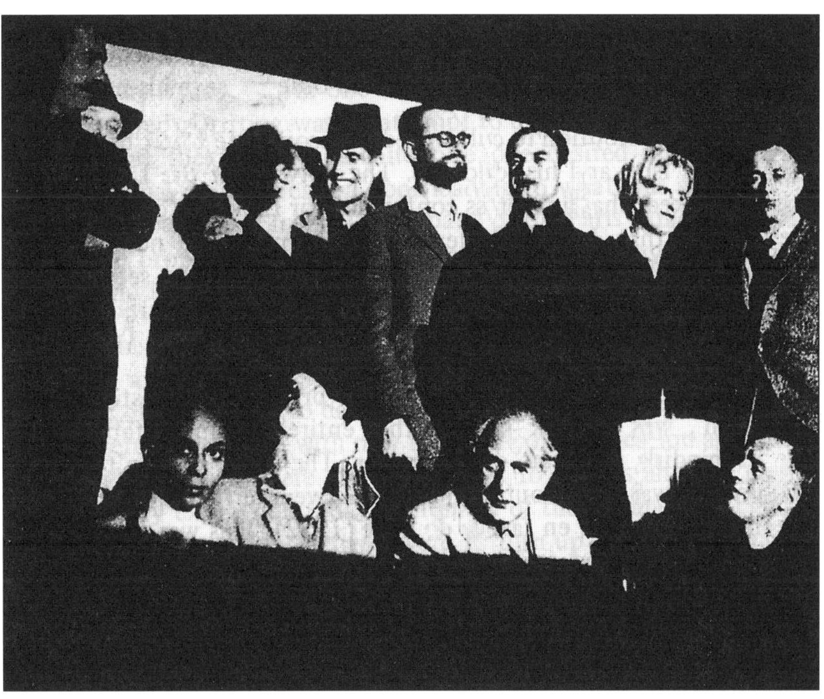

The situationists go to the cinema. London, September 1960.

was a book put together entirely from prefabricated elements, whose happiest touch was its binding in sheets of sandpaper. The book couldn't be put away in bookshelves because whenever it was taken out it ripped the covers of the books on either side. The same period saw his first film 'Hurlements en faveur de Sade' (1952). This was a feature-length film, which, far from being pornographic, lacked any images at all; the audience being plunged into complete darkness from beginning to end, apart from a few short bursts of random monologue, when the screen went white. The last twenty-four minutes were uninterrupted silence and obscurity. In France, there was considerable violence when the film was first 'shown'. In London, however, when the first house came out at the ICA, they didn't even tell the queue for the next performance that there wasn't anything to see. Intellectuals really are a hopeless lot.

Socially, *l'Internationale Lettriste* was defined both by its refusal to work, and thus its penury, and by its grandiose desire to regenerate the nature of immediate experience. The tensions implicit in this are obvious. Total despair was never far away. Debord related how one night they were all drunk and stoned in someone's apartment. It was way into the night and almost everyone had crashed. Debord was smoking kif by himself when suddenly he thought he could smell gas. He walked down a corridor to the kitchen at the far end of the apartment. Two friends were sitting drinking in silence at the kitchen table. All the windows were shut and the gas was turned on full. They had hoped that the whole sick crew would die painlessly in their sleep. This was just symptomatic. They were drinking and doping a lot of the time. There was more than one attempted murder, and several suicides. Someone jumped out of several hotel room windows before finally making it.

Not that their way of life was one of unbroken hippy gloom. Over the whole mid-fifties, there was sustained work on their 'activity to replace art'. In 1953, Ivan Chtcheglov, then aged nineteen and using the pseudonym Gilles Ivain, wrote a short manifesto called *Formula for a New City*. The text was a badly-needed shot in the arm for French Surrealism – increasingly bogged down in virtually conventional art and cultural rehabilitation since the end of the twenties. Chtcheglov's central theme was that the city was itself the total work of art, the total work of real life so long sought for. *Need for total creation has always been inseparable from the need to play with architecture: to play with time and space.* Only in the possibilities offered by the real distribution of time and space can all dreams become true and become one. This manifesto seems one of the most brilliant single pieces of writing produced since the heyday of modern art just after the first world war. Unfortunately, his own visions were to prove too much for Chtcheglov: he ended up in a lunatic asylum a few years later.

Before this, however, he was to play a leading role in developing the two main practical techniques used by the lettrists at this time: *drifting* and *psychogeography*. The first could be described as a sort of free association in terms of city space. The idea was simply to follow the streets, go down the alleys, through the doors, over the walls, up the trees and into the sunlight, etc, that one found most *attractive*; to wander, alone or with one's friends, following no plan but the solicitation of the architecture one encountered. Drifting was an attempt to orient oneself in the absence of any practical considerations: to find the types of architecture one desired unconsciously. Amongst other adventures, they found down by the Seine a door leading to what was supposed to be a small tool store, but was in fact a concealed entrance to those parts of the Paris catacombs that are closed to the public; apparently a large proportion of the total area. Hopefully, many happy hours were spent with the matches, the skulls and the rats.

'Psychogeography' was the study and correlation of the material obtained from drifting. It was used on the one hand to try and work out *new emotional maps* of existing areas and, on the other, to draw up plans for bodies of 'situations' to be interlocked in the new utopian cities themselves. During the same period they were also toying with new forms of communication and deconditioning within the city. *L'Internationale Lettriste* were the first artists to understand the enormous potential of graffiti as a means of literary expression today. A number of the slogans they chalked or painted up – 'Never work', 'Free the passions', 'Let us live' – were to turn up again, more than twenty years later, on the walls of the Latin Quarter in May 1968. They also painted slogans down their trouser-legs and across their ties and shoes. The two latter items they tried to sell.

The actual transition from *l'Internationale Lettriste* to *l'Internationale Situationniste* doesn't seem to have marked any major change in the nature of their activities. 1957 saw Debord's *Rapport sur la construction des situations*, the first theorisation of their new concepts of *situation* and *spectacle*, and they wanted to be dissociated once and for all with Isou and the other art-ridden lettrists. On 28 July 1957, delegates from *l'Internationale Lettriste*, from the largely Scandinavian and German Mouvement pour un Bauhaus Imaginiste and from a dubious London Psychogeographical Committee, met at a formal congress at Coscio d'Arroscia in Italy and decided to amalgamate. *L'Internationale Situationniste* was born.

The first few years of the SI were devoted to a systematic exposition of lettrist philosophy and lifestyle; to getting a magazine out regularly, and distributing it internationally. The number of card-carrying members of the SI at this time seems to have been around thirty or forty, but presumably many more were involved on a less formal basis, or were just very considerably influenced. Most were in their late twenties and were living off the usual expedients of what was still 'bohemian' life: grants, small pockets of bourgeois money, petty crime, hustling and occasional labour in culture or elsewhere.

At this point, the SI was really an international movement. Autonomous groups were functioning over most of Europe. The Scandinavian, Dutch, German and Italian sections organised their own demonstrations and produced their own publications – the German *Spur* ran into trouble with the police, while issues of the Paris magazine appeared steadily, all equally sober, produced equally luxuriously, each with its glowing metal covers of a different colour. The terrorism, wit and general megalomania held good. So did the flow of photographs of girls, soldiers, bombings, comic-strip frames, maps of cities and diagrams of labyrinths, cathedrals and gardens.

In Italy, Pinot-Gallizio invented 'industrial painting' – painting produced mechanically, by the roll. A leaflet by Michèle Bernstein read: *Among the advantages... no more problems with the format, the canvas being cut under the eyes of the satisfied customer; no more uncreative periods, the inspiration behind industrial painting, thanks to a well-contrived balance of chance and machinery, never drying up; no more metaphysical themes, machines aren't up to them; no more dubious reproductions of the Masters; no more vernissages. And naturally, very soon, no more painters, not even in Italy...* (IS no. 2, 1958). Industrial painting was exhibited and sold, pokerfaced, in Turin, Milan and Venice that year.

Their dominant intellectual concern was still with the fusion of all art forms in a new utopian town planning, while their experiments with architecture and the use of cities continued to provide a practical means of self-expression, a real group cohesion on the level of everyday life. Large-scale drifts, sometimes using several teams linked by walkie-talkies, were undertaken; psychogeographic studies and architectural plans were worked out in detail. *We are only at the beginning of urban civilisation... Twentieth century architects should be building adventures...* (IS no. 3, 1959).

Debord made two more films – shorts this time – '*Sur le passage de quelques personnes à travers une assez courte unité de temps*' (1959) and '*Critique de la Separation*' (1960-61). Neither got beyond elitist avant-garde screenings and for good reasons. Close examination of both would show that Resnais knew Debord's films very well and had quite cynically ripped them off.

During this initial period, the SI rose to some sort of underground fame, particularly within northern Europe – though almost exclusively as a group of anti-art theoreticians and revolutionary architects. They were invited to participate in a number of exhibitions and events; generally they refused or just went along to cause trouble. The few attempts they made to work under official patronage invariably ended in disaster. Plans for the conversion of Claude-Nicholas Ledoux's complex of buildings at la Saline-de-Chaux, for the detailed study of Les Halles and for a labyrinth to be built in the Stedelijk Museum in Amsterdam all proved too crazy for the various authorities concerned and had to be scrapped.

What the SI in Paris was trying to work out was a new *revolutionary* critique of society: to discover forms of organisation and activity more effective than the slapstick anarchy of the lettrists. Henri Lefebvre had been their first mentor in social revolution. Once a leading French Communist Party theoretician, Lefebvre had resigned from the Party and become increasingly anarchistic. His basic contention was that contemporary society wasn't suffering from any shortage of consumer goods, but from a new poverty, *a poverty of everyday life*, and that revolution today must be focused on the regeneration of this area. The SI, though they relied increasingly on this concept of *everyday life*, tended to reject Lefebvre's philosophy as being basically academic and personal relations between them deteriorated and finally petered out. In 1960 they passed under the influence of Paul Cardan and *Socialisme ou Barbarie* ('Solidarity', in England). This was a neo-Marxist group devoted largely to redefining the nature of capitalist exploitation during its present bureaucratic and consumer-oriented phase, though also far more involved in the realities of shopfloor agitation and struggle against the unions than either Lefebvre or the SI.

Sex. It's OK, says Mao, but not too much of it.

Graffiti, Censier, 1968.

The working class gradually became something less of an abstraction. The SI began a systematic re-interpretation of European revolutionary history: of Fourier and the utopians, of the young Marx, of the anarchists, of the Commune, of the terrorists, of all the massacred ultra-left social experiments that broke out amidst the proletarian and peasant uprisings of the first third of the twentieth century. Their attack on leaders and all hierarchical political organisations became increasingly savage, as did their insistence on popular spontaneity, violence and the ability of a revolutionary proletariat to evolve adequate political forms on the spot. *Socialisme ou Barbarie* left them with their central, if somewhat summary, political concept: that of the various attempts at workers' total self-management. Workers' councils have emerged from the revolutionary wars of the twentieth century as the most consistent experiments yet made in integrally democratic organisation: St Petersburg 1905, Turin 1920, Catalonia 1936, Budapest 1956.

Socialisme ou Barbarie also left them with the need for developing a new revolutionary critique of political economy: of the commodity form denounced by Marx as the basis of all our social and individual alienation. They developed what was to become their most famous single concept – that of the *spectacle*. Used from the very first as a term to designate contemporary (French) culture, *spectacle* was a spectacle, a circus, a show, an exhibition, a one-way transmission of experience. It was a form of 'communication' to which one side, the audience, can never reply; a culture based on the reduction of almost everyone to a state of abject non-creativity, of receptivity, passivity and isolation. Now they saw that the same structure applied not only to cultural and leisure 'activity', not only to political organisation (whether that of the ruling classes or that of the so-called 'left'). This experience of passivity, isolation and abstraction was the universal experience imposed by contemporary capitalism: an experience radiating from its basic alienation, the commodity. Henceforward, consumer capitalism was to be simply the *society of the spectacle*.

The first thing this meant was that the situationists could no longer see themselves as an art movement of any sort at all. Art was no more than *the* consumer good *par excellence*. Any work of art, however radical, could be digested by modern capitalism and turned into the opposite of all it had meant to those who originally created it. From the point of view of Paris – increasingly that of Debord, whose intransigence was reinforced by the appearance of Raoul Vaneigem (born 1934) – all the other sections were dabbling far too much in 'experimental art' and courting the danger of being separated from what was *essentially* a *total* programme. Modern society wouldn't find any difficulty in reabsorbing individual works of art as the latest, *chic* revolutionary consumer item; and thus the rejection of consumer society made by the whole group would be compromised.

The situation exploded in the first series of the 'exclusions' for which the SI was to become notorious. *The architects Alberts and Oudejans, by accepting a commission to build a church at Volendam, have automatically excluded themselves from the SI.* Exclusion followed exclusion during 1961 and '62 – in the best surrealist manner. The chaos only ended with the virtual disintegration of the Scandinavian, Dutch, Italian and German sections. At the same time a number of situationists who were becoming personally famous as artists – Constant in Amsterdam, Asger Jorn in Scandinavia, Alex Trocchi in London – either dropped out or drifted away to follow individual careers. All these exclusions and break-ups – which set off a whole myth as to the situationists' fanaticism and glacial arrogance – really revolved around whether it was possible to create anything in contemporary society strong enough to withstand the massive pressures brought to bear upon it; or whether the only thing was denunciation, exposé.

The following texts came from this initial, predominantly 'artistic' period of situationist activity.

THE SOUND AND THE FURY

There's been a lot of talk about the 'revolt of contemporary youth' of late. There's been a lot of talk about it because – from the apparently motiveless riots of Swedish teenagers to the would-be literary proclamations of England's 'angry young men' – it is fundamentally such a half-assed and inoffensive sort of revolt. In many ways contemporary youth finds itself in much the same position as the first surrealists. Both are products of the same world of social and intellectual disintegration, of major breakthroughs in the conquest of nature that have failed to make the slightest difference to the same, sometimes brutal, reaction against the whole way of life imposed upon them. But contemporary youth lacks all the surrealists' ability to express themselves in and against culture; and they also lack all the hopes the surrealists pinned on revolution. The tone underlying the spontaneous negativity of American, Scandinavian or Japanese youth is one of resignation. Saint-Germain-des-Prés, immediately after the second world war, had already served as a laboratory for much the same sort of behaviour (abusively labelled 'existentialist' by the press at the time), which is why the intellectual figureheads of this generation in France – Françoise Sagan-Drouet, Robbe-Grillet, Vadim, the awful Buffet – are all such textbook cases, such caricatures of resignation.

If people the same age, outside France, are slightly more aggressive, they certainly aren't any more intelligent. Sometimes it's pure idiocy. Sometimes premature self-congratulation over a singularly spastic rebellion. The smell of rotten eggs broadcast by the idea of God, envelops the mystical cretins of the American 'beat generation', nor is it entirely absent from the statement of the 'angry young men' (cf. Colin Wilson). The latter have discovered, thirty years after the event, a certain moral subversiveness that *England* had managed to hide from them all this time: they really think they are being scandalous if they say they're against the Queen. "People continue to produce plays", writes Kenneth Tynan, "which are based on the absurd idea that people fear and respect the Crown, the Empire, the Church, University and Good Society". The phrase 'continue to produce plays' is indicative of just how tepidly *literary* is the angry young men's point of view. They have simply changed their opinion about a few social conventions without understanding the *change of terrain* of the whole of cultural activity, so obvious in every truly avant-garde movement this century. The angry young men are even more reactionary in the particularly privileged value, almost the sense of redemption, they confer on the act of writing. That is to say, they are defending a mystification which was denounced in Europe before 1920, and whose survival today is of greater counter-revolutionary implications than that of the British Crown.

The whole song and dance reveals one

The greatest spectacle the world has ever seen. An investment of one thousand million dollars (90% of which will have disappeared without leaving the slightest trace in two years' time). A fantastic collection of things and living beings: from the Watusi dancers of His Majesty the King of Burundi, whose sacred drum has never before left its native shore, to the lunar capsule in which man is going to land on the moon. 'Peace through understanding' is the motto of the New York World Fair, due to open on Wednesday...

Visitors can travel into the future in miniature cars. They will drive through future towns where there won't be any parking problems, where motorways will be tunnelled underground, where cars can be parked on the ground floor of massive buildings, shops found on the first floor, residential areas on the second, and parks, open areas of trees and flowers, on the third. Fantasy? The PR men say that at the 1939 New York Exhibition, General Motors had already worked out a system of motorways, flyovers and tunnels which seemed completely fantastic at the time and which has since become part and parcel of American life...

Coca-Cola offers the curious a somewhat unusual 'tour round the world'. They can "feel, touch and taste the most distant spots of the earth", listen to the most exquisite songs and music and undergo a host of other emotions. All these perfumes and tastes will be 'produced' and controlled automatically by computers...

The RAU is trying to attract American sympathy by exhibiting the gold of the Pharaohs; General Franco by the canvases of old and new masters, from Velasquez to Goya, from Picasso to Miro...

For art lovers there is an immense exhibition of modern art. For the more scientific there is a pavilion devoted to recent scientific discoveries. Nor have women been forgotten. In the Clairol pavilion each woman can decide what she wants to be next season: blonde, redhead, brunette, etc. The 'practical beauty' salon allows one to experiment with different things. The pavilion is also equipped with a computer into which all relevant physical data can be fed and which will then give individual advice: what colour you should choose for your powder, your lipstick, your eyeshadow, your eyelashes, your nailpolish, etc.

Le Monde, 22 April 1964

thing very clearly: nobody has any idea what the first surrealists were trying to do (which is hardly surprising in view of the extent to which they have been misrepresented and turned into yet another 'art' movement). Yet, at the same time, it is impossible to try and continue to be a surrealist today: everyone who has tried has found Surrealism's massive pseudo-success an insurmountable obstacle. As a result, many of them have been drawn towards the various reactionary elements that characterised Surrealism from the very first (magic, belief in an age of gold to be found anywhere but in future history, etc). There are even those who congratulate themselves on still being there, so long after the battle, under Surrealism's *arc de triomphe*. There, Gerard Legrand (*Surréalisme même* no. 2) says proudly, they will remain: "a small band of youthful beings resolved to keep alive the true flame of Surrealism".

A movement more liberating than the Surrealism of 1924 – a movement which Breton promised to join as soon as it appeared – is a tricky proposition. Its liberating quality today depends upon its seizure of the more highly-evolved technology of the modern world. And the surrealists of 1958 are not only incapable of joining any such movement – they are actively hostile even to its possibility. On the other hand, it is absolutely necessary that any revolutionary cultural movement today claims as its own, and uses to greater effect, Surrealism's demand for total moral and spiritual freedom.

So far as we are concerned, Surrealism was no more than an initial revolutionary experiment with culture. An experiment that backfired almost immediately – both theoretically and practically. We must go further than the surrealists. Why? *Because we don't want to be bored.*

Degenerate Surrealism, angry and ill-informed young men, well-heeled teenage rebels, may be lacking an overall grasp of things, but far from lacking a cause... boredom is what they all have in common. Contemporary leisure has already judged itself. The situationists have merely to execute this judgement.

IS no. 1, 1958

THE STRUGGLE FOR CONTROL OF THE NEW TECHNIQUES OF CONDITIONING

"Henceforward people can be forced to act in ways pre-determined without their knowledge..." writes Serge Tchakhotine on the means of mass coercion employed by revolutionaries and fascists between the two world wars (*The Rape of Crowds by Political Propaganda*, Gallimard). Technical progress since has been uninterrupted. Experimental study of the mechanisms of behaviour has gone forward; new applications of existing techniques have been discovered, and entirely new techniques have been evolved. For some time now there has been an experiment with subliminal advertising (autonomous images are cut into a film; appearing on the screen for no more than one twenty-fourth of a second, they are seen by the eye but not registered consciously). Also, with the use of infra-sound. In 1957, the Research Service of the Canadian National Defence undertook an experimental study of boredom. A number of individuals were isolated in an environment designed so that nothing could happen (cells with bare walls, neon lights, the only furniture a comfortable couch and without any sounds, smells or variations in temperature). Extensive disturbances in behaviour resulted. The brain, in the complete absence of all sensory stimulation, falls below the pitch of excitation necessary if it is to function normally. The Research Service concluded that a boring environment has destructive effects on human behaviour. Furthermore, that boredom was probably the cause of the unforeseeable accidents that occur in monotonous labour, destined to grow in number with the extension of automation.

The account of a certain Lajos Ruff, published first in the French press, then as a book, in the spring of 1958, goes a good deal further. His story – which, if questionable in some respects, contains no inherent impossibility – describes the 'brainwashing' he underwent at the hands of the Hungarian political police in 1956. For six weeks he was confined to a single cell. While there, he was subjected to a number of tricks and techniques which, while individually quite commonplace, were brought together with sufficient skill as to make him lose all belief in his own personality and the accuracy of his perception of the world. The cell itself was strange enough. The furniture was all transparent. The bed sagged and was difficult to sleep in. Each night, a ray of light moved about the room. He was warned repeatedly about the adverse psychic effects of this ray of light, but there was no way he could avoid seeing it as each night it travelled restlessly about his room. During the day he was interviewed and analysed in interminable detail by a doctor who claimed to be a psychiatrist. A variety of drugs were slipped into his food and drink. As he never even knew whether he was drugged or not, he became increasingly easy to manipulate. Sometimes, though he was quite convinced

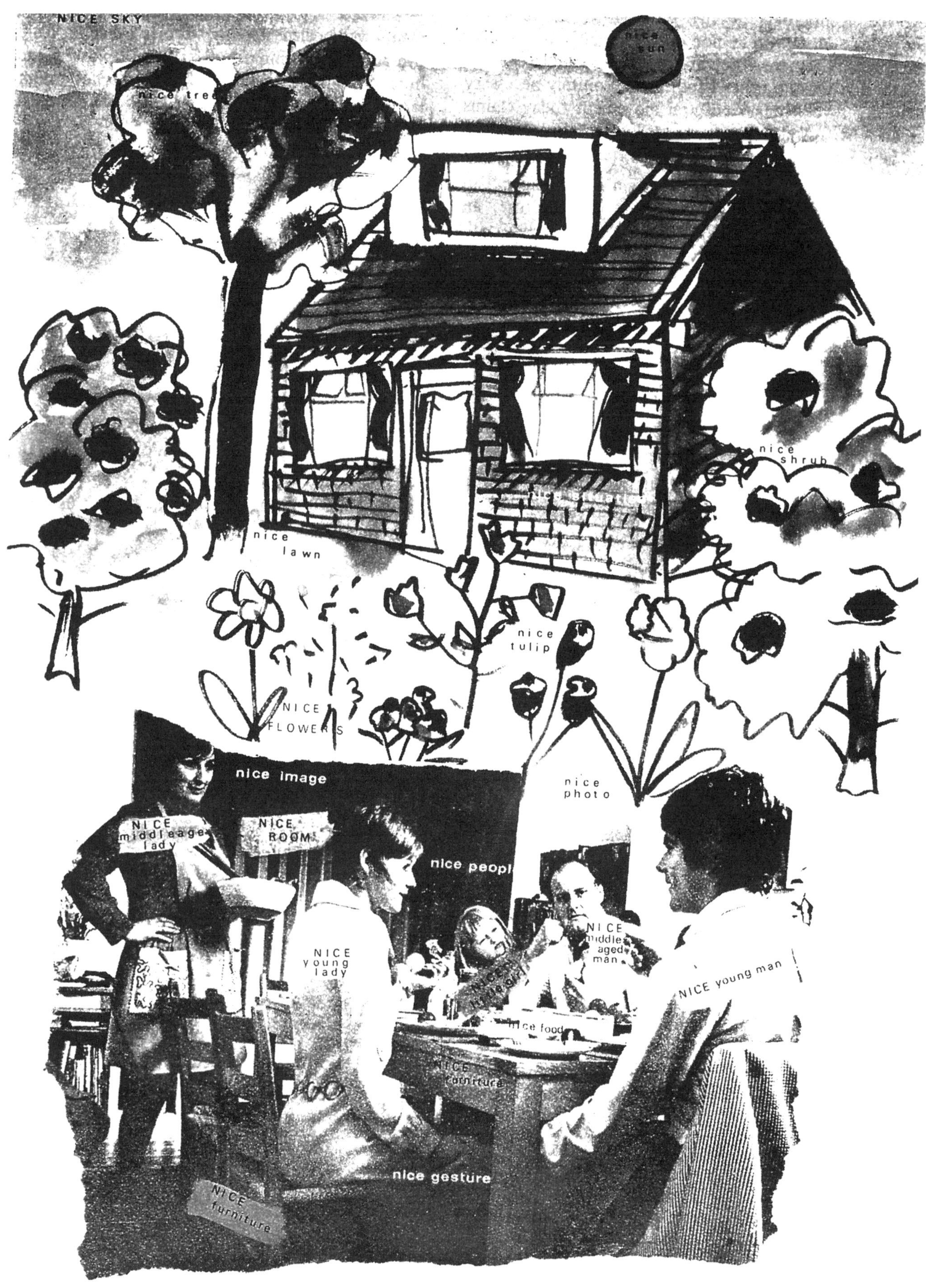
NICE SKY
nice sun
nice tre
nice shrub
nice lawn
nice tulip
NICE FLOWERS
nice image
nice photo
NICE middleage lady
NICE ROOM
nice peopl
NICE young lady
NICE middle aged man
NICE young man
nice food
NICE furniture
nice gesture
NICE furniture

he had never left the cell, he would wake up in the morning with his clothes damp and with traces of mud on his shoes. Meaningless or highly erotic films were back-projected on to the walls of the cell. Visitors came to see him, all of whom acted as though he was the hero of a series of films on the Hungarian resistance he had been shown. The interplay of the details of what he had seen in the films and what had actually taken place in his cell became increasingly complex. He began to feel proud of the role he had played...

This is an example of the *repressive* use of a constructed environment having reached a considerable degree of sophistication. To date, every discovery of disinterested scientific research has been neglected by free artists and promptly seized by the police and the army. When subliminal advertising began to give rise to some misgivings in the States, the whole matter was smoothed over by the statement that the first two slogans broadcast were quite harmless. They were: 'Drive more carefully', and 'GO TO CHURCH'.

It is the whole, humanistic, artistic and juridical conception of the inviolable and unalterable personality that is condemned. Ourselves, we are only too happy to see it go. However, there should be no mistake about the fact that we are all going to be caught up in *a race between free artists and the police in experiment with and developing the use of these new techniques of conditioning*. And the police force already has a considerable lead. On the outcome of this race depends whether we see the appearance of passionate, liberating events or the reinforcement of the old world of repression and horror; and this time reinforced scientifically, without a single slip-up. We talk of free artists, but there isn't any possible artistic freedom before we have seized the body of technology accumulated by the twentieth century – this is for us the true means of artistic production and exclusion from its use prevents one from ever being a truly contemporary artist. If this technology does not fall into the hands of revolutionaries then it is the police-state anthill for all of us. The domination of nature can either be a revolutionary force or it can mean the absolute power of the forces of the past. The situationists want to *forget about the past*. The only force from which they can expect any assistance is the proletariat – theoretically, without a past, permanently forced to reinvent everything, "either revolutionary or it is nothing" (Marx). And will it be revolutionary in our time? The question is of some importance to us: the proletariat must realise art.

IS no. 1, 1958

Where a breath of fresh air costs 12p

Two children homeward bound from school pause at a slot machine for one of the most sought-after commodities in their home city of Tokyo. They are buying oxygen and clean air. The machines dispense three litres of oxygen and two litres of clean air in a minute for around 12p. Which in a city notorious for air pollution could well be considered a bargain.

Evening Standard, 27 November 1973

THE CONSTRUCTION OF SITUATIONS: AN INTRODUCTION

The construction of situations can only begin to be effective as the concept of the spectacle begins to disintegrate. Clearly, the basic principle of the spectacle – non-intervention – is at the heart of all our alienated social life. And, equally clearly, all the most vital features of revolutionary experiment with culture have stemmed from an attempt to break the psychological identification of the spectator with the hero: to sting the spectator into action... Thus the situation is made to be lived by those who made it. The role played by a passive or merely bit-part playing 'public' must steadily diminish while that played by people who cannot be called actors, but rather, to coin a new word, 'livers', must equally steadily augment.

Rapport sur la construction des situations

'Constructing a situation' means more than just bringing together and unifying a number of different artistic techniques in the creation of a single environment – however great the power or the extension in space and time of this environment may be. The situation is also a unified pattern of behaviour in time. It is formed of gestures contained in a transitory décor. These gestures are the product of the décor and of themselves; and in their turn they produce a different décor and different gestures. How can these forces be oriented? Clearly we are not concerned with environments revolving around any kind of mechanically stage-managed 'surprise'. What we consider to be a truly meaningful experiment lies in setting up, on the basis of desires which are already more or less clearly conscious, a temporary field of activity which is favourable to the further development of these desires. This alone can lead to the further clarification of those desires which are already conscious and to the first chaotic appearance of new ones – desires whose material roots lie in the new reality engendered by situationist constructions.

What we should be aiming at is a sort of situationist-oriented psychoanalysis. Those concerned having to discover within themselves desires for particular environments in order to make them real – the diametrically opposed attitude to that taken by the various neo-Freudian groups. Everyone must search for what they love, for what attracts them. (And here again, as against certain recent literary experiments – Leiris, for example – what is important to us is neither the individual structure of our mind, nor the explanation of its genesis, but its possible application to the construction of situations.) In this way the elements out of which situations are to be built can be examined; as can projects to dynamise these elements.

Research of this type can only be meaningful for individuals who have been feeling their way practically towards the construction of situations. All, either spontaneously or in a conscious and organised way, are pre-situationists – that is to say, individuals who have all passed through the same dissatisfaction with culture as it is, through the same acceptance of an experimental sensibility, to find themselves confronted with the objective need for this type of action. All have passed through a specialised training and all, as specialists, have belonged to the same historical avant-garde. Thus it is highly likely that many will share the same desires and variations upon them; which 'themes' will tend to multiply as soon as they come to grips with a period of real action.

The constructed situation is bound to be collective both in its inception and in its development. However, it seems that, at least during an initial experimental period, responsibility for one particular situation must fall on one particular individual. This individual must, so to speak, be the 'director' of the situation. For example, in terms of one particular situationist project – one, say, revolving around an emotionally highly-charged meeting of several old friends one evening. One would expect: a) an initial period of research by a team; b) the election of a director responsible for co-ordinating the basic elements necessary for the construction of the décor, etc, and for working out a number of interventions during the course of the evening (alternatively several individuals can work out differing series of interventions, all of them unaware of all the details planned upon by the others); c) the actual people living the situation who have taken part in the whole project both theoretically and practically, and; d) a few passive spectators not knowing what the hell is going on who should be reduced to action.

Obviously, this specialised relationship between the 'director' and the 'livers' of the situation must never, at any cost, become permanent. It is a purely temporary subordination of a whole team of situationists to one particular individual who has assumed responsibility for the success of one particular project. Furthermore, we'd like to make it very clear that we're not talking about developing the theatre in any sort of way. Both Pirandello and Brecht have analysed the destruction of the theatrical spectacle and pointed out the direction in which 'post-theatrical' demands must lie. You could say the construction of situations will replace the theatre in the same way that the construction of real life tends more and more to replace religion. Really, the main area we want to replace and fulfil is poetry – poetry which destroyed itself utterly at the beginning of the twentieth century.

Both the real fulfilment of the individual, and the fulfilment of what we believe to be a major breakthough in the concept of culture, are impossible without a collective takeover of the world. Until this happens there won't be any real people at all, only shadows haunting things anarchically given by others. From time to time we bump into others as lost as ourselves, travelling intensely in random directions. Our contradictory feelings cancel one another out and reinforce the solid wall of boredom between us. We will wreck this world. We will light the first beacons to herald the coming of a greater game.

Functionalism, the quasi-automatic expression of technical advance, is trying to wipe out the last traces of play among us. The partisans of industrial design complain of the ill effects people's desire to play has upon their work, while modern industry crudely exploits this desire and turns it into a frantic taste for novelty. Art becomes uninterrupted transformation of the design of fridges, etc. The only radical thing to do is to try and free people's desire to play, in other contexts and on a larger scale. The indignation of all the theorists of industrial design in the world won't do anything to change the fact that the private car is in the first place an idiotic game, and only secondarily a means of transport. As against all regressive forms of play – which are always regressions to its infantile stages, and which are also always bound to reactionary politics – we stand for experiment with the great game of social revolution.

IS no. 1, 1958

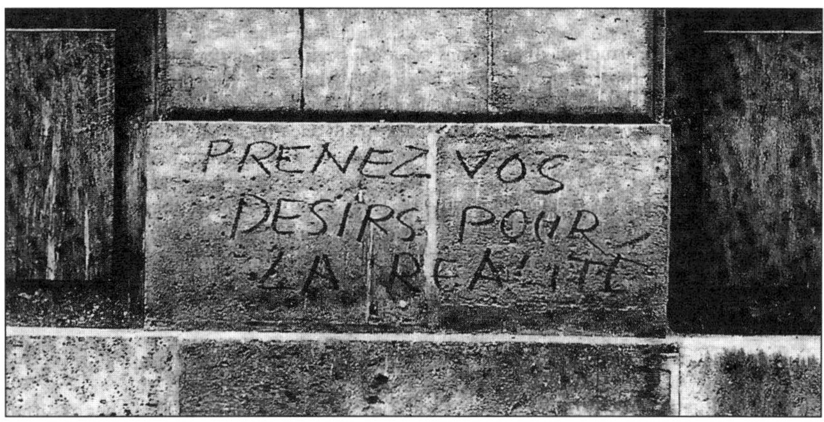

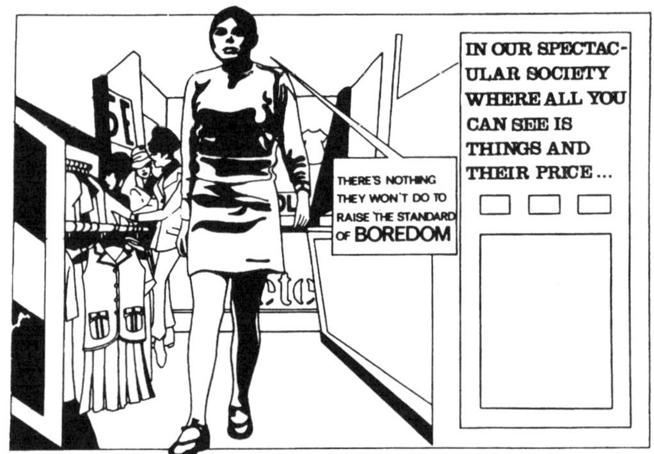
IN OUR SPECTACULAR SOCIETY WHERE ALL YOU CAN SEE IS THINGS AND THEIR PRICE...
THERE'S NOTHING THEY WON'T DO TO RAISE THE STANDARD OF BOREDOM

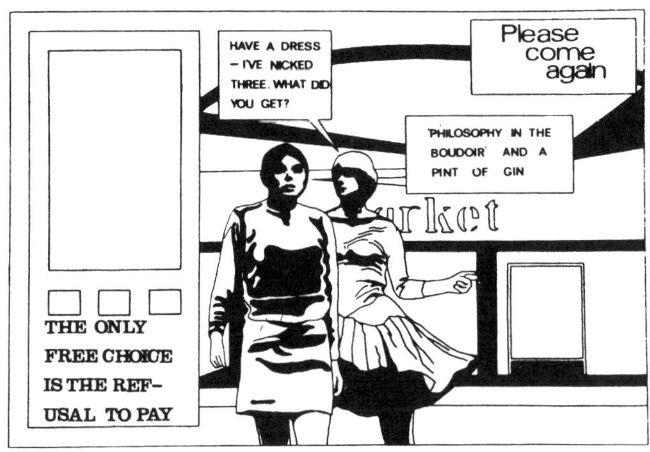
THE ONLY FREE CHOICE IS THE REFUSAL TO PAY
HAVE A DRESS – I'VE NICKED THREE. WHAT DID YOU GET?
'PHILOSOPHY IN THE BOUDOIR' AND A PINT OF GIN
Please come again

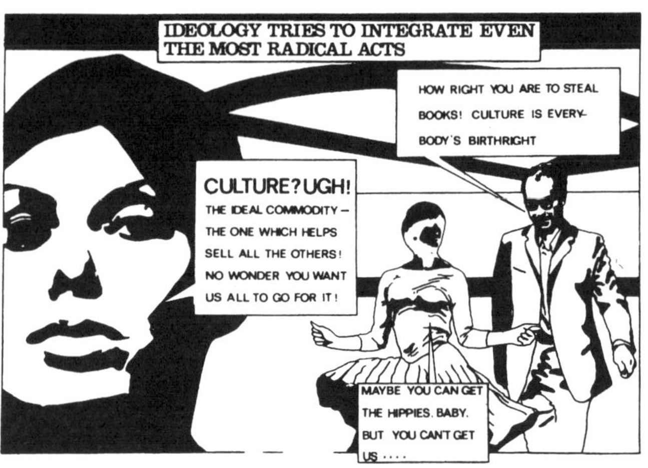
IDEOLOGY TRIES TO INTEGRATE EVEN THE MOST RADICAL ACTS
HOW RIGHT YOU ARE TO STEAL BOOKS! CULTURE IS EVERYBODY'S BIRTHRIGHT
CULTURE? UGH! THE IDEAL COMMODITY – THE ONE WHICH HELPS SELL ALL THE OTHERS! NO WONDER YOU WANT US ALL TO GO FOR IT!
MAYBE YOU CAN GET THE HIPPIES, BABY. BUT YOU CAN'T GET US ....

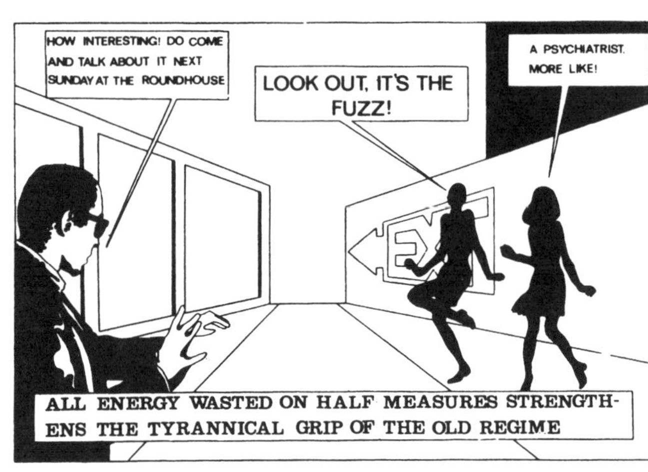
HOW INTERESTING! DO COME AND TALK ABOUT IT NEXT SUNDAY AT THE ROUNDHOUSE
LOOK OUT, IT'S THE FUZZ!
A PSYCHIATRIST, MORE LIKE!
ALL ENERGY WASTED ON HALF MEASURES STRENGTHENS THE TYRANNICAL GRIP OF THE OLD REGIME

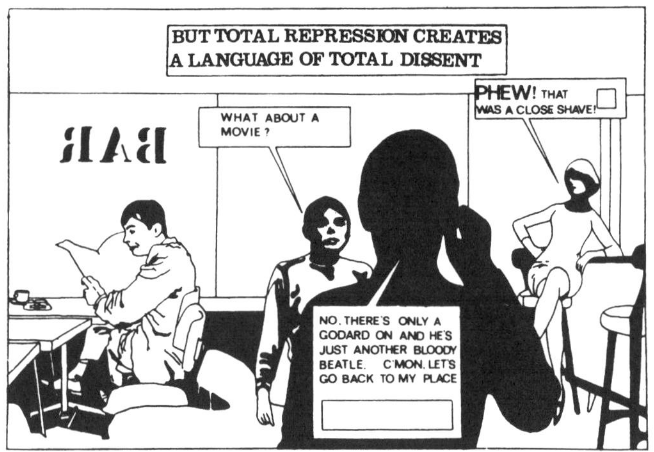
BUT TOTAL REPRESSION CREATES A LANGUAGE OF TOTAL DISSENT
BAR
WHAT ABOUT A MOVIE?
NO, THERE'S ONLY A GODARD ON AND HE'S JUST ANOTHER BLOODY BEATLE. C'MON, LET'S GO BACK TO MY PLACE
PHEW! THAT WAS A CLOSE SHAVE!

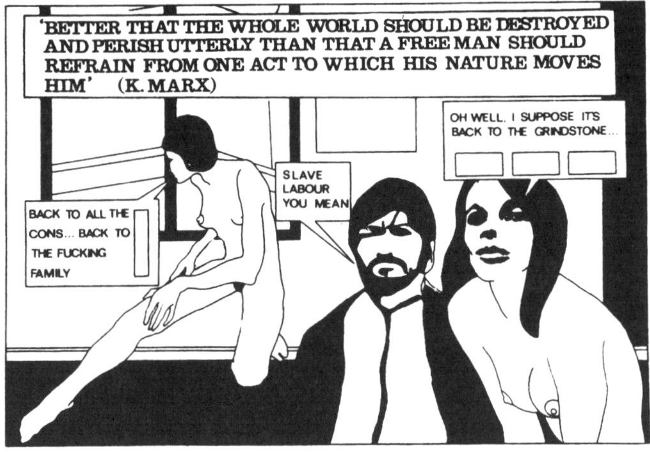
'BETTER THAT THE WHOLE WORLD SHOULD BE DESTROYED AND PERISH UTTERLY THAN THAT A FREE MAN SHOULD REFRAIN FROM ONE ACT TO WHICH HIS NATURE MOVES HIM' (K. MARX)
BACK TO ALL THE CONS... BACK TO THE FUCKING FAMILY
SLAVE LABOUR YOU MEAN
OH WELL, I SUPPOSE IT'S BACK TO THE GRINDSTONE...

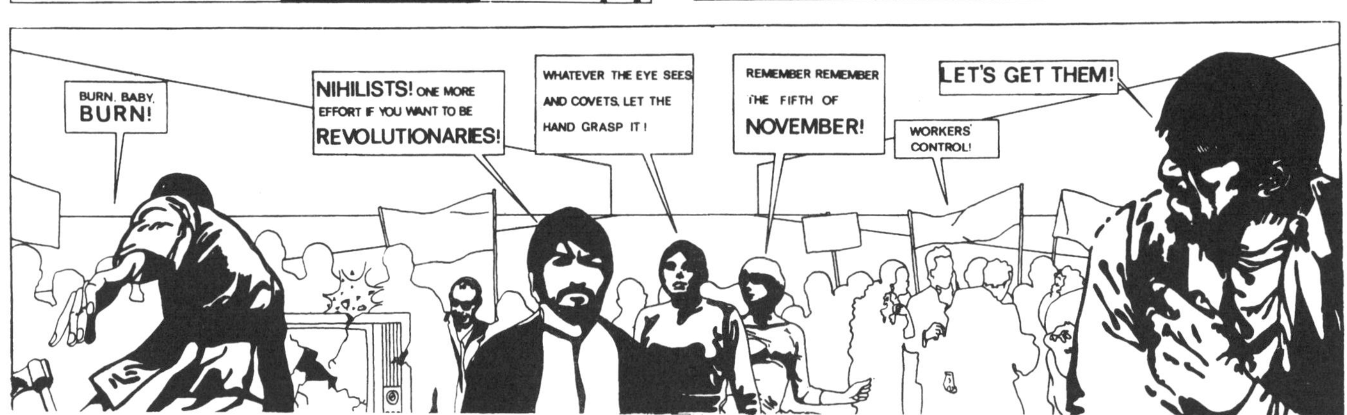
BURN, BABY, BURN!
NIHILISTS! ONE MORE EFFORT IF YOU WANT TO BE REVOLUTIONARIES!
WHATEVER THE EYE SEES AND COVETS, LET THE HAND GRASP IT!
REMEMBER REMEMBER THE FIFTH OF NOVEMBER!
WORKERS' CONTROL!
LET'S GET THEM!

FORMULA FOR A NEW CITY

Milord, I am from another country

We are bored in the town. There is no longer any temple of the sun. The dadaists wanted to see a monkey-wrench between the legs of the girls walking by and the surrealists a crystal bowl. So much for all that. We can read every type of promise into every type of face, concluding phase of morphology. The poetry of commercial advertising has lasted twenty years. We are bored in the town; you really do have to be pretty bored to be still looking for mystery on the hoardings and in the streets, concluding phase of poetry and laughter:

Bain-Douches des Patriarches
Machines à trancher les viandes
Zoo Notre-Dame
Pharmacie des Sports
Alimentation des Martyrs
Béton translucide
Scierie Main-d'or
Centre de récupération fonctionnelle
Ambulance Sainte-Anne
Cinquième avenue café
Rue des Voluntaires Prolongée
Pension de famille dans le jardin
Hôtel des Etrangers
Rue Sauvage

And the swimming pool in the Street of Little Girls. And the police station of Rendezvous Road. The medical-surgical clinic and the free labour exchange of the quai des Orfèvres. The artificial flowers of Sun Street. The Castle Cellars Hotel, the Ocean Bar and the Coming-and-Going Café. The Hotel of the Epoch.

And the strange statue of Doctor Philippe Pinel, benefactor of the insane, the last evenings of the summer. To explore Paris.

And you forgotten, your memories ravaged by all the chaos of the planet, wrecked in the Red Caves of Pali-Kao, without any knowledge of either music or geography, no longer leaving for the hacienda *where the roots dream of the child and where the wine ends in tales from some old almanac*. Well, you've blown it now. You'll never see the hacienda. It doesn't exist anywhere.

The hacienda must be built.

All towns are geological. Wherever we go, we meet a figure from the past, armed with all the prestige of its legend. We grow up in a *closed* landscape, all of whose reference points draw us irresistibly towards the past. A few *variable* angles, a few *receding* perspectives allow us to catch a glimpse of a completely novel conception of space, but these glimpses remain no more than incoherent visions. They are to be found in the magical spots of fairy stories and in some surrealist art: castles, great walls that cannot be climbed, small bars run to seed, caverns with a mammoth frozen in the ice, the mirror behind the pool table.

Even images as dated as these will have some power as a catalyst. Not that they could actually be used in building *a new symbolic town* without being completely transformed, without being given a completely new sense. Our minds, ridden by key-images from the past, have fallen far behind the sophistication of our machinery. The few attempts made to fuse modern science into a new myth have proved abortive. As a result, all contemporary art has been forced to become abstract – contemporary architecture being the worst example of all. Pure plastic art, telling no story and making no movement, cold and soothing to the eye. Elsewhere, other pretty things can be found – can be found as one wanders further and further from the promised land of synthesis. We are all strung out between a past which is still alive emotionally and a future which is as dead as a doornail.

We have no intention of contributing to this mechanical civilisation, to its bleak architecture, to its inevitably catatonic leisure.

We want to create environments that are permanently evolving.

The dark has been driven away by electricity and the seasons by central heating. Night and the summer have lost all their charm and the dawn has gone. Those who live in cities want to withdraw from cosmic reality and all they dream of is ways of doing so. For obvious reasons: dreams begin and end in reality.

Yet, contemporary technology could allow an unbroken contact between the individual and cosmic reality – minus some of whatever one considers its asperities. The stars and the rain can be seen through glass ceilings. The mobile house moves with the sun. Sliding walls allow vegetation to invade life. The house on metal tracks can go down to the sea in the morning and come back to the woods at night.

Architecture is the simplest way of *articulating* time and space; of *modulating* reality; of making people dream. I don't just mean expressing an ephemeral plastic beauty. Rather, a lasting influence, inscribed in the eternal graph of human desires and progress in realising them.

Thus, future architecture will be a means of modifying contemporary conceptions of time and space. It will be a means of *knowledge* and a means of *action*.

The architectural complex will be modifiable, either wholly or in part, by those living there.

Past societies offer an *a priori* Truth and Ethics to the masses. The appearance of the concept of *relativity* in a modern mind allows one to foresee something of an *experimental* nature of the coming civilisation. Experimental isn't quite the right word. Say, more supple; more 'amused'. On the basis of this moving civilisation, architecture, at least initially, will be a tool for experimenting with the thousand different ways of modifying life – modifying it to the ends of a synthesis which will be more glorious a kingdom than anything the world has ever known.

A new form of mental illness has swept the planet: banalisation. Everyone is hypnotised by work and by comfort: by the garbage disposal unit, by the lift, by the bathroom, by the washing machine.

This state of affairs, born of a rebellion against the harshness of nature, has far overshot its goal – the liberation of man from material cares – and become a life-destructive obsession. Young people everywhere have been allowed to choose between love and a garbage disposal unit. Everywhere they have chosen the garbage disposal unit. A totally different spiritual attitude has become essential – and it can only be brought into being by making our unconscious desires conscious and by creating entirely new ones. And by a *massive propaganda campaign* to publicise these desires.

We have already pointed out that desire to construct situations will be one of the main foundations of any new civilisation. This need for *total* creation has always been inseparable from the need to play with architecture: to play with time and space.

Chirico remains one of the most striking precursors of true architecture. What he was dealing with was absence and presence in time.

It has been shown that a particular object, not noticed consciously at the time of a first visit, can, through its absence during succeeding visits, awake an indefinable impression: through a transformation in time, *the absence of the object becomes a presence one can feel*. Furthermore, although generally ill-defined, the quality of this impression can change with the nature of the absent object and with the importance accorded to it by the visitor, ranging from paranoia to serenity (it is irrelevant that in this particular case the memory is the vehicle of these feelings. I only chose this example for its convenience).

In Chirico's painting during the Arcade period, an *empty space* creates a *well-filled time*. It should be clear by now how great the future influence exerted by these architects could be. Today, we have nothing but shit to pour on a century that has relegated *plans* of this magnitude to its so-called museums.

This new vision of time and space, which will be the theoretical basis of future constructions, is still imprecise and will remain so until there has been real, practical experimentation with possible patterns of behaviour in towns designed solely to this end: towns which, apart from the few buildings strictly necessary for some degree of comfort and security, would consist solely of buildings highly charged with emotionally evocative power, buildings one can feel, symbolical buildings representing desires, powers, events from the past, the present and the future. A rational extension of traditional religious experience, of myths, of fairy-tales and, above all, of psychoanalysis, *into architectural expression* becomes more and more urgent every day... as every reason for falling in love disappears.

Everyone will live in their own cathedral. There will be rooms awakening more vivid fantasies than any drug. There will be houses where it will be impossible not to fall in love. Other houses will prove irresistibly attractive to the benighted traveller...

This project could be compared with Chinese and Japanese *trompe-l'oeil* gardens – the difference being that these gardens aren't made to be really lived in – or to the ridiculous labyrinth in the *Jardin des Plates*, at the entry to which, the height of absurdity, Ariadne on strike, is written: "*Games are forbidden in the labyrinth*."

Such a town could be seen as the chance meeting-place of various castles, ravines, lakes, etc... This would be the baroque period of town planning seen as a means of knowledge. Yet, we can go much further than this today. We can build a modern building which doesn't look in the least like a mediaeval castle, but which can radiate even more strongly the poetic power of the *Castle* (keeping to a minimum number of lines, transposing certain others, the positioning of openings, the nature of the surrounding countryside, etc).

The *parts* of such a town could correspond to the *feelings* one normally experiences purely by chance.

The Gothic-Romantic Quarter – the Happy Quarter, the most densely inhabited – the Noble and Tragic Quarter (for good boys) – the Historic Quarter (museums, schools, etc) – the Useful Quarter (hospital, tool depots, etc) – the Sinister Quarter, etc... And an *Astrolaire* which would classify flora in terms of their response to the cosmic rhythms, an astrological garden like the one the astronomer Thomas wanted to build at Laaer Berg in Vienna. Essential if consciousness of the universe is to be kept on the ball. Perhaps a Death Quarter too, not so much for dying in as for having somewhere one can *live in peace*. This makes me think of Mexico and an acceptance of the identity of innocence and cruelty which becomes dearer to me every day.

The Sinister Quarter, for example, would be a distinct improvement on those gaping holes, mouths of the underworld, that a great many races treasured in their capitals: they symbolised the malefic forces of life. Not that the Sinister Quarter need be bristling with traps, *oubliettes* or mines. It would be a Quarter difficult to get into, and unpleasant once one succeeded (piercing whistles, alarm bells, sirens wailing intermittently, hideous sculptures, automatic mobiles with motors called Auto-Mobiles), as ill-lit at night as it glared bitterly during the day. In its heart: the Square of the Monster Mobile. Saturation of the market with any particular product causes demand for this product to fall: as they explored the Sinister Quarter, the child and the grown-up would slowly lose all fears of the anguishing aspects of life and learn to be amused by them.

The main thing people would do would be *to drift around all the time*. Changing landscapes from one hour to the next would end with complete removal from one's habitual surroundings.

Later, as action inevitably stales, this drifting would in part leave the realm of direct experience for that of representation.

Economic difficulties aren't the main

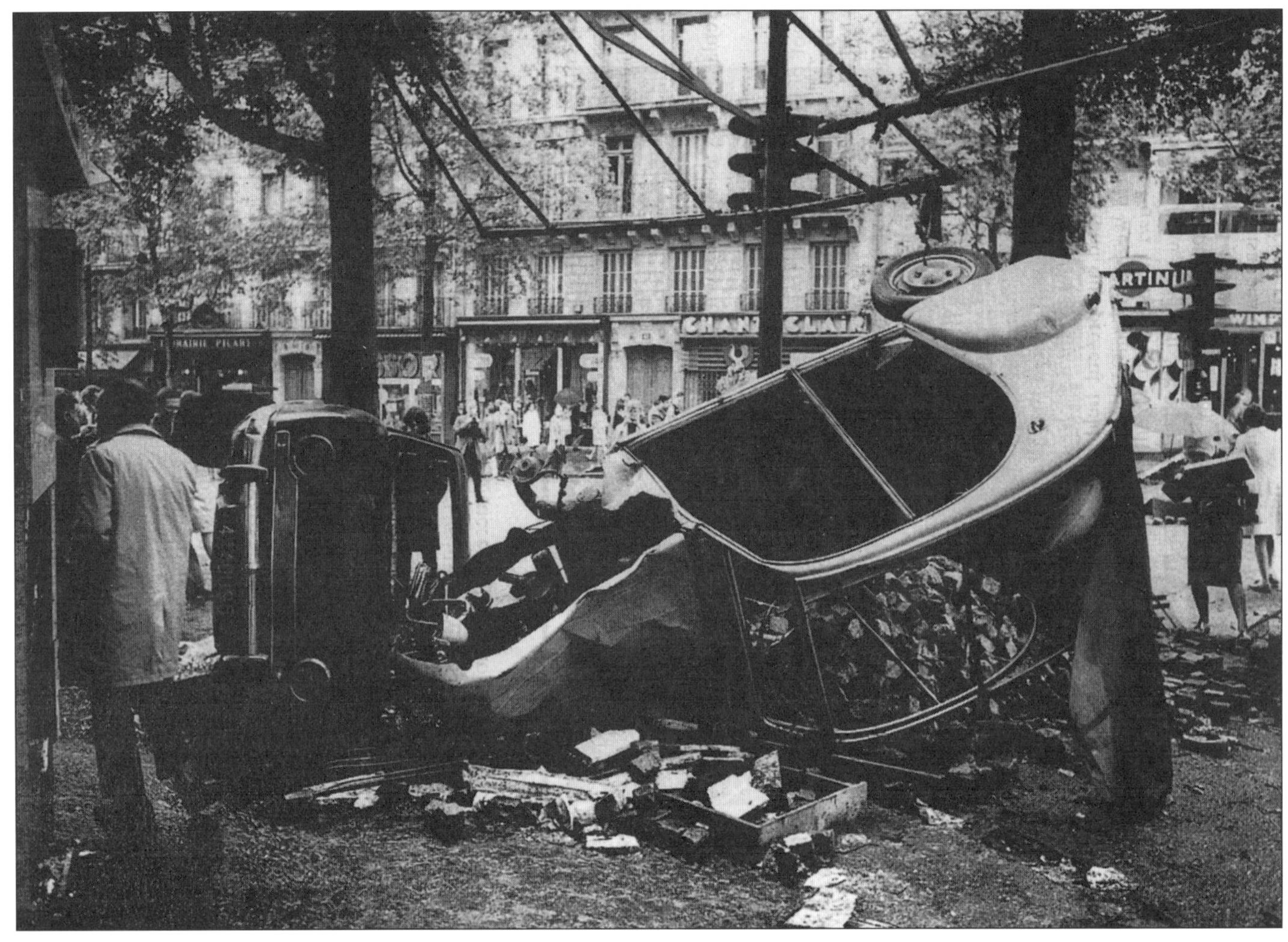

problem at all. It's patently obvious that the more any place is *set apart solely for free play* the more influence it exerts over people's behaviour and the more magnetic its pull becomes. Think of the fame of Monaco or Las Vegas. And Reno, caricature of free love. Nor is it a question of anything as puny as gambling. This initial experimental town will live largely off tolerated and restricted tourism. The next period of intense avant-garde activity will gravitate towards it naturally. Within a short period of time it will become the intellectual capital of the world and will be universally recognised as such.

Gilles Ivain, IS no. 1, 1958

TRAFFIC

The main mistake made by town planners is to see the private car (plus its sub-products, like the motorbike) as being essentially a means of transport. On the contrary, the car is first and foremost the principal manifestation of what happiness is supposed to be, and which is broadcast as such throughout the world by advanced capitalism. In terms of the same global propaganda, the car is both the sovereign good of an alienated life and an essential product of the capitalist market. American economic prosperity this year is said to depend on the success of the slogan: 'Two cars per family'.

The time spent in travel to and from work, as Le Corbusier quite correctly pointed out, is neither more nor less than unpaid labour – labour which still further reduces the amount of 'free' time one has at one's disposal.

We must replace travel as an extension of the working day by travel for pleasure alone.

Cities cannot possibly be rebuilt to suit the needs of the massive, parasitical existence of private cars today. Architecture can only be redesigned in accordance with the development of society as a whole. It must refuse to kow-tow to any values based on forms of social relationships one can see to be condemned (in the first place, the family).

Even if we are forced to accept, for a transitional period, a rigid division between the area where one works and the area where one lives, we must never forget a third area: that of life itself (the area of leisure and freedom – the truth of life). Unitary urbanism acknowledges no frontiers. It asserts that man's environment can be totally unified and that all forms of separation – between work and leisure, between public and private – can finally be dissolved. But even before this, the minimum programme of unitary urbanism is to extend our present field of play to every kind of building we can wish for. The complexity of the field we had in mind would be roughly equivalent to that of an ancient city.

The car isn't any kind of evil *per se*. It is its massive pile-up in towns that has destroyed its role. A balanced town planning would neither suppress the car nor allow it to become a central theme. It would gamble on its gradual disappearance. Even now one can foresee certain new areas being closed to traffic, as in a number of ancient cities.

Those who cannot see beyond the car have never thought, even from a strictly technical point of view, about other forms of transport in the future. For example, certain types of private helicopter being tried out at the moment by the US Army will probably have spread to the public within twenty years.

The breakdown of the dialectic of the human environment to the advantage of cars (there are projected Parisian motorways which will entail the demolition of thousands of houses, while at the same time the housing crisis is getting worse and worse) veils its irrationality under pseudo-practical explanations. It is only practical and necessary in terms of a very specific social set-up. Anyone who believes that the facts of the problem as given are permanent must also acccpt the permanence of contemporary society.

Revolutionary town planners won't just be concerned with the circulation of things, and of human beings trapped in a world of things. They will try to tear these topological chains asunder, paving the way with their experiments for the journey of men through authentic life.

Guy Debord, IS no. 3, 1959

THE SOCIAL SPACE OF LEISURE CONSUMPTION. *The dark, circular area at the top of the photo – Milwaukee Sports Stadium – is occupied by the 18 members of the two baseball teams. In the narrow strip surrounding it there are 43,000 spectators. They, in their turn, are surrounded by a vast car park filled with their empty cars.*

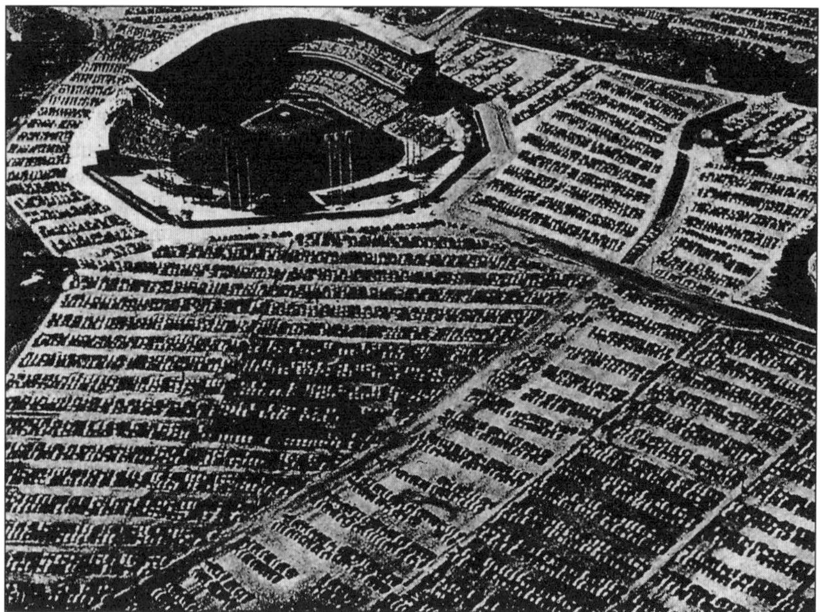

INSTRUCTIONS FOR TAKING UP ARMS

If it seems absurd to talk about revolution, this is because organised revolutionary movements have long since disappeared from the modern countries where the possibilities of a decisive transformation of society are concentrated. But *everything else is even more absurd*, since it is limited to what exists and to the various ways of putting up with it. If the word 'revolutionary' has been debased to the point of being used in advertisements to describe the latest piddling alteration in some ever-changing commodity, this is only because the possibility of a real, of a *desirable* change of the whole of one's experience is no longer being expressed anywhere. Today, the revolutionary project stands accused by the evidence of history: accused of failing and of having led to a new alienation. But all this means is that capitalism has been able to defend itself, on all levels of reality, much better than revolutionaries expected. But it hasn't all become any more tolerable for it. Revolution has to be re-invented, that is all.

This involves a number of problems that will have to be overcome, theoretically and practically, over the next few years. A few particularly important points can be mentioned here.

Out of all the new groupings which are appearing on the far left wing of the European workers' movement, only the most radical are worth preserving: those whose programme is based on *workers' councils*. Nor should we underestimate the number of pure confusionists and other trendies starting to ponce about on the far left.

The most difficult problem before groups who are trying to create a new type of revolutionary organisation is that of creating new, interpersonal relationships within the organisation itself. The remorseless pressure exerted by contemporary society is 100% hostile to any such undertaking. But unless it is carried through successfully by methods that are yet to be tried, we will never be able to escape from specialised politics. For an organisation (and eventually a society) to be really new, universal participation in it is obviously essential. This isn't some abstract theoretical desiderata. It is a *sine qua non*. For even if militants are no longer the mere executors of the decisions made by the leaders of the organisation, they still risk being reduced to the role of spectators of those among them who are the most qualified in politics conceived as a specialised activity; and in this way the passivity of the old world will be reconstituted.

People's creativity and desire to participate can only be awoken by a collective project that is explicitly concerned with every aspect of their own lived experience. The only way to 'stir up trouble' is by calling attention to the atrocious contrast between what life today could be and what it actually is. Without a critique of everyday life, the revolutionary organisation becomes a separated milieu, as conventional

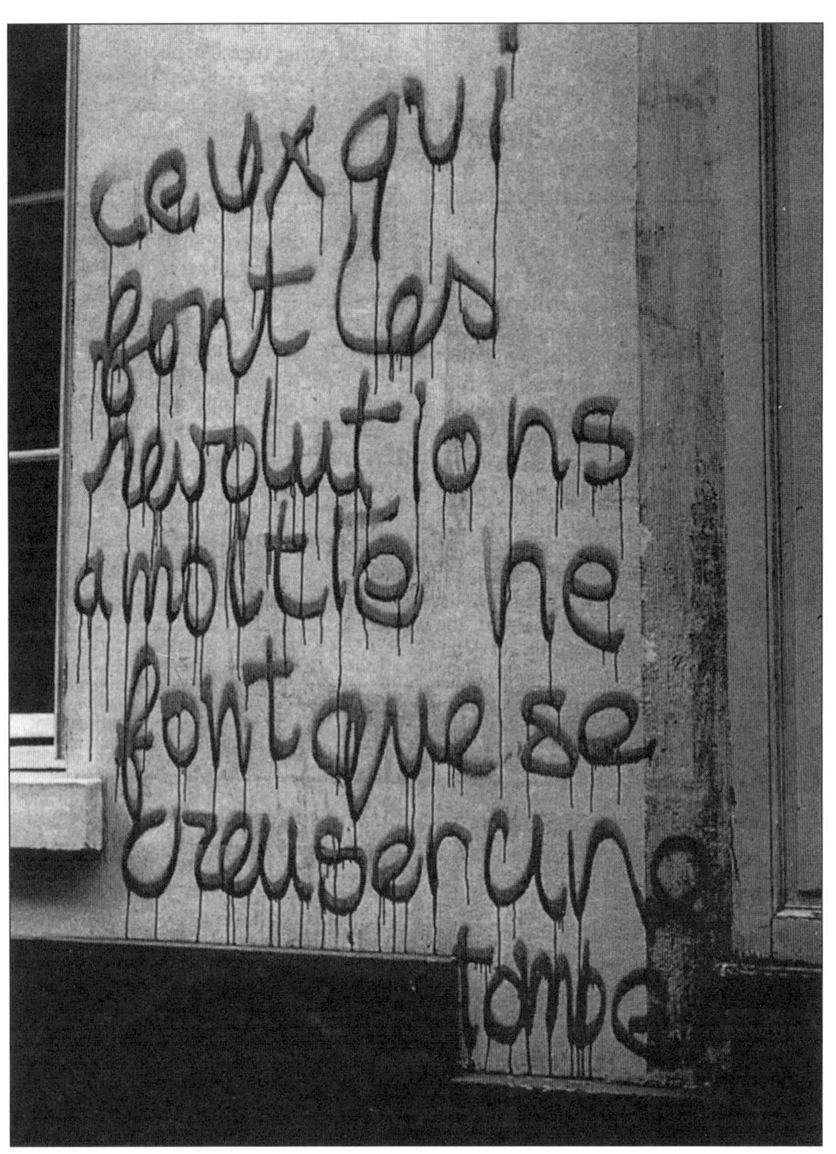

and in the last analysis as passive as a holiday camp: one of those which has been developed into a fully specialised theatre of modern leisure. Henri Raymond, in his study of Palinuro, points out how, in such places, the mechanism of the spectacle merely recreates, in the form of play, the normal relationships prevailing in the outside world. But then he goes on to praise the 'numerous human contacts' which are fostered by such holiday foci, without seeing that a merely quantitative increase in the number of people one meets leaves meetings just as flat and inauthentic as they were before. Even in the most anti-hierarchical and libertarian revolutionary group, communication between people is in no way ensured by a shared political programme. Sociologists usually support attempts to reform everyday life: to organise some consolation for it in leisure time. But the revolutionary project cannot accept the traditional idea of play: of a game limited in space, in time and in qualitative depth. The revolutionary game – the creation of life itself – is utterly different from any game that has ever been played before. To offer a three-week break from a year of work, the *Club Mediterranée* and its holiday villages are forced to rely on shoddy Polynesian ideology (a bit like the French Revolution's Roman fancy-dress or the *militant role*, Bolshevik or other, which today's revolutionaries use to define themselves). The revolution of everyday life, however, can never find its poetry in the past, but only in the future.

Marxist emphasis on the *extension of leisure time* has, quite legitimately, been criticised in the light of the empty leisure produced by modern capitalism. It is true that, if time is ever to become really free, then first and foremost it is work that must be transformed. Its conditions and its purpose must become quite different from those of the forced labour which has prevailed until now (cf. the French journal *Socialisme ou Barbarie*, the English *Solidarity*, the Belgian *Alternative*). But those who put all the stress on the necessity of changing work itself, of rationalising it, of making people interested in it, and who neglect the idea of the free content of life (that is, of developing materially equipped creative power quite apart from the traditional 'working day', however reduced, and quite apart from the time allotted to rest and recreation), run the risk of providing an ideology to cover up for the mere rationalisation of present methods of production in the name of *higher productivity*, without raising the question of the experience of time spent in this production, or of the necessity of this kind of life at all. This must be challenged at the most elementary level. The free construction of the whole space-time of individual life is a demand which will have to be defended against all sorts of dreams of rationalisation in the minds of the aspiring managers of the coming social reorganisation.

The different phases of our own activity up till now can only be understood in terms of the reappearance of revolution. This revolution will be social as well as cultural and right from the start its field of action will have to be far wider than was ever envisaged before. Thus, the IS does not want to recruit disciples or followers, but to bring together people capable of applying themselves to this task in the years to come, in every possible way. Which means, furthermore, that we must reject not only the remains of specialised art but also those of specialised politics; and particularly the post-Christian masochism characteristic of so many intellectuals in this field. We do not claim that we on our own are developing a new revolutionary programme. We say that this programme being formed, will one day become a practical threat to contemporary reality, and that we will take part in this confrontation when it comes. Whatever may happen to us individually, the new revolutionary movement will not be formed without taking into account what we have found out together: and this could be summed up as the supersession of the old theory of permanent but limited revolution by a theory of permanent and universal revolution.

IS no. 6, 1961

An appeal court decision that any holidaymaker who suffers because of a false description in a brochure has the right to compensation, was greeted yesterday as a major victory for consumer protection.

Tour operators reacted less enthusiastically, saying they were appalled and astonished by the court's action in dismissing an appeal by Thomson Holidays, which contended that the firm could be convicted only once for false information about a Greek holiday in their holiday brochure.

Lord Justice Lawton, who roundly dismissed this argument, said two million copies of the brochure had been circulated by Thomson's and prosecutions could be brought against it in respect of every holidaymaker who suffered because of false information.

"An annual holiday", said the judge, "is for many an essential safety valve for the tensions which can build up in the doing of the humdrum, boring and frustrating jobs. It is not in the public interest that the function of this safety valve should be impeded by recklessly making false statements for gain. We are sure that persons in this trade will stop making false statements when it has become obvious to them that recklessness does not pay."

The Guardian

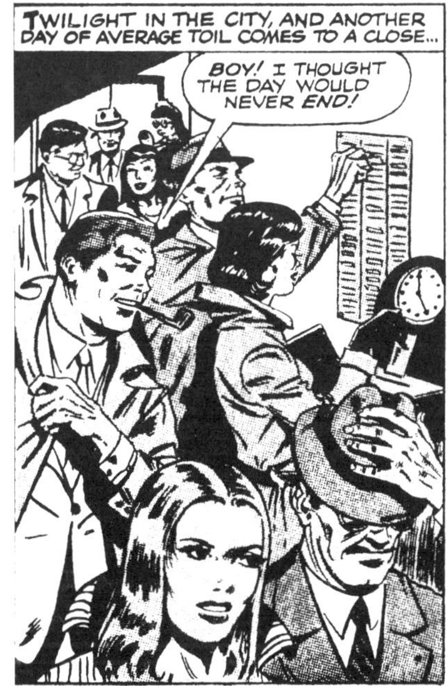

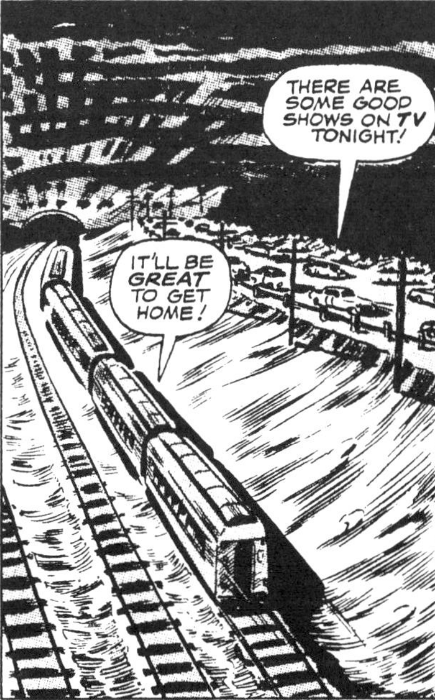

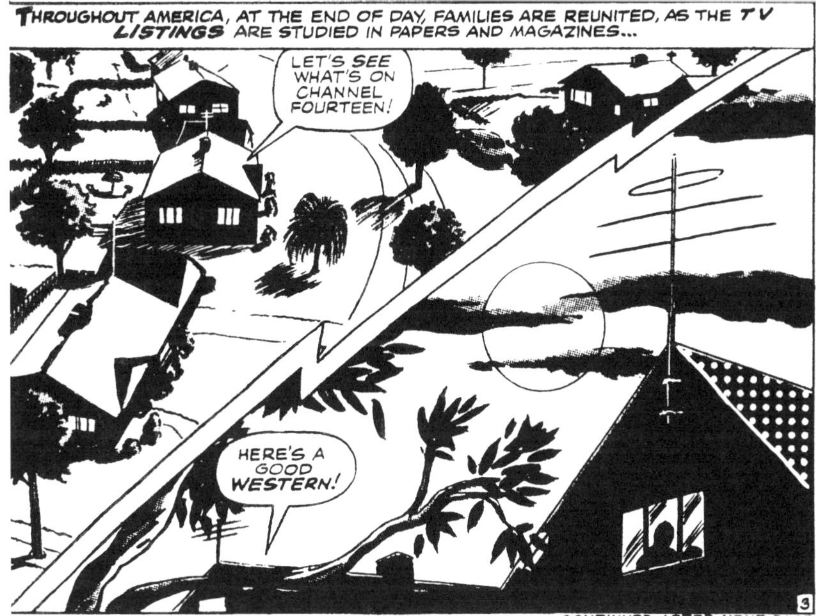

UNITARY URBANISM

1 THE NOTHINGNESS OF TOWN-PLANNING, THE NOTHINGNESS OF THE SPECTACLE

There is no such thing as 'town planning': it is just an ideology in Marx's sense of the word. Architecture, however, is something as real as Coca-Cola: it's a product permeated through and through with ideology, but still real, providing a distorted satisfaction for a distorted need. But 'town planning' is on much the same level as the barrage of advertising surrounding Coca-Cola – pure spectacular ideology. Modern capitalism, organising the reduction of all social life to a spectacle, cannot offer any other spectacle than that of our own alienation. Its vision of the city is its masterpiece.

2 TOWN PLANNING AS CONDITIONING AND PSEUDO-PARTICIPATION

Development of the urban environment is the capitalist education of space. It represents the choice of one specific materialisation of the possible at the expense

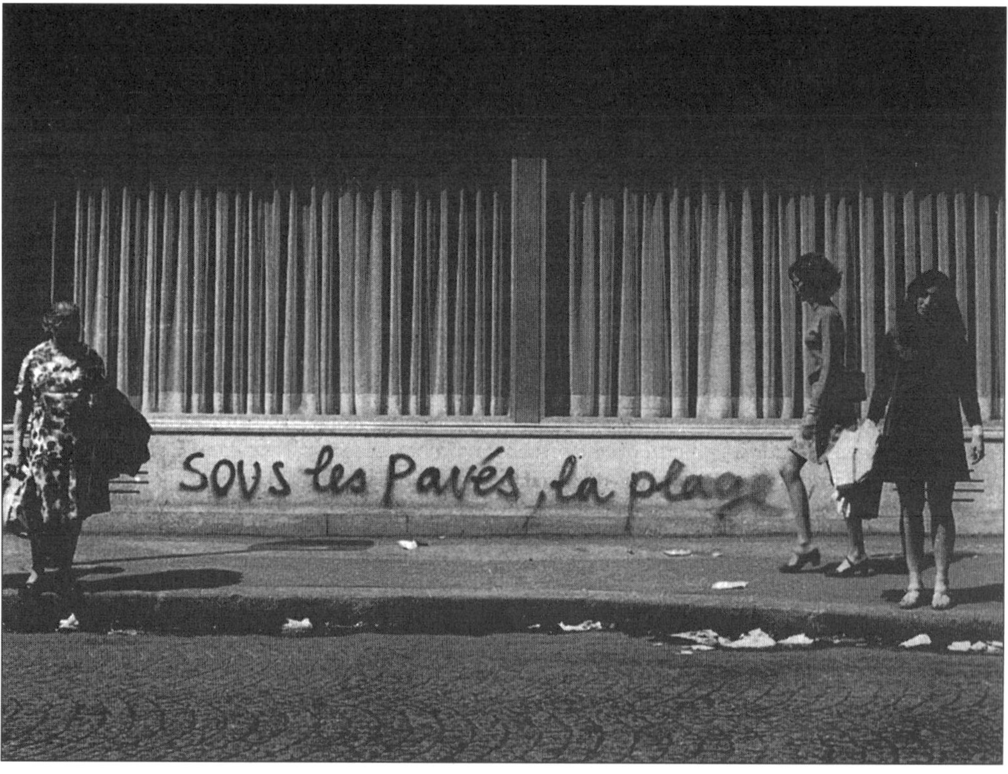

of all others. Like aesthetics – and its disintegration will follow much the same pattern – it could be seen as a somewhat neglected branch of criminology. However, in relation to its purely architectural aspects, its characteristic feature is its insistence on popular consent, on individual integration in the world of bureaucratic conditioning.

People are blackmailed into accepting every abomination on the grounds of its 'necessity'. What exactly this necessity is necessary for is not revealed. And for good reasons. Modern capitalism makes people abandon all criticism simply by arguing that everyone must have a roof over their heads, just as television is accepted on the grounds that everyone must have information and entertainment. Concealing the fact that this information, this amusement and this kind of living-place are not made for people at all but are made without them, are made against them.

Town planning as a whole is no more than contemporary society's sphere of publicity and propaganda – that is to say, the organisation of participation is something in which it is impossible to participate.

3 TRAFFIC FLOW, THE CRUX OF TOWN PLANNING

Keeping traffic moving is essentially organising universal isolation. As such, it is the basic problem of modern cities. Keeping traffic moving is the opposite of allowing people to *meet*; it takes up all the energy which could have been put into such meetings, or into any other kind of participation. Compensation for the resulting emptiness of people's lives is to be found in the spectacle. One's status is assessed by the nature of the place one lives in and by the extent of one's personal mobility. In the last analysis, we no longer live in a part of a city, but in a part of power. We live somewhere in the hierarchy. Our actual rank can be ascertained by the scope of our travel. Power is made manifest by the necessity of being present each day at an increasing number of places – business dinners, etc – situated further and further apart from one another. The people at the top of the modern hierarchy are those who appear in three different capitals in the course of a single day.

4 STANDING BACK FROM THE CITY SPECTACLE

The spectacle, as it makes its bid for total integration, can be seen to lie in both the actual organisation of cities and in the setting up of a stable information system. A cast-iron framework to secure the existing conditions of life. Thus, the first thing to be done is to stop people identifying with their environment and with the stereotyped behaviour patterns thrust upon them. Initially this means setting apart a small number of areas where people are free to relax and to recognise themselves and one another as they really are. We are going to have to accept the period of reified cities for some time yet; but the way in which we accept them can be changed straight away. Mistrust of these air-conditioned, brightly-coloured kindergartens, the dormitory cities of east and west, must be spread. Only when the masses awake can the question of consciously recreating entire cities be raised.

5 FREEDOM

The most important single achievement of contemporary town planning is to have made people blind to the possibility of what we have called *unitary urbanism* – by which we mean a living criticism, fed by all the tensions of the whole of everyday life, of this manipulation of cities and their inhabitants. Living criticism means the setting up of bases for an experimental life: the coming together of those who want to create their own lives in areas equipped to this end. These bases cannot be reserved for any kind of 'leisure' separated from the rest of social life. No spatio-temporal zone can be completely autonomous. Today there is constant pressure from world society on its existing holiday 'reservations'. Pressure from situationist bases will, however, be exerted in the opposite direction: they will function as bridgeheads for an invasion of the whole of everyday life. Unitary urbanism is the opposite of any kind of specialised activity – and to accept a separated sphere of 'urbanism' is to accept all the lies about the city today, all the lies about life in general.

It is happiness that town planning has promised. It will be judged accordingly. Co-ordinating artistic and scientific means of

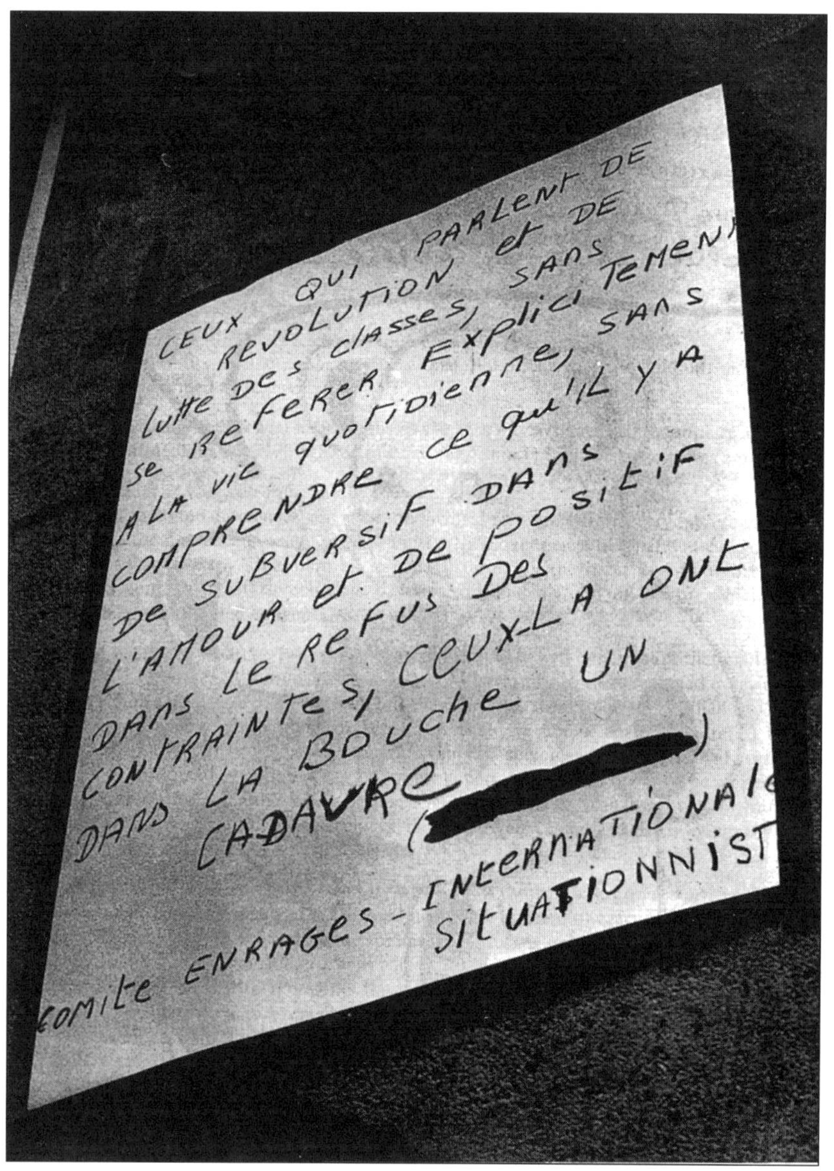

denunciation could lead to a total exposé of contemporary conditioning.

6 INVASION

All space is occupied by the enemy. We are living under a permanent curfew. Not just the cops – the geometry. True urbanism will start by causing the occupying forces to disappear from a small number of places. That will be the beginning of what we mean by construction. The concept of the 'positive void' coined by modern physics might prove illuminating. Gaining our freedom is, in the first place, ripping off a few acres from the face of a domesticated planet.

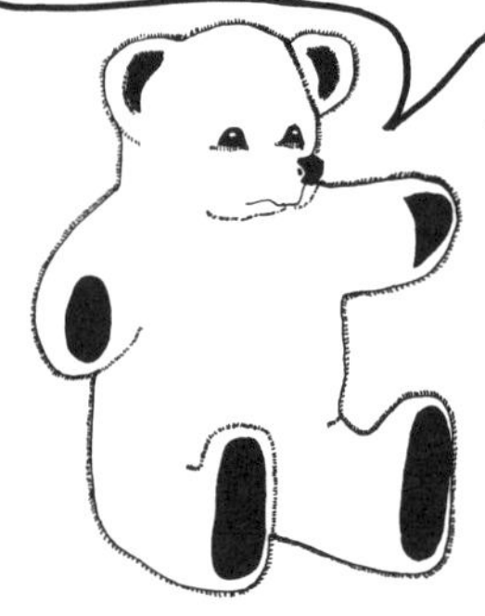

7 SUBVERSION

Unitary urbanism will transcribe the whole theoretical lie of town planning; subvert it as a means of disalienation. We must always be on our guard against the apogee of the bards of conditioning; turn their songs inside out.

8 CONDITIONS OF UNDERSTANDING ONE ANOTHER

The only thing that is of practical importance is the resolution of our fundamental problem: our own self-realisation, our escape from the system of isolation. This is the only thing that's necessary. Nothing else.

9 RAW MATERIALS AND THEIR TRANSFORMATION

The situationist destruction of contemporary conditioning is simultaneously the construction of situations. It is the liberation of the boundless energy trapped under the surface of everyday life. Contemporary town planning, which could be seen as almost geological strata of lies upon lies, will, with the advent of unitary urbanism, be replaced by means of defending an always precarious freedom, starting from the moment when individuals – who as such have yet to be born – will begin to construct, freely, their own lives and their own history.

10 THE END OF PREHISTORY OF CONDITIONING

We are not saying that men must return to any particular stage before conditioning began – but that they must pass beyond it. We have invented an architecture, seen a vision of the city, which cannot be realised without the revolution of everyday life – without the appropriation of the means of conditioning by everyone, the endless enrichment of these means and their fulfilment.

Kotanyi/Vaniegem, IS no. 6, 1961

THE TRANSFORMATION OF EVERYDAY LIFE

To study everyday life with any other purpose than that of changing it would not only be pointless – it would be condemned to failure.

Reading and writing theoretical articles, insofar as it is an extremely commonplace form of human relationship throughout a fairly large sector of society, should itself be criticised as a part of everyday life.

Specialists in the 'human sciences' are only too inclined to extract from everyday life what is actually happening to them at each moment and to transfer their experience to separated categories which are said to be value-free. It is habit in all its forms, primarily the habit of employing a number of *professional* concepts – that is, concepts produced by the division of labour – which hides reality behind a body of privileged conventions.

In fact, the reality of what we are calling 'everyday life' may well remain hypothetical for a considerable number of people. Everyone agrees, however, that various gestures repeated every day – opening a door or filling a glass – are perfectly real. But these gestures seem to be so trivial and so unimportant that, not unreasonably, it could be objected that they are not of sufficient interest to merit still further specialisation of sociological research. And few sociologists seem inclined to pursue Henri Lefebvre's definition of everyday life as "whatever experience remains once all specialised activity has been eliminated". Sociologists, being arch-specialists themselves, can see nothing but specialised activities everywhere. Everyday life is always somewhere else. Someone else is living it. And whoever they may be, they are certainly not sociologists.

This betrays a chronic need for the security of a way of thought based on the artificial separation of the whole of life into divided and subdivided areas. The concept of everyday life embarrasses, and it has to be rejected as 'useless' and 'crude' precisely because it rescues all that is left of reality once it has been classified and catalogued. It calls attention to a residue a number of people don't want to face, because this residue also represents the point of view of the *whole* of experience. It means we must make an all-inclusive judgement, and even proceed to do something about it. It is because of their possession of one or more forms of cultural specialisation that various intellectuals pride themselves on what they fondly believe to be their personal participation in the dominant sector of society. However, at the same time, their specialisation has put them in a position where they cannot avoid seeing the alarming extent to which this culture has decayed and fallen apart. Whatever one may feel about the value of this culture as a whole or about the value of certain parts of it, the alienation it has imposed on these intellectuals is to have made them believe they hold an important position in the hierarchy of power and that they are set apart from the everyday life of the rest of the population, *as though they themselves were not proletarians too*.

There can, however, be no doubt about the existence of specialised activities. At a particular time, they can even offer positive advantages that should be acknowledged in a demystified way. Everyday life is not everything, even though its permeation of specialised activities is such that no one can ever really get away from it. Everyday life – to use a facile image – is at the centre of everything else. Everyday life is the measure of all things: of fulfilment, rather the failure of human relationships; of the use of lived time; of artistic experiment; of revolutionary politics.

It is no good just repeating that the Enlightenment image of the disinterested 'scientific' observer is pure nonsense in any case: 'objective' observation is even less possible in this context than anywhere else. The refusal to accept the existence of everyday life stems not only from the fact that it is the inevitable meeting-place of empirical sociology and conceptual elaborationary reconstruction of culture and politics.

Today, to fail to criticise everyday life can only mean to accept the continued existence of forms of culture and politics which are rotten to the core and whose crisis, far advanced in the most highly-industrialised countries, is expressed by mass neo-illiteracy and by mass political apathy. Alternatively, radical criticism of everyday life as it stands – and criticism *in acts* could lead to a supersession of culture and politics in their traditional sense, that is to say, to more highly-evolved forms of controlling experience.

If our everyday life is the only real life we lead, then why is its importance so instinctively and so categorically denied by the experts? After all, they have no particular reason to do so. Many of them would even claim to be in favour of recreating the revolutionary movement.

It is because everyday life is so thoroughly impoverished. And furthermore, because this poverty is in no way accidental. It is enforced at every moment by the repression and the violence of class society; it is a poverty organised historically to meet the demands of the history of exploitation.

The use of everyday life, seen as the consumption of lived time, is dictated by scarcity: the scarcity of free time itself, and the scarcity of the possible uses of this free time.

Just as the accelerated history of our time is the history of accumulation and industrialisation, the backwardness of everyday life – its tendency to remain static – is produced by the laws and the vested interests presiding over this industrialisation. Until now, everyday life has proved resistant to history. *This is, in the first place, a judgement of history*, insofar as it has been the heritage and the project of a society based on exploitation.

The utter poverty of conscious organisation, of human creativity in everyday life expresses the fundamental necessity of unconsciousness and mystification to a society based on exploitation, to an alienated society.

In this context, Henri Lefebvre has extended the idea of unequal development and applied it to everyday life, characterising it as a backward sector of history, out of joint but not completely separated from its context. The level of everyday life could indeed be described as a colonised sector. In terms of world economy we know that underdevelopment and colonisation are interrelated factors. Everything suggests that the same applies to the socio-economic structure.

Everyday life, mystified in every possible way, supervised by the cops, is a sort of reservation for the placid, good niggers who, although they cannot understand it, actually manage to keep contemporary society running, with the rapid growth of its technological power and the irreversible expansion of its market. History – that is to say, the conscious transformation of reality – cannot at present be used in everyday life because the men living it are the product of a history over which they have absolutely no control. They themselves are making this history, but not freely.

Consciousness of modern society exists in specialised and more or less hermitic fragments. Thus, everyday life, where every question tends to be posed in terms of life as a whole, is inevitably the kingdom of complete ignorance.

This society, through the nature of its

industry, has made work lose any sense it ever had. No given pattern of behaviour has retained any true relevance to everyday life.

This society is tending towards the reduction of everyone to isolated consumers, between whom communication has been made completely impossible. So, everyday life is private life: the realm of separation and spectacle.

Thus, the underdevelopment of everyday life cannot be characterised solely by its relative inability to put technology to use. This factor is an important, but only partial, consequence of the alienation of everyday life as a whole – an alienation that could be summed up as the inability to invent a technique for freeing everyday existence.

Technology has in fact already modified various aspects of everyday life: the domestic arts, the telephone, television, long-playing records, mass air-travel, etc, etc. These factors come into play by chance, anarchically, without anyone having foreseen their interaction or their consequences. But, as a whole, there can be little doubt that this introduction of technology – whose context is, in the last analysis, one of rationalised, bureaucratic capitalism – is tending to impoverish still further what little independence and creativity people had left. The New Towns exemplify the blatantly totalitarian nature of neo-capitalistic social organisation: isolated individuals – generally isolated within the framework of the family cell – can watch their own lives being reduced to endless repetitions of the same trivial gesture, on top of which they are forces to consume an equally-repetitive spectacle.

One can only conclude that people censor the subject of their own everyday lives because they are well aware just how terrifyingly empty they are, and at the same time because, sooner or later, whether they admit it or not they feel that everything which really interested them, everything they really wanted and which they were forced to sacrifice to the way society functions, was focused *there*, and had nothing whatsoever to do with specialised activities and distractions. Consciousness of the energy wasted in everyday life and of its possible richness is inseparable from consciousness of the poverty of the prevailing organisation of life. Only the visible existence of this wasted wealth can enable one to define everyday life as penury and incarceration.

In these circumstances, to evade the political problem posed by the poverty of everyday life can only mean to evade the complete boundlessness of one's own demands to live life to the full – demands which could not lead to anything less than a reinvention of revolution itself. Needless to say, an evasion of politics on this level is in no way incompatible with being an active Labour Party worker or a cheery militant in some Marxist, Trotskyist or 'anarchist' faction.

In fact, everything depends on the intransigence with which one is prepared to ask oneself: How am I living? How satisfied am I with my life? How dissatisfied? And this means refusing the solicitation of every form of advertising, whether it is designed to persuade us that we can be happy because of the existence of God, or because of Fairy Snow, or because of free Largactil.

The expression 'critique of everyday life' could, and should, also be understood as the critique which everyday life would make, in absolute terms, of everything exterior and irrelevant to itself.

The question of the use of technology in everyday life and anywhere else is inevitably a political question (of all the possibilities of technology, those which are being developed at the moment have all been selected as a means of strengthening the position of the ruling class). Science fiction's version of a future, where interstellar adventure coexists with a terrestrial everyday life bogged down in the same material squalor and the same antediluvian morality, means purely and simply that there will still be a class of specialised rulers using the proletarian masses of factory and office to their own ends. In this perspective, the exploration of space, far from being an adventure, is no more than the enterprise these rulers have chosen, the way they have found to universalise their crazy economy and give the division of labour a cosmic dimension.

What is private life deprived of? Of life itself, which is cruelly absent. People could not be any more deprived of communication and self-realisation than they are. They are, in a word, deprived of the opportunity to make their own history. Hypotheses about the nature of this penury can only be worked

And yet everybody wants to breathe and nobody can breathe and a lot of people say "we'll be able to breathe later". And most people don't die, because they are already dead.

Graffiti, Nanterre, 1968

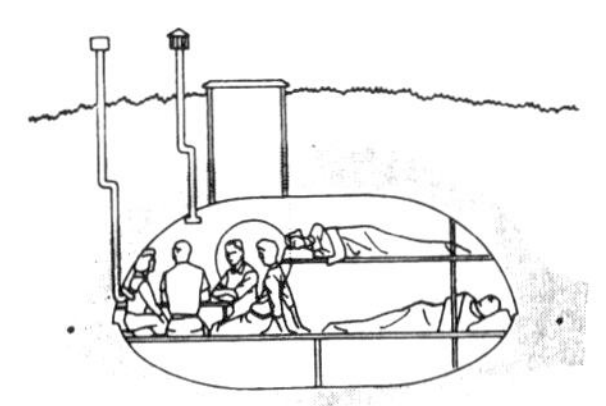

I love you!!! Oh, say it with cobblestones!!!

Graffiti, Nanterre, 1968

out in the form of actual projects of enrichment; the project of a different lifestyle; the project, in fact, of any sort of style at all... Alternatively, if we see everyday life as the frontier between the dominated and the non-dominated sectors of life, and therefore as its most problematic area, then it is vitally important we succeed in replacing the present ghettos by a frontier constantly expanding in every direction, ceaselessly creating new possibilities.

Today, whenever the question of the intensity of lived experience arises – over the use of drugs, for example – it is posed in the only terms an alienated society is capable of using – in terms of a deluded espousal of a falsified project, in terms of fixation and dependence. This applies equally to the prevailing conception of love, which is seen very much the same way as drugs. Passion in general is conceived as a *singular obsession*, directed towards one, and only one, object. Even in this narrow definition it is frustrated and its *élan* diverted into the phoney compensations of the spectacle. La Rochefoucauld once observed: "Often, what prevents us devoting ourselves exclusively to any one vice is the fact that we have several others." An extremely constructive statement if its moral presuppositions are rejected and it is stood back on its feet as the basis of a programme for the full realisation of human capacities.

All these problems concern us directly because the nature of our time is determined both by the appearance of the proletarian project – the abolition of class society and the initiation of human history – and also, inevitably, by the intense resistance which this project has called forth and reinforced by its mistakes and failures.

The crisis of everyday life is part and parcel of the new forms of capitalism's crisis – forms which go unnoticed by those Weary Willies who are still religiously computing the date of the next cyclical crisis of the economy.

Modern capitalism's vast riches have been accumulated at the expense of all former values and all the common references of previous communication. It is impossible to replace them by any others, whatever their nature, until the vast powers of modern industry, erratic from the very first and all but berserk today, are controlled rationally and placed in the service of everyday life. The malaise of contemporary civilisation, most acutely felt by the young, is *officially* admitted, invoked and 'analysed' at every moment. In this context, the crisis of modern art is no accident. Artistic activity had always been alone in its understanding of the secret problems of everyday life, although this understanding was largely mystified and deformed. 'Modern art' has of necessity been the theatre of a complete destruction of all forms of artistic expression.

It is now leisure that defines everyday life as much as, if not more than, work. This is borne out by any examination of the recent development of the conception of 'wasted time'. For classical capitalism, wasted time is time that is not devoted to production, to accumulation and to thrift. The lay morality taught in bourgeois schools ingrafted this as a rule of life. It so happens, however, that modern capitalism, through an unexpected turn of events, has been forced to flood the market with consumer goods and to 'raise the standard of living' (of course this expression is quite strictly meaningless). As the conditions of production – atomised and clocked to the nth degree – have become so nauseating that they can no longer be justified at all, the new morality which runs through advertising, dominates the media and determines the spectacle as a whole, confesses with disarming candour that the time which is wasted is the time spent at work. Work can only be justified by the amount of the money you earn, allowing you to buy, consume and enjoy a passive leisure ('free time'), manufactured and controlled by capitalism.

To admit the phoniness of the consumer needs that modern industry conjures up to maintain its frantic expansion – to admit the emptiness of leisure and the impossibility of *ever* getting any satisfaction – is to pose the question: What sort of time would not be wasted? What exactly is the wealth of a truly affluent society?

Take, for instance, the outraged cries on the left at the supposed threat to socialist principles posed by Russian concessions to private consumption *à l'américaine*. There really isn't any need to have digested Hegel and the whole of Marx to realise that any socialism which is being driven back by family cars invading its markets has nothing whatsoever to do with the socialism for which the workers' movement was fighting. The bureaucratic rulers of Russia should not be attacked on their tactics nor on their dogmatism, but on the only fundamental issue, the fact that people's lives remain exactly the same as they always were. Nor is this some occult curse dogging an everyday life that is doomed to remain reactionary. It is a fate imposed on everyday life by a precise external force – by the power structure and its specialists, whatever the trademark under which they busily plan poverty in all its guises.

The fact that many former left-wing activists have dropped out of politics, that they have withdrawn from the alienation of politics to the alienation of private life, doesn't just mean that they have returned to privacy as an escape from the 'duty of the revolutionary'. They have dropped out because politics is a specialised activity manipulated by other people. A sphere where the only real responsibility anyone ever had was that of delegating all responsibility to leaders over whom they had no control; the very sphere in which the original communist project was betrayed and alienated. The private and public cannot be crudely opposed to each other for the very good reason that both sectors are equally alienated. The task of the new revolutionary movement will be precisely to transcend their antagonism. The problem of alienation must be seen dialectically and the possibility of new forms of alienation occurring constantly in the very struggle against alienation must be emphasised.

Nowhere has capitalist civilisation been surmounted, though it continues to produce its own enemies everywhere. Consciousness of its own past defeats will make the next upsurge of the revolutionary movement far more radical than ever before; its programme must become more audacious as the productive strength of modern civilisation increases. Already, this civilisation contains, in a latent state, the material basis missing from all previous 'utopian' projects. The next attempt to attack capitalism as a whole will have already invented and put into practice a completely new use of everyday life. It will already be based on a different lifestyle (because we now realise that any traces of the kind of relations between people which characterise contemporary society within the revolutionary movement itself will lead, imperceptibly, to the recreation of this society itself, or to the creation of something very close to it).

Just as the bourgeoisie during its ascendant phase, was forced to liquidate everything transcending life on earth (heaven, eternity...), the revolutionary proletariat – which, by definition, cannot acknowledge either a past or models to be followed – must liquidate, even more systematically, everything transcending everyday life. Or rather, everything which claims to transcend it: the spectacle, the 'historic' gesture or remark, the 'grandeur' of leaders, the mysteries of specialisation, the 'immortality' of art and its importance separated from life. In other words, it must repudiate all the sub-products of eternity that have survived as weapons of the ruling class.

Revolution, shattering the present resistance of everyday life to history, will create conditions allowing *the present to dominate the past* and ensuring the constant domination of the creative over the repetitive. The aspects of everyday life expressed by the concepts of ambiguity – misunderstanding, compromise or misuse – will decline in importance as that of their opposites ascends: conscious choice and gamble.

The criticism of language characteristic of modern art – appearing at the same time as the meta-language of machines: the bureaucratic language of bureaucratic hegemony – will then be superseded by more highly-evolved forms of communication. The contemporary concept of the decipherable social text will lead to new ways of actually writing the social text itself. A new lifestyle, a new use of the urban environment, are among the first areas of experiment for a revolutionary group. The primary production of a revolutionised industry could only be the enrichment of everyday life by means of permanently-evolving games.

Today, the permanent recreation of everyday life cannot happen spontaneously as a natural activity. It must be part of a conscious project, undertaken amidst blatantly repressive conditions – and undertaken to wreck them.

THE HEAVEN OF THE SPECTACLE AND DESIRE

A European Leisure Centre is about to be set up in Strasbourg in order to investigate the possibilities of a better utilisation of leisure time... A thorough study has been devoted to television which, according to the delegates, offers new possibilities for leisure activities at home, always providing that the family masters this new form of technology and uses it rationally.

Le Monde, 15 April 1962

Feuerbach starts out from the fact of religious self-alienation, the duplication of the world into a religious, imaginary world and a real one... But the fact that the secular foundation detaches itself from itself and establishes itself in the clouds as an independent realm is really only to be explained by the self-cleavage and self-contradictoriness of this secular basis. The latter must itself, therefore, first be understood in its contradiction, revolutionised in practice. Thus, for instance, once the earthly family is discovered to be the secret of the holy family, the former must then itself be criticised in theory and revolutionised in practice.

Marx, 1845

No cultural avant-garde, not even one with revolutionary sympathies, can accomplish this. No more can any revolutionary party conceived in traditional terms, not even if it accords crucial importance to the critique of culture (ie the body of artistic and conceptual tools with which a society defines its own nature and the purpose of life). The time is up for this type of culture and politics. They interest nobody, and no wonder! The revolutionary transformation of everyday life is not reserved for some hazy future: the nightmare of life today makes it everyone's most desperate, most visceral problem. The alternatives are hardly attractive. Either immediate self-destruction with the elegance of a Jacques Vaché, or, far worse, just giving up and going to sleep once and for all. This transformation will mark the end of all one-way artistic expression, stored in the form of commodities, at the same time as it will mark the end of all specialised politics.

IS no. 6, 1961

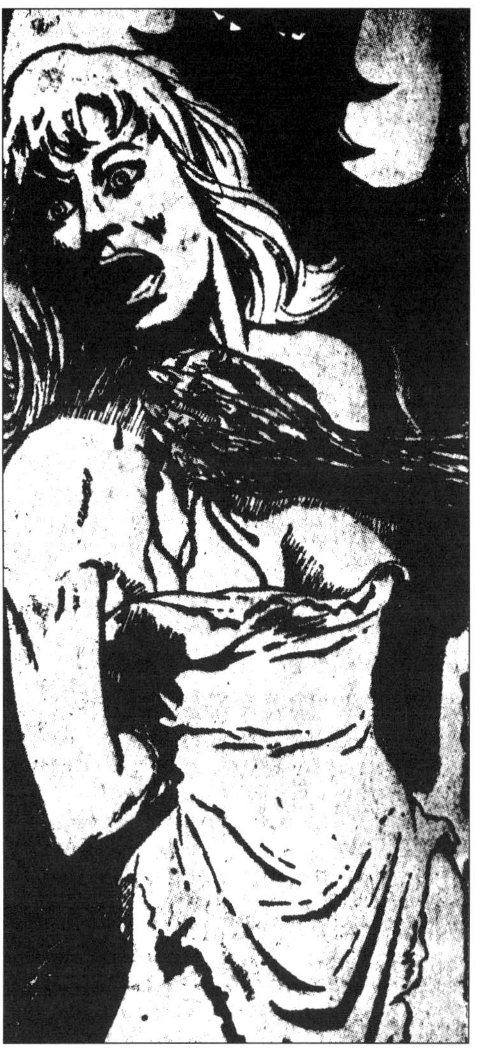

THE BAD OLD DAYS WILL END

The world of the spectacle has reached its apogee. New forms of resistance are beginning to break out everywhere. These are anything but well known, since the whole point of the spectacle is to portray universal and hypnotic submission. But resistance exists, and it is spreading.

Everyone knows about the rebellion of youth in the highly-industrialised countries, even if they don't understand much about it. Militant journals such as *Socialisme ou Barbarie* in Paris and *Correspondence* in Detroit have published well-documented articles on the permanent resistance of workers at work (against the whole organisation of work), on depoliticisation and on the loss of faith in trade unions, which have become no more than a mechanism for integrating workers into society and an additional weapon in the economic arsenal of bureaucratic capitalism. As the old forms of opposition reveal their ineffectiveness, or, more often, turn right round and become part of the existing order, dissatisfaction is spreading underground, irreducible, eating away the foundations of the affluent society. Marx's 'Old Mole' is still grubbing away, the ghost still haunts all the nooks and crannies of our televised Elsinore Castle, whose political mists will melt away the moment workers' councils exist and wield power.

The first attempts to organise the classical proletariat, around the end of the eighteenth and beginning of the nineteenth centuries, were preceded by a period of isolated, 'criminal' actions, aiming to destroy the machines which were doing people out of their work. We are now in a similar period of vandalism against the *machines of consumption*, which are just as effective in doing us out of our life. It is not destruction itself that is valuable, of course, but the refusal to submit, which will ultimately be capable of transforming itself into a positive project of converting these machines in such a way that they increase the real power of men. Quite apart from the havoc wrought by teenage gangs, we can mention several outbreaks on the part of workers that are quite incomprehensible from the point of view of traditional demands.

On 9 February 1961 in Naples, factory workers coming out of the day shift found no trams to take them home; the drivers were all out on a wildcat strike because several of them had been sacked. The workers showed their solidarity with the strikers by throwing various projectiles at the offices of the tram company, followed by petrol bombs which set fire to part of the tram station. Then they burned several buses and successfully held off police and firemen. Numbering several thousand, they spread out through the city, smashing shop windows and neon signs. Later that night, troops had to be called in to restore law and order, and tanks moved into Naples. This totally spontaneous and aimless demonstration was obviously a direct revolt against the time wasted in travelling to and from work, which is such a substantial addition to the time spent in wage slavery in modern cities. After breaking out in response to a minor aggravation, the revolt immediately began to spread to the whole décor of consumer society, newly pasted over the traditional poverty of southern Italy. As 'juvenile delinquents' have shown us, shop windows and neon signs are at the same time the most symbolic and the most fragile items in this décor.

On 4 August in France, striking miners at Merlebach attacked twenty-one cars parked in front of the management buildings. Everyone pointed out with amazement that these cars nearly all belonged *to the miners themselves* or to their own friends. Who can fail to see in this, quite apart from the reasons which always justify aggression on the part of the exploited, a gesture of self-defence against the central object of consumer alienation?

When the men on strike in Liege decided, on 6 January 1961, to destroy the presses of the newspaper *La Meuse*, they acted with exceptional clear-mindedness in choosing to attack the *information system* wielded by their enemies. Every way of transmitting information was either in the hands of the government or in those of the bosses of the trade union and socialist party bureaucracies, and this proved to be precisely at the crucial point in their struggle: their systematic exclusion from popular consciousness, their condemnation to disappear without a trace. Another symptom of the same attitude towards the media is to be found in the following statement from the union of French journalists and radio and television technicians, dated 9 February: "Our fellow reporters and technicians who were covering the demonstration on Thursday night *were set upon by the crowd as soon as they saw the sign RTF*. This fact is significant. It is why the SJRT and the SUT feel they must state once again that *the lives of our fellow reporters and technicians depend on the respect in which their reports are held...*" However, despite these first attempts to fight back against the forces of conditioning, we cannot afford to close our eyes to the extent to which the latter continue to prove successful. For example, when, at the beginning of the year, the Decaseville miners delegated twenty of their number to go on hunger strike, they chose to fight according to the spectacular rules of the enemy by relying on the tear-jerking potential of twenty 'stars'. They failed, as they were bound to do. Their only chance of success had lain in their extending their collective action, at whatever cost, beyond the one mine whose production they were holding up. Capitalism and all the forms of pseudo-opposition to it have so effectively spread *parliamentary* and *spectacular* ideas that revolutionary workers tend to forget that *representation* must always be kept to the barest minimum: used as little as possible. At the same time, however, it isn't only industrial workers who are beginning to fight back against the general sloth. Last January, the actor Wolfgang Neuss placed a small ad in the Berlin newspaper *Der Abend*, giving away the identity of the killer in a television detective serial which had been keeping the masses in suspense for weeks. This was a truly beautiful piece of sabotage.

The attack which the first workers' movement launched against the whole organisation of the old world finished long ago, and nothing can bring it back to life. It failed, not without achieving immense results, but these were not the aim it originally had in mind. No doubt this diversion to partly-unexpected results is the general rule for human actions, but what forms the exception to this rule is the true revolutionary moment, the moment of the qualitative leap, of all or nothing. We must study the classical workers' movement again without any illusions, particularly with respect to its various political and pseudo-theoretical heirs, since all they have inherited is its failure. The apparent successes of this movement are its fundamental failures (reformism or coming to power of a state bureaucracy) and its failures (the Commune or the Asturian revolt) represent for us and for the future its open successes. This subject must be precisely located in time. One could say that the classical workers' movement began twenty years before the official founding of the International, with the first link-up of communist groups in different countries which Marx and his friends organised from Brussels in 1845. And that it was completely finished after the failure of the Spanish revolution, ie immediately after the May Days in Barcelona in 1937.

We must rediscover the whole truth about this period. All the main tactical and strategic debates between different groups of revolutionaries, all the possibilities they neglected at the time, should be re-examined: re-examined in the light of the failure of the whole traditional revolutionary movement. Marx is obviously the first person whose thought must be rediscovered; nor should this present much difficulty in view of the extent of the documentation and the enormity of the lies that have been told about him. We must also reassess the attitude of the anarchists in the First International, Blanquism, Luxembourgism, the Council movement in Germany and Spain, Kronstadt, the Makhnovists, etc. Nor should there be any mistake about the practical importance of the utopian socialists. Nor, as should be obvious, is this just a question of a whole lot more books to read. Its sole purpose is to help in the construction of the new revolutionary movement – the new revolutionary movement of which we have seen so many signs over the last few years, including last but not least ourselves. It will be utterly different. We must understand these signs by reference to the classical revolutionary project, and vice versa. We have to rediscover the history of the movement of history itself, which has been so well concealed and distorted. Besides, when all is said and done, it is only the revolutionary project – plus a few experimental artistic groups which are, in any case, generally pretty closely linked to it – that offers any hope of truly living at all today: which allows us to take an objective interest in modern society and in the possibilities it contains.

There is no other way to be faithful to, or even to understand, our comrades of the past than to reinvent the problem of revolution. Why does this seem so difficult? Starting from the experience of a free everyday life – that is, from the search for freedom in everyday life – it isn't so difficult as all that; and moreover it seems to us that a number of young people today are quite acutely aware of this. And to feel it strongly enough enables us to rediscover, to redeem, *our own lost history*. It is not difficult for this kind of thought, which is prepared to question everything that exists. It is enough not to have *abandoned* philosophy, as almost all philosophers have – or not to have abandoned real opposition to *contemporary reality*, as almost all political activists have. And those who have not abandoned philosophy, art and politics will find that all three lead to the same transcendence. It is only specialists, whose individual power depends on the power of a whole society of specialisation, who have abandoned the *critical* truth of their various disciplines in order to enjoy the more positive wages of their *function*. But all real forms of research flow together into one totality, just as real people get together one more time to try to escape from their prehistory.

Many people cannot believe in the possibility of a new revolutionary movement. They keep on repeating that the proletariat has been integrated or that the working class is quite happy with the way things are today. This means one of two things. Either that they themselves are quite happy with the way things are – in which case we will give them something to be unhappy about, and that without further ado. Or, alternatively, that they think they are 'artists' or something – in which case we will dispel their illusions by showing them that the new proletariat includes almost everybody.

In the same way, apocalyptic fears or hopes as to revolutionary movements appearing in colonised or semi-colonised countries neglect one vital fact: the revolutionary project can only be realised in the highly-industrialised countries. And until it is highly-industrialised, every mass movement in the underdeveloped zone will be doomed to follow the model of the Chinese revolution, whose birth coincided with, and whose subsequent evolution was determined by, the liquidation of the classical workers' movement. What is true is that these wars of national liberation, even if they are canalised by the bureaucratic Chinese model, prevent equilibrium in the confrontation of the two great power-blocs and make any division of the world by their rulers unstable. But the safety of the stakes in the global poker-game is challenged just as effectively by the internal disequilibrium of the factories of Manchester and East Berlin...

The small groups of rebels who somehow

managed to live through the destruction of the traditional workers' movement (through the horrible irony that turned its virility into the mainstay of a totalitarian state) managed to hand down the truth of what this movement really had been, but only in a historical and almost academic form. An honourable resistance to violence has kept its traditions intact but has not been able to readjust and become a living force once more. The formation of new organisations depends on a more radical critique: a critique expressed in action. It is a question of breaking completely with *ideology* – ideology whose safekeeping so many revolutionary groups see as their main function and *raison d'être* – that is to say, Marx's critique of the role played by ideologies must be redeveloped. It is essential to get away from specialised revolutionary activity – from the self-mystification of 'scrious' politics – because, as anyone can see, mastery of any one form of specialisation leads even the most intelligent people to become stupid about everything else; so that they lose any hope of success in the political struggle itself, since it is inseparable from the problems of our society as a whole. Specialisation and pseudo-seriousness are among the main defence mechanisms that the old world has built in everyone's head. A revolutionary association of a new type will mark its break with the old world by allowing, in fact by demanding, an authentic and creative participation on the part of all its members – instead of merely asking its *militants* for a participation measured solely in terms of *time*, which comes down to re-establishing the basic form of control imposed by contemporary society: the quantitative criterion of how long one works. This passionate participation on the part of everyone is vitally necessary, both because the militant of traditional politics, the responsibly-minded individual who 'devotes himself', is condemned to disappear along with traditional politics itself, and even more because devotion and sacrifices are always rewarded by *authority* (even if it is purely moral authority). *Boredom is always counter-revolutionary*. Always.

Groups who accept that all forms of traditional politics have failed, not circumstantially but fundamentally, must also accept that they can only claim to be a *permanent avant-garde* if they themselves exemplify a new lifestyle – a new falling in love with life again. Nor is this making of lifestyle a basic criterion some wild utopianism: whenever the traditional workers' movement appeared or it exploded, it can be seen time after time. And today it isn't just a question of trying to go as far as people did in the nineteenth century: it's a question of trying to go a damn sight further. Otherwise the militants of any future organisation will form no more than dull propaganda groups with, no doubt, very just, very important ideas – but without any audience to speak of. Whatever the internal dynamic or external action of any organisation, unilateral, spectacular transmission of revolutionary doctrine has lost any hope of proving effective in the society of the spectacle, a society that organises massive spectacles about anything at all and simultaneously makes any spectacle whatsoever a distinctly stomach-turning experience. This means that any form of specialised propaganda is highly unlikely to spark off any action when the time for it comes, to play its real part in real struggles when the masses no longer have any alternative.

We must resurrect what in the nineteenth century was meant by the social war of *the poor*. The feeling of *penury* was everywhere, in all the pop-songs of the time, in everything said by those actively taking part in the traditional working class movement. One of the most urgent tasks before the IS and before any comrades working in the same direction, is to define our *new poverty*. Over the last few years a number of American sociologists have played almost the same role in exposing this new poverty as that played by the first utopian philanthropists *vis-à-vis* factory conditions during the last century. The disease has been revealed, but only in an idealistic and artificial way. Since understanding is granted by praxis alone, one can only really understand the nature of the enemy by fighting them (v. for example, G Keller and R Vaneigem's projects *to transfer the aggression of the 'blousons noirs' into the plane of ideas*).

Our new poverty cannot be defined without defining our new (possible) wealth.

We must oppose the image broadcast by contemporary society – according to which capitalism has evolved (both naturally and owing to the pressure of legitimate reformist demands) from an economy based on profit to an economy based on need – by publicising the idea of *an economy based on desire*. This could be formulated as technological society plus the imagination to see what could be done with it. Moreover, contemporary economy is not based on needs, it is based on habits – habits that were never needs in the first place, but were quite blatantly manufactured by contemporary society.

Accepting phoney opposition to the world goes hand in glove with believing in its phoney riches (and therefore with an almost deliberate refusal to see its new poverty). Sartre's disciple Gorz is a case in point. In no. 188 of his *Temps Modernes*, he confesses how embarrassed he is that, thanks to his career as a journalist, which in truth is nothing to write home about, he can afford to buy the consumer goods offered him: taxis and trips abroad, he says respectfully – and this at a time when taxis are forced to inch forward behind the solid mass of cars that everyone has been forced to buy; and when journeys abroad reveal no more than the same boring spectacle of the same boring alienation spread over the whole face of the earth. At the same time he really gets carried away about 'the youth' – like Sartre once upon a time with his 'total freedom of criticism of the USSR' – of the only 'revolutionary generations' of Yugoslavia, Algeria, Cuba, China and Israel. The other countries are old, says Gorz, to justify his own debility. And so he sidesteps having to make any of the revolutionary decisions which 'the youth' of such countries are forced to make, just as they are in the West where not everyone is so old nor so much in the limelight: where every rebel isn't quite such a Gorz.

Fougeyrollas, the latest philosopher to have 'transcended' Marx, is somewhat worried that while all previous major breakthroughs in world history have been characterised by a change in the mode of production, the communist society heralded by Marx would seem to be, were it even feasible, no more than an extension of our own industrial society. Back to the bottom of the class for Fougeyrollas. The coming society will not be based on industrial production at all. It will be a world of art made real. What is his "integrally new type of production, with which our society is pregnant" (*Marxisme en question*)? It is the construction of situations: the free creation of immediate experience itself.

IS no. 7, 1963

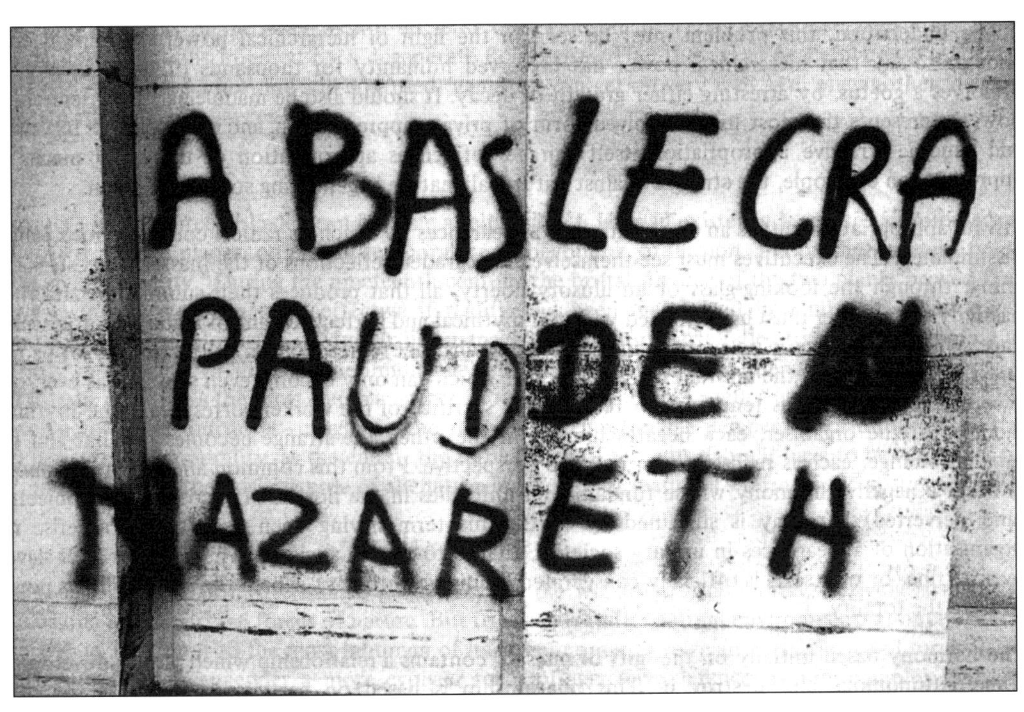

THE TOTALITY FOR KIDS

Almost everyone has always been excluded from *lifc* and forced to devote the whole of their energy to *survival*. Today, the *welfare state* imposes the elements of this survival in the form of technological comforts (cars, frozen foods, Welwyn Garden City, Shakespeare televised for the masses).

Moreover, the organisation controlling the material equivalent of our everyday lives is such that what in itself would enable us to construct them richly, plunges us instead into a luxury of impoverishment, making alienation even more intolerable as each element of comfort appears to be a liberation and turns out to be a servitude. We are condemned to the slavery of working for freedom.

To be understood, this problem must be seen in the light of hierarchical power. Perhaps it isn't enough to say that hierarchical power has preserved humanity for thousands of years as alcohol preserves a foetus, by arresting either growth or decay. It should also be made clear that hierarchical power represents the most highly-evolved form of private appropriation, and historically is its alpha and omega. Privative appropriation itself can be defined as appropriation of things by means of appropriation of people, the struggle against natural alienation engendering social alienation.

Private appropriation entails an *organisation of appearances* by which its radical contradictions can be dissimulated. The executives must see themselves as degraded reflections of the master, thus strengthening, through the looking-glass of an illusory liberty, all that produces their submission and their passivity. The master must be identified with the mythical and perfect servant of a god or a transcendence, whose substance is no more than a sacred and abstract representation of the *totality* of people and things over which the master exercises a power that can only become even stronger as everyone accepts the purity of his renunciation. To the real sacrifice of the worker corresponds the mythical sacrifice of the organiser. Each negates himself in the other, the strange becomes familiar and the familiar strange. Each is realised in an inverted perspective. From this common alienation a harmony is born – a negative harmony whose fundamental unity lies in the notion of sacrifice. This objective (and perverted) harmony is sustained by myth; this term having been used to characterise the organisation of appearances in unitary societies, that is to say, in societies where power over slaves, over a tribe, or over serfs is officially consecrated by divine authority, where the sacred allows power to seize the totality.

The harmony based initially on the '*gift* of oneself' contains a relationship that was to develop, become autonomous and destroy it. This relationship is based on partial *exchange* (commodity, money, product, labour force...), the exchange of a part of oneself on which the bourgeois conception of liberty is based. It arises as commerce and technology become preponderant within agrarian-type economies.

When the bourgeoisie seized power they destroyed its unity. Sacred, privative appropriation became secularised in capitalistic mechanisms. The totality was freed from its seizure by power and became concrete and immediate once more. The era of fragmentation has been a succession of attempts to recapture an inaccessible unity, to shelter power behind a substitute for the sacred.

A revolutionary movement is when 'all that reality presents' finds its immediate *representation*. For the rest of the time, hierarchical power, always more distant from its magical and mystical regalia, endeavours to make everyone forget that the totality (no more than reality!) exposes its imposture.

1

Bureaucratic capitalism has found its legitimate justification in Marx. We are not concerned here with assessing the role of orthodox Marxism in reinforcing the structures of neo-capitalism, whose present reorganisation testifies to the greatest respect for Soviet totalitarianism. The point is to stress the extent to which Marx's most profound analyses of alienation have been vulgarised in the most commonplace facts, which robbed of their magic and embodied in every gesture, have become the sole substance, day after day, of the lives of a growing number of people. Bureaucratic capitalism contains the self-evident truth of alienation; it has brought it home to everybody far more successfully than Marx could ever have hoped to do. It has become commonplace as the disappearance of material poverty has merely revealed the mediocrity of existence itself. The extent of our impoverishment may have been reduced in terms of mere material survival, but it has become more profound in terms of our way of life – at least one widespread feeling that dissociates Marx from all the interpretations imposed by a degenerate Bolshevism. The 'theory' of peaceful coexistence has spelt it out to those who were still confused: gangsters can get on very well with one another, despite their spectacular divergences.

2

"Any act", writes Mircea Eliade, "can become a religious act. Human existence is realised simultaneously on two parallel planes, on that of temporality, of becoming, of illusion, and on that of eternity, of substance, of reality". During the nineteenth century, the brutal divorce of the two planes proved that power would have been more effective if reality had been maintained in a mist of divine transcendence. To give reformism its due, it has managed where Bonaparte failed, to dissolve, becoming in eternity and reality an illusion; the union may not be as satisfactory as the sacrament of marriage, but it *lasts*, and that's the most the managers of social peace and coexistence can ask of it. And it also leads us to define ourselves – caught in the illusory but inescapable perspective of duration – as the end of abstract temporality, as the end of the reified time of our acts. Does it have to be spelt out: to define ourselves at the positive pole of alienation as the end of mankind's term of social alienation?

3

The socialisation of primitive human groups reveals the will to struggle more effectively against the mysterious and terrifying forces of nature. But to struggle in the natural environment, at once against and with it, to submit to the most inhuman of its laws in order to seize an extra chance of survival – to do this could only engender a more evolved form of aggressive defence, a more complex and less primitive attitude, manifesting on a more evolved level the contradictions that the forces of nature, which could be influenced while they could not be controlled, never cease to impose. As it became social, the struggle against the blind domination of nature succeeded in the measure that it gradually assimilated primitive and natural alienation, but in another form. Alienation became social in the struggle against natural alienation. Is it by chance that a technical civilisation has developed to the point where social alienation has been revealed by its conflict with the last areas of natural resistance that technical power hadn't managed (and for good reasons) to destroy? Today, the technocrats propose to put an end to primitive alienation: overcome with brotherly love, they exhort us to perfect the technical means which 'in themselves' would enable us to conquer death, suffering, sickness and boredom. But the miracle wouldn't be to get rid of death, the miracle would be to get rid of suicide and the desire to be dead. There are ways of abolishing the death penalty which make one miss it. Until now, the specific application of technics to society, while reducing quantitatively the number of occasions of suffering and death, has allowed death itself to eat like a cancer into the heart of life.

4

The prehistoric period of food gathering was succeeded by the period of hunting during which the clans formed and struggled to ensure their survival. Hunting grounds and reserves were established and used for the benefit of the group as a whole. Strangers were banned absolutely as the welfare of the whole clan depended on the observation of its boundaries. So that the liberty won by settling more comfortably in the natural environment, by more effective protection against its hazards, itself engendered its own negation outside the frontiers laid down by the clan and forced the group to moderate its customary activities by organising its relations with excluded and menacing tribes. From the moment it appeared, economic survival on a social basis engendered boundaries, restrictions and conflicting rights. It should never be forgotten that until now both our own nature and the nature of history have been produced by the development of private appropriation: by a class, by a group, a caste or an individual seizing control of a collective power of socio-economic survival, whose form is always complex, from the ownership of land, of territory, of a factory, of capital, to the 'pure' exercise of power over men (hierarchy). Even beyond the struggle against regimes whose vision of paradise is the cybernetic welfare state, lies the necessity of a still vaster struggle against a fundamental and initially natural condition in the development of which capitalism plays only an episodic role, and which will only disappear with the last traces of hierarchical power; or else, of course, the '*marcassins de l'humanité*'.

5

To be a proprietor is to arrogate a good from whose enjoyment one excludes other people; at the same time it is to grant everyone the *potential* right of possession. By excluding them from the *de facto* right of ownership, the proprietor makes those he excludes themselves a part of his property (annexing the non-owners absolutely, annexing the other proprietors relatively): without whom, moreover, he is nothing. Those without property have no choice in the matter. The proprietor appropriates and alienates them as the producers of his own power, while the necessity of physical survival forces them despite themselves to collaborate in their own alienation, to produce it. They *survive* as those who cannot *live*. Excluded, they participate in possession through the mediation of the proprietor, a mystical participation since originally all clan and social relationships evolved on a mystical basis, slowly replacing the principle of involuntary cohesion in terms of which each member functions as part of the group as a whole ('organic interdependence'). Their activity within the structure of private appropriation guarantees their survival. They consolidate a right to property from which they are excluded and, owing to this ambiguity, each of them sees himself as participating in property, as a living fragment of the right to possess, although the development of any such belief can only reveal his own exclusion and possession. (Chronic cases of this alienation: the faithful slave, the cop, the bodyguard, the centurion, who through a sort of union with their own death confer on death a power equal to the forces of life, identifying in a destructive energy the negative and the positive poles of alienation, the absolutely obedient slave and the absolute master.) It is of vital importance to the exploiter that this appearance is maintained and made more sophisticated: not because he is especially Machiavellian, but simply because he wants to stay alive. The organisation of appearances is dependent on the survival of the proprietor, a survival dependent in its turn on the dispossessed, it creates the possibility of staying alive while one is exploited and excluded from human life. Thus, initially, privative appropriation and domination are imposed and experienced as a positive right, but in the form of a negative universality. Valid for everyone, justified in everyone's eyes by divine law or natural reason, the right of privative appropriation is objectified in general illusion, in a universal transcendence, in an essential law under which everyone, individually, manages to tolerate the limits assigned to his own right to live and to the conditions of life in general.

6

The function of alienation as *the condition of survival* should be understood in this social context. The labour of the dispossessed obeys the same contradictions as the right of privative appropriation. It transforms them into the possessed, into those who produce their own appropriation and are responsible for their own exclusion, but it is the only chance of survival for slaves, for serfs, for workers – so much so that the activity which allows existence to continue by emptying it of all content, finally, through a reversal of perspective that is both comprehensive and sinister, takes on a positive sense. Not only has work been valorised (in the form of sacrifice under the *ancien régime*, in its brutalising aspects in bourgeois ideology and in the so-called popular democracies), but moreover, from a very early stage, to work for a master, to alienate oneself with the best will in the world, became the honourable – and virtually indisputable – price of survival. The satisfaction of basic needs remains the best safeguard of alienation; it is best dissimulated on the grounds of its 'necessity'.

Alienation multiplies needs because it can satisfy none; today, lack of satisfaction is measured in numbers of cars, fridges, TVs: the alienating objects have lost the ruse and the mystery of transcendence, they are there in their concrete poverty. To be rich today is to possess the greatest *number* of impoverished objects.

So far, surviving has stopped us living. This is why the impossibility of survival is so important. That it is impossible can only become more and more obvious as comfort and over-abundance of the elements of survival reduce life to a single choice: suicide or revolution.

7

The sacred even presides over the struggle against alienation. As soon as the violence of the relationship between exploiter and exploited is no longer concealed by the panoply of mysticism, the struggle against alienation is suddenly revealed as a ruthless hand-to-hand fight with naked power, discovered in its brutal strength and its weakness, a vulnerable giant whose slightest wound confers on the aggressor the notoriety of an Erostratus. Since power survives, the event remains ambiguous. Destruction – sublime moment when the complexity of the world becomes tangible, transparent, within everyone's grasp, revolts for which there can be no expiation – those of the slaves, of the *Jacques*, of the iconoclasts, of the *Enragés*, of the *Fédérés*, of Kronstadt, of Asturias, and – a promise of things to come – the hooligans of Stockholm and the wildcat strikes... Only the destruction of all hierarchical power will allow us to forget these. We intend to make sure that it does.

The deterioration of mystic structures and their slowness to regenerate themselves have not only made possible the *prise de conscience* and the critical penetration of insurrection. They are also responsible for the fact that once the 'excesses' of revolution are past, the struggle against alienation is grasped on a theoretical plane, as an extension of the demystification preceding revolt. It is then that revolt in its purest and most authentic features is re-examined and disavowed by the 'we didn't really mean to do that' of theoreticians whose job it is to explain an insurrection to those who created it, to those who intend to demystify by acts, not just by words.

All acts opposing power today call for analysis and tactical development. Much can be expected of:

a The new proletariat, discovering its penury amidst abundant consumer goods (viz. the development of the working class struggles beginning in England; equally, the attitudes of rebel youth in all the highly-industrialised countries).

b Countries that have had enough of their partial and tricked-up revolutions and are consigning past and present theoreticians to the museum (viz. the role of the intelligentsia in the East).

c The underdeveloped nations, whose mistrust of technical myths has been kept alive by the cops and mercenaries of colonisation, the last and over-zealous militants of a transcendence against which they are the best possible vaccination.

d The vigour of the SI ("Our ideas are in everyone's mind"), capable of forestalling remote-controlled revolts, 'crystal nights' and sheepish resistance.

8

Privative appropriation is bound to the dialectic of particular and general. In the realm of the mystic, where the contradictions of slave and feudal systems dissolve, the dispossessed, excluded in particular from the right of possession, endeavours to assure his survival through his labour: the more he identifies with the interests of the master, the more successful he will be. He only knows the other dispossessed through their common predicament: the compulsory surrender of labour force (Christianity recommended voluntary surrender – once a slave offered his labour 'of his own accord' he was no longer a slave), the search for optimum conditions of survival and mystical identification. Struggle, though born of a universal will to survive, is engaged on the level of appearances where it brings into play identification with the desires of the master, and introduces a certain individual rivalry of the masters amongst themselves. Competition will develop on this plane for as long as a mystical opacity continues to envelop the structure of exploitation, and for as long as the conditions producing this confusion continue to exist; or, alternatively, for as long as the state of slavery determines consciousness of the state of reality. (By objective consciousness we still understand consciousness that is conscious of being an object.) The proprietor, for his part, is forced to acknowledge a right from which he alone is not excluded but which, however, is apprehended on the level of belief, and on it a strength which is essential if he is to hold his own amongst the other proprietors; it is his strength. If, in his turn, he seems to renounce the exclusive appropriation of everything and everybody, if he seems to be less a master than a servant – a servant of the public good, a defender of the faith – then his strength is crowned with glory and renown and to his other privileges he adds that of denying on the level of appearances – the only level of reference of unilateral communication – the very idea of personal appropriation. He denies that anyone has this right, he repudiates the other proprietors. In the feudal perspective, the proprietor is not integrated in appearances on the same level as the dispossessed, slaves, soldiers, functionaries, servants, etc. The lives of the latter are so squalid that the majority can only live as a caricature of the Master (the feudal, the prince, the major-domo, the taskmaster, the high priest, God, Satan...). Yet the master himself is also forced to play the part of a caricature. He can do so without especial effort: his imitation of total life is already caricatural, completely isolated as he is among those who can only survive. He is already one of our own kind, with the added grandeur of a past epoch, with its strength and its nostalgia. He too was waiting, just as we are waiting today, longing for the adventure where he could become one with himself, where he could find himself once more on the pathway to his total perdition. Could the master, at the moment he alienates the others, suddenly realise he was only an exploiter, a purely negative being. This is neither likely nor desirable. By ruling the greatest possible number of subjects, doesn't he allow them to stay alive? Doesn't he offer them their only hope? (Whatever would happen to the workers if someone didn't employ them? as Victorian 'thinkers' liked to ask.) In fact, what the proprietor does is to exclude himself officially from all claim to private appropriation. To the sacrifice of the dispossessed, who through his work exchanges his real life for an apparent one (for the life that stops him killing himself and allows the master to kill him instead), the proprietor replies by appearing to sacrifice his nature as proprietor and exploiter. He excludes himself mythically, he puts himself at the service of everyone and of myth (at the service, for example, of God and his people). With an additional gesture, with an act whose gratuity bathes him in an other-worldly radiance, he gives renunciation its pure form of mythical reality. Renouncing common life, he is the poor man amidst illusory wealth, he who sacrifices himself for everyone while other people only glory. The more powerful he is the more spectacular his sacrifice. He becomes the living reference point of the whole of illusory life, the highest point which can be reached in the scale of mythic values. Withdrawn 'voluntarily' from more common mortals, he is drawn towards the world of the gods and, on the level of appearances (the only general level of reference), it is faith in his participation in the divinity which consecrates his position in the hierarchy of the other proprietors. In the organisation of transcendence, the feudal – and, through osmosis, the proprietors of power or of production material, in varying degrees – is led to play the principal role, the role he really does play in the economic organisation of the survival of the group. So the existence of the group is bound on every level to the existence of the proprietors as such, to those who, owning everything since they own everybody, also force everyone to renounce their lives on the pretext of their own renunciation, absolute and divine. (From the god Prometheus, punished by the gods, to the god Christ, punished by men, the sacrifice of the proprietor becomes vulgarised, loses its sacred aura, is humanised.) Myth unites proprietor and dispossessed. It envelops them in a common form where the necessity of survival, as an animal or as a privileged being, forces them to live on the level of appearances and under the inverted sign of real life, which is that of everyday praxis. We are still there, waiting to live before or after a mystique against which our every gesture protests in its very submission.

9

Myth, the unitary absolute in which the contradictions of the world find an illusory resolution, the harmonious constantly-harmonised vision that reflects and strengthens order – this is the sphere of the sacred, the extra-human zone where, among so many other wonderful revelations, the revelation of private appropriation is not to be found. Nietzsche was very much to the point when he wrote: "All becoming is a criminal emancipation from eternal being, and its price is death." The bourgeoisie claimed to replace the pure Being of feudalism with Becoming, while in fact all it did was to deconsecrate Being and to reconsecrate Becoming to its own advantage. It elevated its own Becoming to the status of Being, no longer that of absolute property but that of relative appropriation: a petty democratic and mechanical Becoming, with its notion of progress, of merit and causal succession. The life of the proprietor hides him from himself. Bound to myth by a pact of life or death, he can only become conscious of his own positive and exclusive enjoyment of any good through the lived appearance of his own exclusion – and isn't it through this mythic exclusion that the dispossessed will discover the reality of their own exclusion? He accepts the responsibility of a group, he assumes the proportions of a god. He submits himself to its benediction and its punishment, he swathes himself in his austerity and wastes away. The master is the model of the gods and the heroes. The face of the proprietor is the true face of Prometheus and of Christ – the face of all those whose spectacular self-sacrifice has made it possible for 'the vast majority of men' to continue to sacrifice themselves to an extreme minority, to their masters. (Analysis of the proprietor's sacrifice should be worked out more subtly: isn't the case of Christ really the sacrifice of the proprietor's son? If the proprietor can only seem to sacrifice himself on the level of appearances, then Christ stands for the real immolation of his son when the circumstances leave no other alternative. As a son he is only a proprietor at an early stage of development, an embryo, little more than a dream of future property. In this mythic dimension belongs the celebrated remark of the journalist Barres, at the moment when the 1914 war had made his dreams come true at last: "Our youth, as is fitting, has gone to yield *our blood*.") This rather distasteful little game, before it took its place in the museum of rites and folklore, knew a heroic period when kings and tribal chieftains were ritually put to death according to their 'will'.

ASPIS-PRONIA
Greek Insurance Company Ltd

THE FIRST ASTROPOLICY
IN THE WORLD

SPECIAL SPACE RISKS

Article 2. Proceeds will be payable in the event of loss of life or disappearance in space and permanent total disability resulting from:

a Aggression by extra-terrestrial or human beings in space.

b Suicide or attempted suicide committed while of sound or unsound mind.

c War of any nature, waged on Earth or in space.

SPACE RISKS EXCLUDED

Article 3. No proceeds will be payable:

a In the event that the insured astronauts, under circumstances allowing them to survive in space, should deliberately and against the instructions of the National Aeronautics and Space Administration (NASA) refuse for any reason whatsoever to return to Earth.

b In the event of kidnapping of the insured astronauts by extra-terrestrial beings, and their detention alive, away from Earth, for a minimum period of three years.

c In the event of kidnapping of the insured astronauts by human beings, and their detention alive, either on Earth or away from Earth for a minimum period of three years.

Historians assure us that these august martyrs were soon replaced by prisoners, slaves and criminals. They may not get hurt any more, but they've kept the halo.

10

The concept of a common fate is based on the sacrifice of proprietor and dispossessed. In other words, the concept of the human condition is embodied by an ideal and tormented image whose function is to resolve the irresolvable opposition between the mythical sacrifice of a minority and the real sacrifice of everyone else. The function of myth is to unify and make immortal, in a succession of static instants, the dialectic of 'will-to-live' and its negation. This universally dominant factitious unity attains its most tangible and concrete representation in communication, particularly in language. Ambiguity is most obvious on this level, it reveals the absence of real communication, it leaves the analyst at the mercy of ridiculous phantoms, at the mercy of words – eternal and changing instants – whose content changes with the person who uses them, just as the notion of sacrifice does. When language is put to the test it can no longer dissimulate the basic misunderstanding and the crisis of participation becomes inevitable. The traces of total revolution can be followed through the language of a period, always menacing and never fulfilled. They are intoxicating and chill signs of the tumult they foreshadow, but who is prepared to take them seriously? The discredit of striking language is as deep-rooted and instinctive as suspicion towards myths – not that everyone doesn't remain as fond of them as ever. How can key words be defined by other words? What phrases can show the signs giving the lie to the phraseological organisation of appearances? The best texts still await their justification. Only when a poem by Mallarmé becomes the sole reason for an act of revolt will the relationship between poetry and revolution lose its ambiguity. To await and prepare for this moment is not to manipulate information as the last shock wave whose significance escapes everyone, but as the first repercussion of an act still to come.

11

Born of man's will to survive the uncontrollable forces of nature, myth is a policy of public welfare that has outlived its necessity. It has consolidated itself in its tyrannical strength, reducing life to the sole dimension of survival, denying it as movement and totality.

Attacked, myth will unify all that attacks it. It will engulf and assimilate it sooner or later. Nothing can withstand it, no image, no concept that attempts to destroy the dominant spiritual structures. It reigns over the expression of facts and lived experience, on which it imposes its interpretative structure (dramatisation). Private consciousness is the consciousness of lived experience that finds its expression on the level of organised appearances.

Myth is sustained by rewarded sacrifice. As every individual life is based on its own renunciation, lived experience must be defined as sacrifice and recompense. As a reward for his asceticism, the initiate (the promoted worker, the specialist, the manager – new martyrs canonised democratically) receives a niche carved in the organisation of appearances. He is made to feel at home in alienation. But collective shelters disappeared with unitary societies, and all that's left today is their concrete translation as a public service: temples, churches, palaces... memories of a universal protection. Shelters are private nowadays and even if their protection is far from certain, there can be no mistaking their price.

12

'Private' life is defined primarily in a formal context. Obviously it is created by the social relationships based on privative appropriation, but its essential form is created by the expression of these relationships. Universal, beyond opposition but always exposed, this form makes appropriation a right acknowledged universally from which everyone is excluded, *a right to which renunciation is the only access*. If it fails to break free of the context imprisoning it (a secession which is called revolution) the most authentic experience can only become conscious, can only be expressed and communicated by a movement of inverting the sign by which its fundamental contradiction is dissimulated. In other words, if any positive project fails to revitalise the praxis of radical overthrow of the conditions of life – conditions that, in their entirety, are those of privative appropriation – then it will not stand the slightest chance of escaping the negativity that reigns over the expression of social relationships. It will be recuperated in inverse perspective, like the image in a mirror. In the totalising perspective in which it conditions the whole of everybody's life, and in which its real and its mythic power can no longer be distinguished (both being real and both mythic) the movement of private appropriation has made negativity the only possible form of expression. Life in its entirety is suspended in a negativity that erodes it and defines it formally. To talk of life today is like talking of rope in the house of a hanged man. Since the key of will-to-live has been lost, we have wandered through the corridors of an endless mausoleum... Those who still accept their exhaustion, their squalor and stagnation, can imagine they just couldn't care about life as easily as they can fail to see a living denial of their despair in each of their everyday gestures, a denial which should make them despair only of the penury of their own imagination. These images, as though life had fallen into a trance, offer a field of possibilities with the conquering and the conquered animal at one pole and the saint and the pure hero at the other. The smell in this shithouse is really too much. The world and man as representation reek of carrion, and there's no longer any god around to turn the butchery into beds of lilies. After all the ages men have died having accepted without appreciable change the answers of the gods, of nature, of biology, it wouldn't be unreasonable to ask if we don't die because so much death comes, and for specific reasons, into every moment of our lives.

13

Privative appropriation can be defined essentially as the appropriation of things by means of the appropriation of people. It is the spring and the troubled water where all reflections mingle and blur. Its field of action and of influence, spanning the whole of history, seems to have been characterised until now by being based on a double determination of behaviour: by an ontology founded on self-negation and sacrifice (its subjective and objective aspects respectively) and by a fundamental duality, a division between particular and general, between individual and collective, between private and public, between theoretical and practical, between spiritual and material, between intellectual and manual, etc, etc. The contradiction between universal appropriation and universal expropriation postulates that the master has been seen for what he is and isolated. This mythic image of terror, impotence and renunciation occurs to slaves, to servants, to all those who cannot stand to go on living as they are. It is the illusory reflection of their participation in property, a natural illusion since they really do participate in it through the daily sacrifice of their energy (called pain or torture in antiquity, and labour or work today) since they themselves produce the property that excludes them. The master himself can only cling to the notion of work-as-sacrifice, like Christ to his cross and his nails; it is up to him to authenticate sacrifice, to appear to renounce his right of exclusive enjoyment and no longer to expropriate with a purely *human* violence (violence without mediation). The grandeur of the gesture obscures its initial violence, the nobility of sacrifice absolves the warrior, the brutality of the conqueror shines in the light of a transcendence whose reign is immanent, the gods are the intransigent guardians of law, the cantankerous shepherds of the meek and law-abiding flock of 'being and Wanting-to-be-Proprietor'.

The gamble of transcendence and the sacrifice entailed are the masters' greatest achievement, their most accomplished submission to the necessity of conquest. Anyone, be he brigand or tyrant, who intrigues for power unpurified by renunciation will sooner or later be tracked down and killed like a mad dog, or even worse – like someone who pursues no other ends than his own and whose conception of 'work' has been formed without giving a damn what anyone else may think. Tropmann, Landru, Petiot, balancing their budget without taking into account the defence of the free world, the state or human 'dignity', didn't stand a sporting chance. Freebooters, gangsters, outlaws, refusing to play by the rules of the game, disturb those whose conscience is at peace (whose consciousness is a reflection of myth) but the masters when they kill the criminal or enrol him as a cop re-establish the omnipotence of 'eternal truth': those who don't sell themselves lose their right to survive and those who do sell themselves lose their right to live. The sacrifice of the master is the matrix of humanism, and let it be understood once and for all that this makes humanism the grotesque negation of all that is human. Humanism is the master taken seriously at his own game, acclaimed by those who see his apparent sacrifice as a reason to hope for salvation and not just the caricatural reflection of their own real sacrifice. Justice, dignity, honour, liberty... these words that yap or squeal, are they any more than household pets whose masters have calmly awaited their homecoming since the time when heroic domestics fought for the right to walk them on the street? To use them is to forget that they are the ballast that allows power to rise, to rise out of reach. A future regime might well decide against promoting sacrifice in such universal forms and begin to track these words down and to wipe them out. If so, one could well foresee the left wing engaged in one more plaintive battle of words whose every phrase extols the 'sacrifice' of a previous master and calls for the equally mythical sacrifice of a new one (a left-wing master, a power mowing down workers in the name of the proletariat). Bound to the notion of sacrifice, humanism is born of the fear of both masters and slaves: it is the solidarity of a shit-scared humanity. But those who have rejected all hierarchical power can use any word as a weapon to beat out the rhythm of their action. Lautréamont and the illegalist anarchists were well aware of it; so were the dadaists.

Thus, the appropriator becomes a proprietor from the moment he puts ownership of people and of things in the hands of God, or of a universal transcendence, whose omnipotence streams down on him as a grave sanctifying his slightest gesture. To oppose the proprietor thus consecrated is to oppose God, Nature, the nation, the people. In short, to exclude oneself from the world in its entirety. "There can be no question of governing and even less of being governed", writes Marcel Havrenne so prettily. For those who add violence to his humour, there can no longer be either salvation or damnation. There can be no position in the universal comprehension of things, either with Satan, the great recuperator of the faithful, nor in any form of myth since they are the living proof of its redundance. They were born for a life yet to be invented; insofar as they lived, it was on this hope that they finally came to grief.

Two corollaries of the singularisation of transcendence:

a If ontology implies transcendence, any ontology justifies *a priori* the being of the master and of hierarchical power wherein the master is reflected in degraded, more or less faithful images.
b Upon the distinction between manual and intellectual work, between practice and theory, is superimposed the distinction between work-as-real-sacrifice

and its organisation in the form of apparent sacrifice.

It is tempting to explain fascism – amongst other reasons – as an act of faith, and *auto-da-fé* of a bourgeoisie haunted by the murder of God and the destruction of the great, sacred spectacle, vowing itself to the Devil, to an inverted mysticism, a black mysticism with its rituals and holocausts. Mysticism and high finance.

It should never be forgotten that hierarchical power cannot exist without transcendence, ideologies and myths. Demystification itself could be turned into a myth: it would be sufficient to 'omit', most philosophically, *active* demystification. After which, all demystification, separated hygenically into little pieces, becomes painless, euthanatic, in a word, humanitarian. Were it not for the movement of demystification which will end by demystifying the demystifiers.

14

When the bourgeois revolutionaries attacked the mythical organisation of appearances, they attacked, quite despite themselves, not only the key points of unitary power, but the key points of any hierarchical power whatsoever. Can this inevitable mistake explain the guilt-complex so typical of bourgeois mentality? The mistake was undoubtedly inevitable.

In the first place a mistake because once the cloud of lies dissimulating private appropriation was pierced, myth itself disintegrated and a vacuum was revealed which could only be filled by poetry and delirious liberty. Certainly, orgiastic poetry to date has not destroyed power. Its failure is easy to explain and its ambiguous signs reveal the blows struck at the same time as they heal the wounds. Historians and aesthetes can keep their collections: one has only to pick at the scab of memory and the cries, words and gestures of the past make the whole body of power start to bleed freshly once more. The whole organisation of the survival of memories will not stop them being forgotten as soon as they come to life again and begin to dissolve in experience. The same applies to our survival in the construction of our everyday lives.

An inevitable process: as Marx showed, the appearance of exchange value and its symbolic substitution by money split open a radical crisis latent in the heart of the unitary world. Commodities introduced a universal character into human relationships (a dollar bill represents all I can buy with this sum) and an egalitarian character (equal things are exchanged). This 'egalitarian universality' partly escapes both the exploiter and the exploited while both accept it as a common measure. They discover themselves face-to-face, no longer confronted in the mystery of divine birth and ascendance, as the nobility once was, but in an intelligible transcendence, that of Logos, a body of laws that *can be understood by everybody*, even if any such understanding remains cloaked in mystery. A mystery with its initiates, first of all priests, struggling to maintain the Logos in the limbo of divine mysticism, soon yielding to philosophers then to technicians both their position and the dignity of their sacred mission. From Plato's *Republic* to the cybernetic state.

Thus, under the pressure of exchange value and technology (which could be called the 'do-it-yourself-mediation-kit'), myth was gradually secularised. However, two facts are to be noted:

a As the Logos frees itself from mystic unity it affirms itself at once in and against it. Upon magical and analogical structures of behaviour are superimposed rational and logical structures that negate while conserving them (mathematics, poetics, economics, aesthetics, psychology, etc).

b Each time the Logos or the 'organisation of intelligible appearances' becomes more independent, it tends to break away from the sacred and to become fragmented. As such it presents a double danger to unitary power. We have already seen that the sacred expresses the seizure of the totality by power, and that anyone wanting to accede to the totality must do so through the mediation of power: the interdict striking mystics, alchemists, gnostics is sufficient proof. This also explains why power today 'protects' specialists, in whom it can sense – but without really trusting them – the missionaries of a reconsecrated Logos. There are historic signs that testify to the attempts made within mystic unitary power to found a rival power asserting its unity in the name of Logos: amongst which, Christian syncretism, the psychological explanation of God, the Renaissance, the Reformation and the *Aufklarung*.

The masters who tried to retain the unity of the Logos were well aware that only unity can stabilise power. Examined closely, their efforts have not been as vain as the fragmentation of the Logos in the nineteenth and twentieth centuries would seem to prove. In the general movement of atomisation, the Logos has been broken down into specialised techniques (physics, biology, sociology, paprology, etc, etc) but at the same time the need to re-establish the totality has become more and more imperative. It should never be forgotten that an all-powerful technocratic power could not begin to plan the totality: the Logos would succeed myth as the seizure of the totality by a future unitary (cybernetic) power. In this perspective, the vision of the *Encyclopaedistes* (strictly rationalised progress stretching into the indefinite future) would only have known a period of indecision lasting two centuries before its realisation. This is the direction in which the Stalino-cyberneticians are preparing the future. In this perspective, peaceful co-existence should be seen as the basis of totalitarian unity. Everyone must realise that they have already rebelled.

15

We know the battlefield. The problem now is preparing for battle. Otherwise the pataphysician, armed with his totality without a technique, and the cybernetician, armed with his technique without a totality, will consummate their political coitus. And they will be duly blessed.

From the point of view of hierarchical power, myth could only be deconsecrated if the Logos was reconsecrated, or if at least its deconsecrating elements were reconsecrated. To attack the sacred was at the same time to liberate the totality, thus to destroy power. But the power of the bourgeoisie, broken, impoverished, constantly harassed, maintains a relative stability by its use of this ambiguity: technology, which deconsecrates objectively, appears subjectively as an instrument of liberation. Not a real liberation, which could only be won by deconsecration – that is to say, by the end of the spectacle – but a caricature, an ersatz, an induced hallucination. What the unitary vision of the world transferred to the beyond (the image of elevation), fragmentary power inscribes in a future state of increased well-being (the image of the project), of

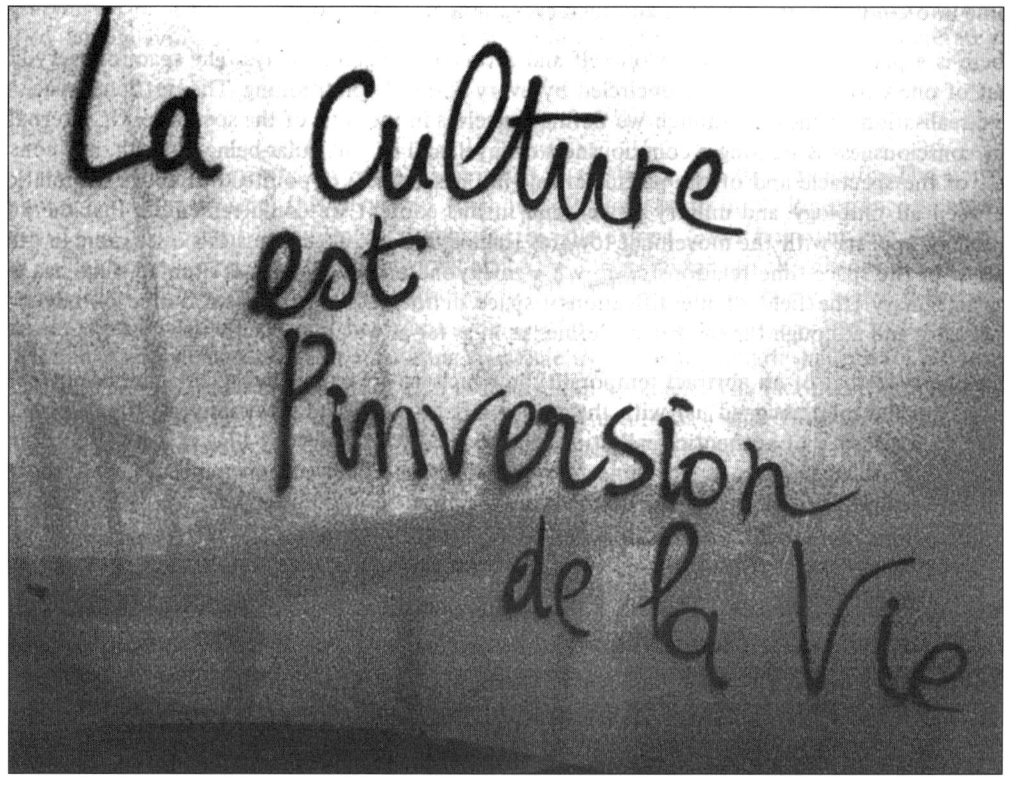

tomorrows-that-will-be-another day, but which will really be no more than today multiplied by the number of gadgets to be produced. From the slogan 'Live in God' we have gone on to the humanistic motto 'Survive as long as you can', which means 'Stay young at heart and you'll live a long time'.

Myth, deconsecrated and fragmented, loses its grandeur and its spirituality. It becomes an impoverished form, retaining former characteristics but revealing them as something concrete, brutal and tangible. God doesn't run the show any more and until the day of the Logos taking over, armed with technology and science, the spectres of alienation will materialise everywhere, sowing disorder in their path. Pay attention to them: they are the first manifestations of a future order. We must start to *play* from this moment if the future is not to be ruled by the principle of survival, or if even survival itself is not to become impossible (the hypothesis of humanity destroying itself). And with it, obviously, the whole experiment of constructing everyday life. The vital objectives of struggle for the construction of everyday life are the key points of all hierarchical power. To construct one is to destroy the other. Caught in the vortex of deconsecration and reconsecration, essentially we stand for the negation of the following elements: the organisation of appearances as a *spectacle* where everyone denies themselves; the *separation* on which private life is based since it is there that the objective separation between proprietors and dispossessed is lived and reflected on every level; and *sacrifice*. The three are obviously interdependent, just as their opposites – participation, communication, realisation. The same applies to their context – non-totality (a bankrupt world, a controlled totality) and totality.

16

The human relationships previously dissolved in divine transcendence (in the totality crowned by the sacred) decanted and became solid as soon as the sacred stopped acting as a catalyst. Their materiality was revealed and, as the capricious laws of economy succeeded those of providence, the power of men began to appear behind the power of the gods. Today, endless roles correspond to the mythical role everyone once played under the divine spotlights. Though their masks are human faces, they still force both actor and extra to deny their real life, to fulfil the dialectic of real and mythical sacrifice. The spectacle is nothing but deconsecrated and fragmented myth. It forms the armour of a power (which could also be called essential mediation) that is exposed *to every blow* once it no longer succeeds in dissimulating in the cacophony where all cries drown one another out and become harmonious, the nature of privative appropriation. And just how much shit it heaps on everyone.

Roles have become impoverished in the context of a fragmentary power eaten away by deconsecration just as the spectacle betrays its impoverishment in comparison with myth. They betray its mechanisms and its artifice so clumsily that power, to defend itself against popular denunciation of the spectacle, has no alternative but to denounce it first itself. Even more clumsily, it changes actors and ministers, it organises pogroms of putative or prefabricated producers of the spectacle (agents of Moscow, Wall Street, the judeocracy or *les deux cent familles*). Which is to say that the whole cast has been forced to become hams, that style has been replaced by manner.

Myth, as an immobile totality, encompassed all movement (the pilgrimage, for example, as fulfilment and adventure within immobility). On the one hand, the spectacle can only conceive the totality by reducing it to a fragment inserted in a series of fragments (psychological, sociological, biological, philological, mythological visions of the world), while, on the other hand, it is situated at the point where the movement of deconsecration converges with the attempt to reconsecrate. Thus it can only succeed in imposing immobility within the movement of reality, the movement changing it despite its resistance. In the era of fragmentation, the organisation of appearances makes movement a linear succession of immobile instants (this progress from notch to notch is perfectly exemplified by Stalin's 'diamet'). Under what we have called 'the colonisation of everyday life', the only possible change is a change of fragmentary roles. In terms of more or less inflexible conventions one is successively citizen, father, sexual partner, politician, specialist, businessman, producer, consumer. Yet what supervisor doesn't feel watched himself? You may get a fuck, but you'll always get fucked. The proverb is universal.

The epoch of fragmentation has at least eliminated all doubt on one point: everyday life is the battlefield where the battle between totality and power takes place, power using all its strength to control it.

What do we demand in pitting the power of everyday life against hierarchical power? We demand *everything*. We have taken our place in the general conflict stretching from domestic squabbles to revolutionary war and we have gambled on the will to live. This means we must survive as anti-survivors. Fundamentally, we are only concerned with the moments when life shatters the glaciation of survival (whether these moments are unconscious or theorised, historic – like the revolution – or personal). But we must also realise we are *also* prevented from following the course of these moments freely (apart from the moment of revolution itself) not only by the general repression exercised by power, but also by the exigencies of our own struggle, of our tactics, etc. It is equally important to find the means of balancing this additional 'percentage of error' by widening the scope of these moments and by showing their qualitative importance. Our remarks on the construction of everyday life cannot be recuperated by cultural or sub-cultural establishments (*New Left Review*, etc – thinkers with three weeks' paid holiday), for the very good reason that all situationist ideas are no more than the development of acts attempted constantly by countless people to try and prevent another day being no more than twenty-four hours of wasted time. Are we an avant-garde? If we are, to be avant-garde means to keep abreast of reality.

17

It's not the monopoly of intelligence we hold but that of its use. Our position is strategic, we are at the heart of every possible conflict. The qualitative is our *force-de-frappe*. People who half understand this review ask us for an explanatory monograph thanks to which they will be able to convince themselves they are intelligent and cultured – that is to say, idiots. Someone who gets fed up and chucks it in the gutter has more sense. Sooner or later it will have to be understood that the words and phrases we use are still outdated by reality. The distortion and clumsiness of the way we express ourselves (that someone with taste called, not inaccurately, "a somewhat irritating kind of hermetic terrorism") comes from our central position on the ill-defined and shifting frontier where language sequestrated by power (conditioning) and free language (poetry) fight out their complex war. To those who can't keep up with us we prefer those who reject us impatiently because our language isn't yet authentic poetry – the free construction of everyday life.

Everything related to thought is related to the spectacle. Almost everyone lives in a state of terror at the possibility they might awake to themselves, and their fear is carefully kept alive by power. Conditioning, the poetry of power, has subjected so much to its control (all material equipment belongs to it: the press, television, stereotypes, magic, tradition, economy, technics – what we call sequestered language) that it has almost succeeded in dissolving what Marx called the non-dominated sector of nature to replace it by another (viz. our identikit picture of 'the survivor'). Lived experience, however, cannot be reduced to a series of empty configurations with such facility. Resistance to the exterior organisation of life, to the organisation of life as survival, contains more poetry than any volume of verse or prose, and the poet, in the literary sense of the word, is the person who has sensed or understood that this is so. But the life of any such poetry hangs on a thread. Certainly, as the situationists understand it, it is irreducible and cannot be recuperated by power (as soon as an act is recuperated it becomes a stereotype, conditioning, the language of power). However, it is encircled by power. It is by isolation that power encircles the irreducible and pins it down; yet complete isolation is not feasible. The pincer movement has two claws: first the threat of disintegration (insanity, illness, destitution, suicide) and secondly, remote-controlled therapeutics; the first granting death, the second no more than survival (empty communication, the cohesion of friends or families, psychoanalysis prostituted to alienation, medicare etc). Sooner or later the SI must define itself as a therapy: we are ready to defend the poetry created by everyone against the false poetry manipulated solely by power (conditioning). Doctors and psychoanalysts had better get it straight too unless they are prepared, one fine day, to take the consequences for what they have done along with architects and other apostles for survival.

18

All antagonisms that have not been resolved, integrated and superseded are losing their significance. These antagonisms can only evolve while they remain imprisoned in previous forms that have not been superseded (anti-cultural art in the cultural spectacle, for example). Any radical opposition that has either failed or been partially successful – which comes down to the same thing – wastes away gradually into reformistic opposition. Fragmentary opposition is like the teeth on a cogwheel – they marry another and make the wheel go round, the machine of the spectacle, the machine of power.

Myth held all antagonisms in the archetype of Manicheanism. But what can function as an archetype in a fragmented society? In fact, the memory of previous antagonisms, utilised in a patently devalued and non-aggressive form, appears today as the last attempt to bring some coherence to the organisation of appearances, so great is the extent to which the spectacle has become a spectacle of undifferentiated confusion. We are ready to wipe out all trace of these memories, harnessing all the energy contained in previous antagonisms for a radical conflict yet to come. A river will burst from all the springs blocked up by power; a river which will change the face of the world.

A travesty of antagonism, power insists that everyone be for or against the Rolling Stones, *le nouveau roman*, the obscenity laws, Chinese food, LSD, short skirts, the United Nations, pop art, nationalisation, thermonuclear war and hitch-hiking. Everyone is asked their opinion of every detail to stop them having one of the totality. The manoeuvre, however inept, might have worked were the commercial salesmen involved not waking up to their own alienation. To the passivity imposed on the dispossessed masses is added the growing passivity of directors and actors submitted to the abstract laws of the market and the spectacle, exercising a less and less effective power over the world. Already, signs of revolt are breaking out among the actors; stars who try and escape publicity, or rulers who criticise their own power; Brigitte Bardot or Fidel Castro. The tools of power wear out. Their desire for their own freedom, as instruments, should be calculated on.

19

The spectacular reformism of Christianity appeared at the moment when the slave revolt threatened to overthrow the structure of power and to reveal the relationship between transcendence and the mechanism of privative appropriation. Its central democratic demand was not that slaves accede to the reality of a human life – impossible without denouncing appropriation as a movement of exclusion – but, on the contrary, to an existence whose source of happiness is mythical (the imitation of Christ as the price of the hereafter). What has changed? Waiting for the hereafter has become waiting for the tomorrow-that-will-be-another-day; the sacrifice of real and immediate life is the price at which the illusory liberty of an apparent life is bought. The spectacle is the sphere where forced labour is transformed into voluntary sacrifice. There is nothing more suspect than the formula 'to everyone according to his work' in a world where work is the blackmail of survival; to say nothing of the formula 'to each according to his needs' in a world where needs are determined by power. Any construction attempting to define itself in an autonomous, and therefore partial, way can be relegated to reformism. It is unaware of its real definition by the negativity in which everything is suspended. It tries to build on quicksand as though it were rock. Contempt and misunderstanding of the context fixed by hierarchical power can only end by strengthening this context. On the other hand, the spontaneous acts we can see forming everywhere against the power and its spectacle must be warned of all the obstacles in their path and must find tactics corresponding to the strength of the enemy and to its means of recuperation. These tactics, which we are about to popularise, are those of diversion.

20

Sacrifice must be rewarded. In exchange for their real sacrifice, the workers receive the instruments of their liberation (comfort, gadgets) which, however, are a purely fictitious liberation since power controls the ways in which all material equipment can be used, since power utilises to its own ends both the instruments and those who use them. The Christians and bourgeois revolutions democratised mythical sacrifice or the 'sacrifice of the master'. Today, there are countless initiates who receive the crumbs of power for having put to public service the totality of their partial knowledge. They are no longer called 'initiates' and not yet 'priests of the Logos': they are just known as specialists.

On the level of the spectacle their power is incontestable: the candidate on 'Double your money' or the post office clerk, itemising the mechanical subtleties of his Anglia, both identify with the specialist, and we know how production managers can use these identifications to bring skilled labourers to heel. Essentially, the true mission of the technocrats would be to unify the Logos, if only – through one of the contradictions of fragmentary power – they weren't all so pathetically isolated. Alienated realisation escapes them. What real control can the atomic technician, the strategist or the political specialist exercise over nuclear weapons? What absolute control can power hope to impose on all the gestures forming against it? The stage is so crowded that only chaos reigns as master. "Order reigns and doesn't govern" (Editorial notes, IS no. 6).

Insofar as the specialist takes part in the construction of the instruments that condition and transform the world, he initiates the *revolt of the privileged*. Previously, any such revolt has been called fascism. It is essentially an operatic revolt – didn't Nietzsche see Wagner as a precursor? – when actors who for a long time have been pushed to the side suddenly demand to hold the leading roles. Clinically speaking, fascism is the hysteria of the spectacular world as it reaches a paroxysm. In this paroxysm the spectacle momentarily assures its unity and at the same time it reveals its radical inhumanity. Through fascism and Stalinism, its romantic crisis, the spectacle betrays its true nature: it is a disease.

We are poisoned by the spectacle. All the elements necessary for a cure (that is, for the construction of our everyday lives) are in the hands of specialists. Thus, from one point of view or another, we are highly interested in all of them. Some are chronic cases: we don't intend, for example, to try and show the specialists of power, the rulers, just how far their delirium has carried them. On the other hand, we are ready to take account of the rancour of specialists imprisoned by roles that are constricted, grotesque or infamous. We must confess, however, that our indulgence has its limits. If, despite all we do, they continue stubbornly to put their guilty conscience and their bitterness at the service of power, to fabricate the conditioning that colonises their own everyday lives; if they continue to prefer an illusory representation in the hierarchy to the reality of realisation; if they continue to brandish their specialisation (their painting, their novels, their equations, their sociometry, their ballistics); finally, if they know perfectly well – and very soon *it won't be possible to ignore it* – that only the SI and power hold the key to their specialisation, if then they still choose to serve power because power, battening on their inertia, has so far selected them for its service, then *fuck them!* No-one could be more generous. Above all, they should understand that henceforth the revolt of non-ruling actors is a part of the revolt against the spectacle.

The general abhorrence excited by the lumpenproletariat comes from the use to which it is put by the bourgeoisie. It served both as a means to regulate power and as a source of recruits for the more equivocal forces of law and order: cops, informers, hired guns, artists… Despite which, its implicit critique of *the society of work* is remarkably radical. Its open contempt for both employers and employees contains a valid critique of work as alienation, a critique that hasn't been taken seriously until now both because the lumpenproletariat was essentially the sector of all that was ambiguous in society, and also because during the nineteenth and the beginning of the twentieth centuries the struggle against natural alienation and the production of well-being still seemed to be valid pretexts for work.

Once the abundance of consumer goods is known to be no more than the other side of an alienated production, the lumpenproletariat acquires a new dimension. It liberates a contempt for organised work that, in the age of the welfare state, is gradually taking the proportions of a demand that only the ruling classes still refuse to acknowledge. Despite the constant attempts of power to recuperate it, every experiment affected on everyday life, that is, every attempt to construct it – an illegal activity since the destruction of feudal power, where it was restricted and reserved for a minority – becomes concrete today through its critique of alienating work and its refusal to submit to forced labour. So much so that the new proletariat tends to be defined negatively as a 'front against forced labour', bringing together all those who resist their annexation by power. This is our field of action. It is here that we gamble on the ruse of history against the ruse of power. It is here that we back the worker, be he steelworker or artist, who – consciously or not – rejects organised work and life, against the worker who – consciously or not – accepts work at the orders of power. In this perspective it is not unreasonable to foresee a transitional period during which automation and the will of the new proletariat leave work solely to the specialists, reducing managers and bureaucrats to the rank of temporary slaves. In the context of complete automation, the 'workers', instead of supervising machines, would be free to humour cybernetic specialists whose sole task was to increase production – a production that had been radically transformed, a production serving life and not survival.

22

Unitary power endeavoured to dissolve the individual existence in a collective consciousness, so that each social unity defined itself subjectively as a particle with a clearly-determined weight suspended as though in oil. Everyone had to feel blinded by the evidence that the hand of God, shaking the recipient, used everything for designs of his own which transcended the understanding of each particular human being, and appeared as the emanations of a supreme will bestowing sense on the slightest change. (In any case, all perturbation was an ascending or descending movement towards harmony – the Four Reigns, the Wheel of Fortune, the trials sent by the gods.) One can speak of a collective consciousness in the sense that it was simultaneously for each individual and for everyone: consciousness of myth and consciousness of a particular-existence-within-myth. The power of the illusion is such that authentic life draws its significance from what it is not; from this stems the clerical condemnation of life, reduced to pure contingence, to squalid materiality, to vain appearances and to the lowest level of transcendence becoming increasingly debased to the extent that it escapes mythic organisation.

God was the guarantor of space and time, whose co-ordinates defined unitary society. He was the common reference-point for all men; space and time came together in him as in him all beings become one with their destiny. In the era of fragmentation, man is torn apart between a space and a time that no transcendence can unify through the mediation of a centralised power. We live in a space and time that are out of joint, deprived of all reference point and all co-ordinates, as though we were never to come into contact with ourselves, although everything invites us to.

There is a place where one makes oneself and a time in which one plays. The space of everyday life, that of one's true realisation, is encircled by every form of conditioning. The restricted space of our true realisation defines us, though we define ourselves in the time of the spectacle. Or, alternatively: our consciousness is no longer consciousness of myth and of particular-*being*-in-myth, it is consciousness of the spectacle and of the particular-*role*-in-the-spectacle. (I pointed out above the relationship between all ontology and unitary power, and in this context we could remember that the crisis of ontology appears with the movement towards fragmentation.) To express this once more in different terms: in the space-time relationship in which everyone and everything is situated, time has become the imaginary (the field of identifications); space defines us, although we defined ourselves in the imaginary and although the imaginary defines us insofar as we are subjectivities.

Our liberty is that of an abstract temporality in which we are *named* in the language of power (these names are the roles assigned us) with the choice left to us of finding *synonyms* officially registered as such. The space of authentic realisation (the space of our everyday life) is, on the contrary, the kingdom of silence. There is no name to name the space of lived experience, if not in poetry, in language struggling to be free of the domination of power.

23

When the bourgeoisie deconsecrated and fragmented myth, its primary demand was for independence of consciousness (demands for freedom of thought, freedom of the press, freedom of research and refusal of dogma). So consciousness stopped being more or less consciousness-reflecting-myth. It became consciousness of successive roles played in the spectacle.

Above all, what the bourgeoisie demanded was the freedom of actors and extras in a spectacle no longer organised by God, by his cops and his priests, but by natural and economic laws, 'inexorable and capricious laws': cops and specialists on the payroll once again.

God has been torn aside like a useless bandage and the wound has stayed raw. The bandage may have stopped the wound healing up, but it justifies suffering, it gave it a sense well worth a few shots of heroin. Now, suffering has no justification whatsoever and heroin is far from cheap. Separation has become concrete. Anyone at all can put their finger on it and the only answer cybernetic society can offer us is to become spectators of putrescence and decay, spectators of survival.

Hegel's drama of consciousness is more exactly consciousness of drama. Romanticism echoes like the cry of the soul torn from the body, a suffering made even more intolerable because we all find ourselves alone to face the collapse of the sacred totality, and of all the Houses of Usher.

24

The totality is objective reality in the movement of which subjectivity can only participate as realisation. Anything apart from the realisation of everyday life belongs to the spectacle where survival is frozen (hibernation) and served out in slices. There can be no authentic realisation except in objective reality, in the totality. All the rest is caricature. The objective realisation that functions in the mechanism of the spectacle is nothing but the success of power-manipulated objects (the 'objective realisation in subjectivity' of famous artists, of film stars, of the celebrities of *Who's Who*). On the level of the organisation of appearances, every success – and even every failure – is inflated until it becomes a stereotype, and is broadcast by the information media as though it were the only possible success or failure. So far, power has been the only judge, though pressure has been brought to bear on its judgement. Its criteria alone are valid for those who accept the spectacle and are satisfied with playing a role within it. And there are no more artists on that scene, there are only extras.

25

The space and time of private life were harmonised in the space and time of myth. The universal harmony of Fourier answers this perverted harmony. As soon as myth no longer encompasses the individual and the partial in a totality dominated by the sacred, each fragment erects itself as a totality. The fragment erected as a totality is, in fact, the *totalitarian*. In the dissociated space and time that makes private life, time – made absolute in the form of abstract liberty, which is that of the spectacle – consolidates by its very dissociation the spatial absolute of everyday life, its isolation and constriction. The mechanism of the alienating spectacle exerts such strength that private life reaches the point of being defined as something that is deprived of spectacle. The fact that it escapes spectacular roles and categories is experienced as an additional privation, as a sense of sickness which power uses as a pretext to reduce everyday life to insignificant gestures (to smoke a joint, read a book or make a cup of tea).

26

The spectacle that imposes its norms on lived experience itself stems from lived experience. The time of the spectacle, lived in the form of successive roles, makes the space of authentic experience the area of objective impotence while, at the same time, objective impotence – resulting from the conditioning of privative appropriation – makes the spectacle the absolute of virtual liberty.

Elements born of lived experience are only acknowledged on the level of the spectacle where they are expressed in the form of stereotypes, although any such expression is constantly opposed in lived experience and denied by authentic lived experience. *The identikit picture of the survivors* – to whom Nietzsche refers as the 'little people' or the 'last men' – can only be conceived in terms of the following dialectic of possibility/impossibility:

a The possible on the level of the spectacle (variety of abstract roles) reinforces the impossible on the level of authentic experience.
b The impossible (that is, the limits imposed on real experience by privative appropriation) determines the field of abstract possibilities.

Survival has two dimensions. As against this reduction, what forces can focus attention on the everyday problem of all human beings: the dialectic of survival and of life? Either the specific forces on which the SI has gambled will allow these contraries to be superseded, reuniting space and time in the construction of everyday life; or life and survival will become locked in their antagonism, growing weaker and weaker until the point of ultimate confusion and ultimate poverty is reached.

27

Lived experience is shattered and labelled spectacularly in categories, biological, sociological, etc, which, while being related to the communicable, never communicate more than facts emptied of their authentically experienced content. Thus it is that hierarchical power, imprisoning everyone in the objective mechanism of privative appropriation (admission-exclusion, viz. section 3) also dictates the nature of subjectivity. Insofar as it does so it forces, with a varying degree of success, each individual subjectivity to objectify himself – that is to say, to become an object it can manipulate. This forms an extremely interesting dialectic which should be analysed in greater detail (cf. the objective realisation in subjectivity – that of power – and the objective realisation in objectivity – which comes into the praxis of constructing everyday life and of destroying power).

Facts are deprived of content in the name of the communicable, in the name of an abstract universality, in the name of a perverted harmony in which everyone realises themselves in an inverted perspective. In this context, the SI belongs to the tradition of dissent which encompasses de Sade, Fourier, Lewis Carroll, Lautréamont, Surrealism and Lettrisme – at least in its less well-known forms, which are also the most radical.

Within a fragment erected as a totality, each further fragment is itself totalitarian. Sensibility, desire, will, taste, the subconscious and all the categories of the ego were treated as absolutes by individualism. Today, sociology is enriching the categories of psychology, but the introduction of variety into the roles merely emphasises the monotony of the reflect of identification. The liberty of 'the survivor' will be to assume the abstract constituent to which he has 'chosen' to reduce himself. Once there is no question of true realisation, only a psycho-sociological dramaturgy is left, in which subjectivity functions as an overflow to get rid of the effects one has worn for the daily exhibition. Survival becomes the final stage of life organised as the mechanical reproduction of memory.

28

Until now, the approach to the totality has been falsified. Power has been inserted parasitically as an indispensable mediation between men and nature. But the relationship between men and nature is founded only by praxis. It is praxis that is always breaking the veneer of lies that myth and its substitutes try to substantiate. It is praxis, even alienated praxis, that maintains contact with the totality. By revealing its fragmentary character, praxis reveals at the same time the real totality (reality): it is the totality being realised through its opposite, the fragment.

In the perspective of praxis, every fragment is the totality. In the perspective of power, which alienates praxis, every fragment is totalitarian. This should be enough to wreck the attempts cybernetic power will make to envelope praxis in a mystique, although the seriousness of these attempts should not be underestimated.

All praxis belongs to our project. It enters with its share of alienation, with the dross of power: however we can purify it. We will clarify the manoeuvres of subjection and the strength and purity of the acts of refusal. We will use our strategy, not in a Manichean vision but as a means of developing this conflict in which, everywhere at the moment, adversaries are seeking one another and only clashing accidentally, lost in irremediable darkness and confusion.

29

Everyday life has always been emptied to substantiate apparent life, but appearances, in their mythical cohesion, were powerful enough to ensure that no-one ever became conscious of everyday life. The poverty and emptiness of the spectacle betrayed by every type of capitalism, by every type of bourgeoisie, has revealed the existence of everyday life (a shelter life, but a shelter for what and from what?) and simultaneously its poverty. As reification and bureaucratisation eat deeper and deeper into life, the exhaustion of the spectacle and of everyday life become increasingly evident to everyone. The conflict between the human and the inhuman has also been transferred to the plane of appearances. As soon as Marxism became an ideology, Marx's struggle against ideology in the name of the richness of life was transformed into an ideological anti-ideology, a spectacle of the anti-spectacle (just as, within the avant-garde, the fate of the anti-spectacular spectacle is its restriction to the actors, anti-artistic art being created and understood only by artists; the relationship between this anti-ideological ideology and the function of the professional revolutionary in Leninism should be studied). Thus, Manicheanism was resuscitated for a time. Why did St Augustine attack the Manicheans with such acerbity? Because he knew the danger of a myth offering only one solution, the victory of the good over the evil; he knew that this impossibility threatened to wreck the whole structure of myth and to focus attention of the contradiction between mythic and authentic life. Christianity offers the third way, the way of sacred confusion. What Christianity accomplished by the strength of myth is accomplished today by the strength of *things*. There isn't any longer the slightest antagonism between Soviet workers and capitalist workers, or between the bomb of the Stalinist bureaucrats and the bomb of the non-Stalinist bureaucrats: there is only unity in the chaos of reified beings.

Who is responsible? Who should be shot? We are dominated by a system, by an abstract form. Degrees of humanity and inhumanity are measured by purely quantitative variations of passivity. The quality is the same everywhere. We are all proletarianised, or well on the way to being so. What are the traditional 'revolutionaries' doing? They are eliminating certain distinctions, they are making sure that no proletarians are any more proletarian than everyone else. But what party wants to end the proletariat? The perspective of survival has become intolerable. What we are suffering from is *the weight of things in a vacuum*. That's what reification is: everyone and everything falling at an equal speed, everyone and everything stigmatised with their equal value. The rein of equal values has realised the Christian project, but it has realised it without Christianity (as Pascal understood it) and, above all, it has realised it over God's dead body, contrary to Pascal's expectations.

The spectacle and everyday life coexist in

the reign of equal values. People and things are interchangeable. The world of reification is a world without a centre, like the new towns are its décor. The present withdraws before the promise of a perpetual future that is no more than a mechanical extension of the past. Time itself is deprived of a centre. In this concentration camp universe, victims and torturers wear the same mask and only the torture is real. No fresh ideology will be able to soothe the pain, neither that of the totality (the Logos), nor that of nihilism, which will be the crutches of the cybernetic state. They condemn all hierarchical power whatever its organisation and dissimulation. The antagonism the SI is about to renew is the oldest of all: it is radical antagonism and that is why it can assimilate all that has been left by the great individuals and insurrectionary movements of the past.

30

So many other banalities could be examined and reversed. The best things never come to an end. Before rereading the above – even the most mediocre intelligence will understand by the third attempt – it would be wise to concentrate very carefully on the following text for these notes, as fragmentary as the preceding, must be discussed in detail. The central point is the question of the SI and revolutionary power.

The SI, being aware of the crisis of both mass parties and of 'élites', must embody the supersession of both the Bolshevik central committee (supersession of the mass party) and of the Nietzschean project (supersession of the intelligentsia).

a Whenever any power has set itself up to direct revolutionary will, it has *a priori* undermined the power of the revolution. The Bolshevik central committee was defined both as concentration and representation. Concentration of a power antagonistic to bourgeois power and representation of the will of the masses. This double characteristic made sure that it rapidly became no more than an empty power, a power of empty representation, and that it soon rejoined bourgeois power in a common form (bureaucracy), forced to follow a similar evolution. The conditions of concentrated power and of mass representation exist potentially in the SI since it monopolises the qualitative and since its ideas are in everyone's mind. Nevertheless, we refuse both concentrated power and the right of representation, conscious that we are taking the only *public attitude* (we cannot avoid being known to some extent in a spectacular manner) that we can give those who discover revolutionary power through our theoretical and practical positions, power without mediation, power entailing the direct action of everyone. Our guiding image could be Durutti's brigade moving from village to village, liquidating the bourgeois elements and leaving the workers to see to their own organisation.

b The intelligentsia is power's hall of mirrors. Opposing power, it never offers more than cathartic identifications playing on the passivity of those whose every act reveals real dissent. The radicalism – of gesture, obviously, not of theory – which could be glimpsed in the Committee of 100 and in the 'Declaration of the 121' suggests, however, a number of different possibilities. We are capable of precipitating this crisis, but only by entering the intelligentsia as a power (against the intelligentsia). This phase – which must precede and be contained within the phase described in a) will put us in the perspective of the Nietzschean project. We will form a small, almost alchemical, experimental group within which the realisation of the total man can be started. Nietzsche could only conceive an undertaking of this nature within the framework of the hierarchical principle. It is, in fact, within this framework that we find ourselves. Therefore it is of the utmost importance that we present ourselves without the slightest ambiguity (on the level of the group, the purification of the centre and the elimination of residues now seem to be completed). We accept the hierarchical framework in which we are placed, waiting impatiently to abolish our domination of others, others we can only dominate on the grounds of our criteria against domination.

c Tactically, our communication should be

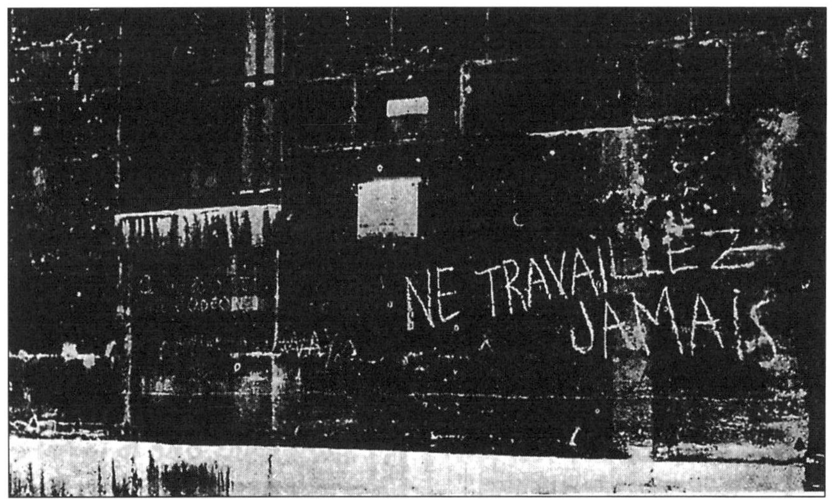

'NEVER WORK'

Preliminary programme to the situationist movement

This inscription, on a wall of the rue de Seine, can be traced back to the first months of 1953 (an adjacent inscription, inspired by more traditional politics, allows one virtually one hundred per cent accuracy in dating the graffiti in question: calling for a demonstration against General Ridgeway, it cannot be later than May 1952). The inscription reproduced above seems to us to be one of the most important relics ever unearthed on the site of Saint Germain-des-Prés, as a testimonial of the particular way of life which tried to assert itself there.

diffused from a centre that remains more or less occult. We will set up a non-materialised network (direct relationships, episodic contacts without ties, development of embryonic relations based on sympathy and understanding, in much the same way as the red agitators before the arrival of the revolutionary armies). We will claim as our own, through their analysis, various radical gestures (acts, writings, political attitudes, works) and we will consider that our own acts and analyses are demanded by the majority of people.

In the same way as God formed the reference point of past unitary society, we are preparing to create the central reference point of a unitary society now possible. This point cannot be fixed. As against the ever-renewed confusion that cybernetic society draws from the past of inhumanity, it stands for the game that everyone will play, 'the moving order of the future'.

Raoul Vaneigem, IS nos. 7-8, 1962-63.

La survie et sa fausse contestation

TRAITE DE SAVOIR-VIVRE A L'USAGE DES JEUNES GENERATIONS
par Raoul Vaneigem

(Gallimard)

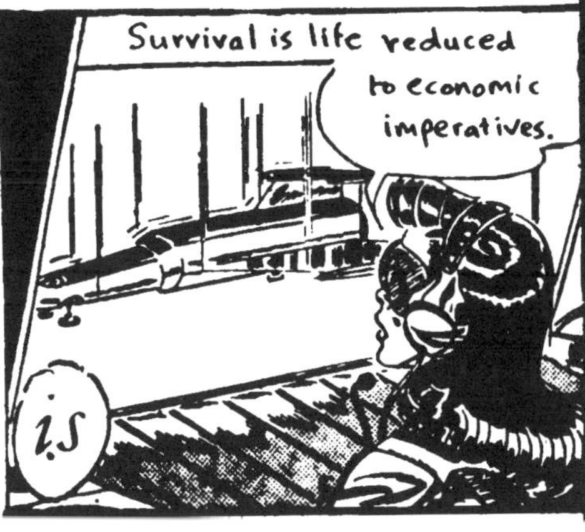

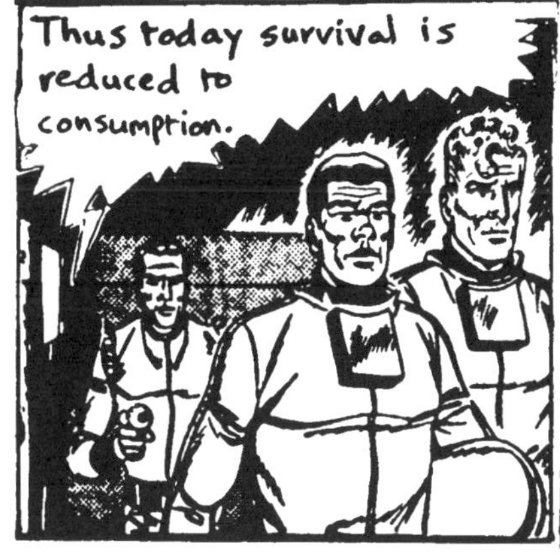

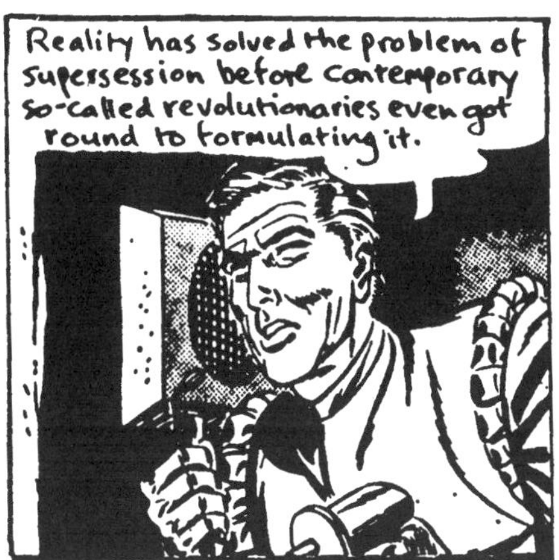

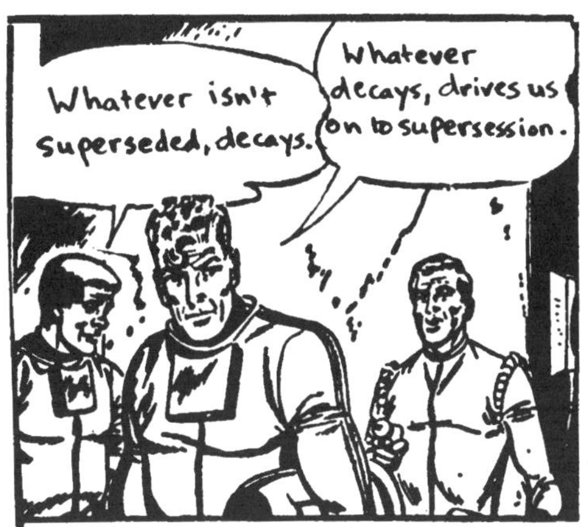

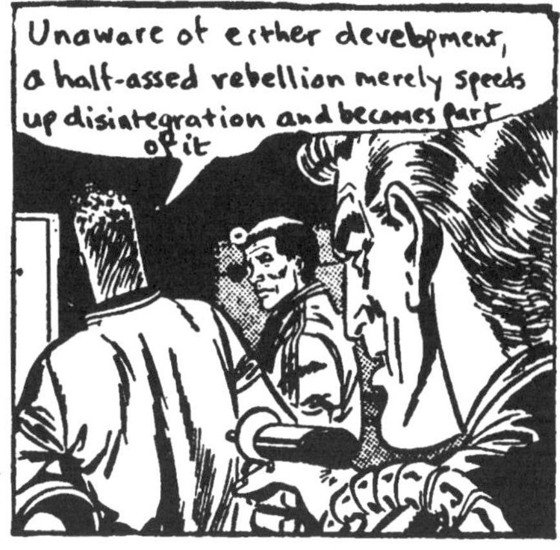

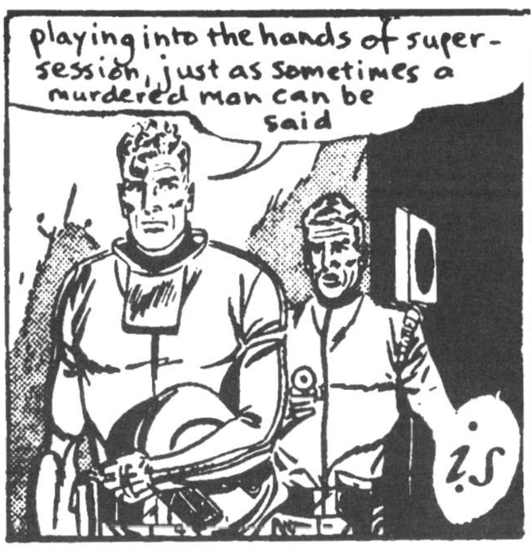

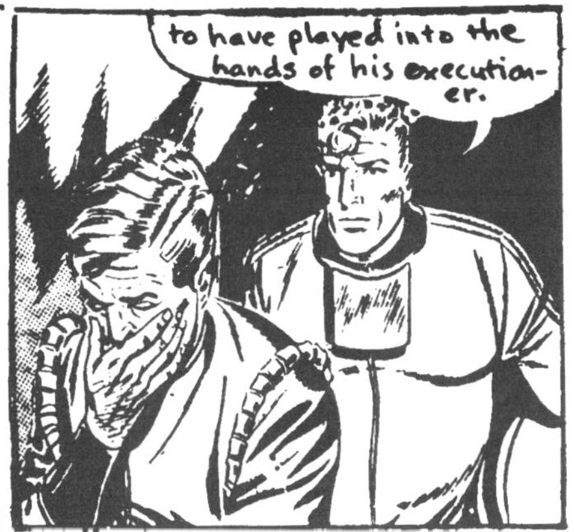

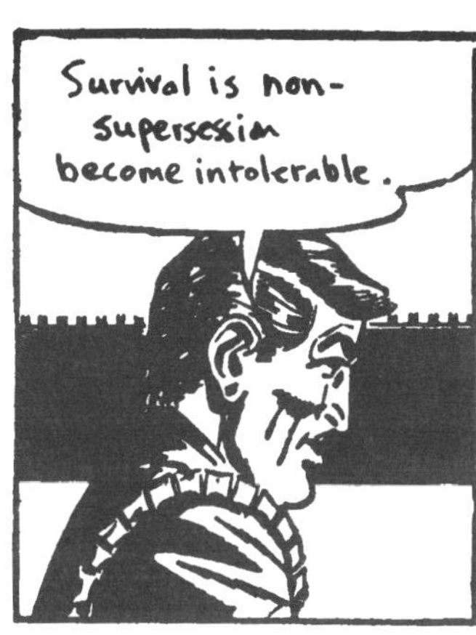

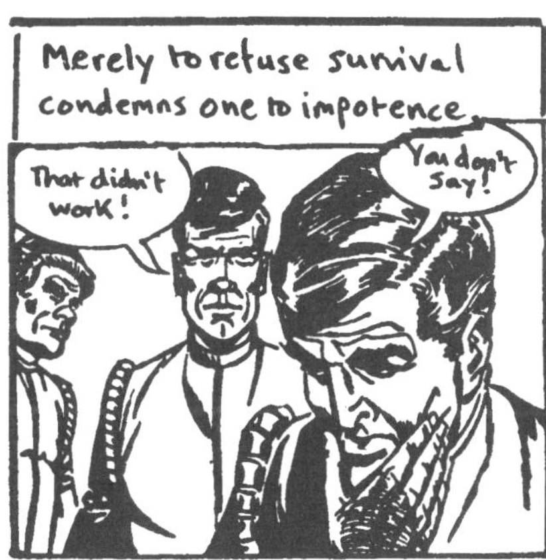

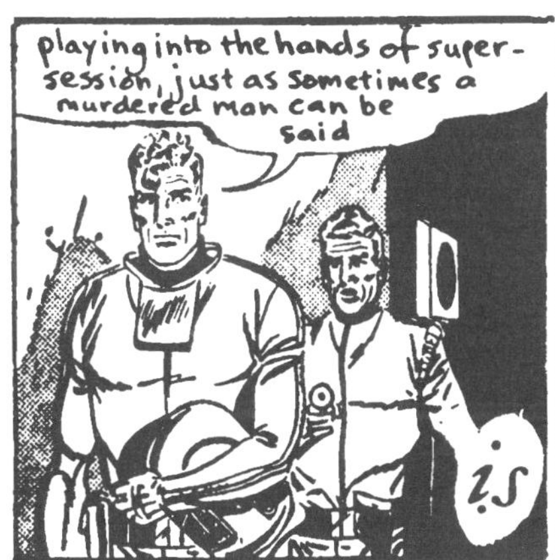

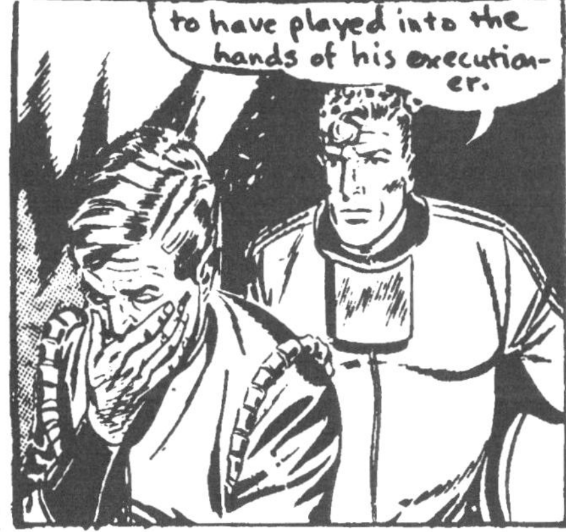

THESES ON THE COMMUNE

I

"The traditional working class movement must be re-examined without any illusions; particularly without any illusions as to its various political and pseudo-theoretical heirs, since all they have inherited is its failure. The apparent successes of this movement are its fundamental failures (reformism or coming to power of a state bureaucracy) and its apparent failures (the Commune or the Asturian revolt) represent for us and for the future its greatest success."

IS no. 7

II

The Commune was the biggest rave-up of the nineteenth century. Underlying everything was the Communards' conviction that they had become masters of their own history, not on the level of 'governmental politics', but on the level of everyday life. Look, for example, at the *games* they played with their weapons – that is to say, the games they played with their power. It is in this sense that we understand Marx's remark that "the most important social measure of the Commune was its own existence in activity".

III

Engels' *Study the Paris Commune – that was the Dictatorship of the Proletariat* should also be taken perfectly seriously, because it reveals what the dictatorship of the proletariat is *not* – the 57 varieties of dictatorship of the proletariat in the name of the proletariat.

IV

Obviously, the Commune was incoherent. No systematic form of organisation was evolved. But today the problems of political organisation seem considerably more complex than they did to the abusive heirs of the bolshevik-type system, and it is high time the Commune was studied, not only as an extremely primitive example of general insurrection, whose mistakes have all been left far behind, but as a positive experiment whose whole truth has not been discovered, let alone fulfilled, to this day.

V

The Commune had no leaders. This was at a time when the idea that nothing could be done without leaders held undisputed sway over the working class movement. And it is this lack of leadership that explains the Commune's paradoxical mixture of success and failure. Its official spokesmen were plain incompetent (at least if they are measured up against Marx, Lenin or even Blanqui). It is, on the contrary, its anonymous 'irresponsible' acts and 'outrages' that are truly valuable and that one would want to see reappearing again today, even if, at the time, most of them were forced to be purely destructive. The best known example being the Communard who, when confronted by a suspect bourgeois who insisted he'd never had anything to do with politics, replied: "That's exactly why I'm going to kill you."

VI

The general arming of the masses was crucially important both practically and symbolically throughout the Commune. For the most part, the right to impose popular will, by force if necessary, was not surrendered to any specialised military body. As against this exemplary autonomy and independence of armed groups stands their lack of co-ordination. At no point, either in attack or in defence, did the Communards reach real military efficiency. However, let us not forget that the Spanish revolution, and in the last analysis the Spanish civil war itself, were lost by failure to transform autonomous groups into an integrated 'republican army'. Everything suggests that the resolution of the contradiction between autonomy and co-ordination depends largely on the degree of technological skill achieved by any period.

VII

To date, the Commune represents *the only realisation of a revolutionary urbanism* – attacking, on the spot, the petrified symbols of the dominant organisation of life, understanding social space in political terms, denying the innocence of a single monument. Anyone who dismisses such activity as being an eruption of lumpenproletariat nihilism, the work of some small, half-crazy gang of petrol bombers, should be forced to state exactly what they think is valuable in present-day society – and it will probably turn out to be a whole crock of shit. "All space is occupied by the enemy... True urbanism will start by causing the occupying forces to disappear from a small number of places. That will be the beginning of what we mean by construction. The concept of the 'positive void' coined by modern physics might prove illuminating." ('Unitary urbanism', IS no. 6.)

VIII

The Commune was defeated more by force of habit than by force of arms. The most disgraceful example of this was the Communards' mental block against using cannon to loot the French National Bank when everyone was so short of funds. Throughout the entire period of the Commune, the National Bank remained a pro-Versailles enclave, defended by a few rifles and by the myth of property and theft. Various other ideological habits proved equally disastrous: the resurrection of Jacobinism, the defeatist strategy of barricades, a throwback to '48, etc, etc.

IX

The Commune shows very clearly how the defenders of the old world always benefit from a secret complicity on the part of the revolutionaries; especially on the part of those who *think* the revolution. This complicity revolves around the points where *they think alike*. In this way, the old world retains strongholds (ideology, language, morality, taste) within the developing new world: strongholds it can use to recapture the territory it has lost. Only *active thought*, the thought natural to the revolutionary proletariat, can escape it forever: the public records office went up in flames. The fifth column one should really dread lies in the minds of the revolutionaries themselves.

X

During the last days of the Commune, a group of arsonists went to blow up Notre Dame. When they got there, they found a cathedral defended by an armed battalion of Communard artists. The story is revealing. It's a fine example of direct democracy and also an example of the sort of problems that the workers' councils will have to face. Were these solid artists right to defend the cathedral in the name of the eternal, aesthetic values (in the last analysis, in the name of museum culture), when others wanted nothing more than to express themselves, freely, just for that one day: to make this demolition job a symbol of their complete defiance of a society which was about to consign their whole lives to oblivion and silence? The artists, acting as specialists, already found themselves trying to repress a really decisive act in the struggle against alienation. The Communards should be criticised for not having replied to the totalitarian terror of power with the sum total of the weapons at their disposal. Everything indicates that the arsonists, the poets who, at that moment, expressed the poetry in suspense throughout the Commune *were simply rubbed out*. The fact that the Commune as a whole was repressed has meant that various aborted acts, deprived of what would have been their context, can now be passed off as 'atrocities'. Thus time is censored. The remark that "those who make half a revolution only dig their own graves" also explains the total silence in which Saint-Just passed his last days on earth.

XI

The theoretician, who surveys life with the traditional novelist's God-like omniscience, can very easily prove that the Commune never stood a chance in the first place, that nothing could ever have come of it. But for those who actually lived through the Commune, the supersession *was there*.

XII

The audacity and inventiveness of the Commune can only be assessed in relation to the political, intellectual and moral life of its own time – in relation to the *interdependence* of all the crap over which it splashed the petrol and to which it put its match. So, considering the solidarity of all the crap around today (to the right and to the left), one can assess the audacity and inventiveness one might reasonably expect from a comparable holocaust now.

XIII

The class war, of which the Commune was one episode, is still with us (although its superficial characteristics have changed considerably). As to the matter of "making the Commune's unconscious tendencies conscious" (Engels), the last word is still to be said.

XIV

For the last 30 years in France, left-wing Christians and Stalinists (remembering the anti-Nazi front) have agreed to treat the Commune as an expression of national disarray, of wounded patriotism, of the masses, having finally despaired of the bourgeois right wing, 'petitioning someone to govern them well' (presumably along the lines of the current Stalinist 'policy'). All that's necesssary to demolish this particular piece of Holy Writ is an examination of the role played by the foreigners who came to fight for the Commune. Above all, it was the inevitable test of strength towards which, since 1848, every action in Europe undertaken by "our party" (Marx) had been leading.

Debord/Kotanyi/Vaneigem (broadsheet, 1963)

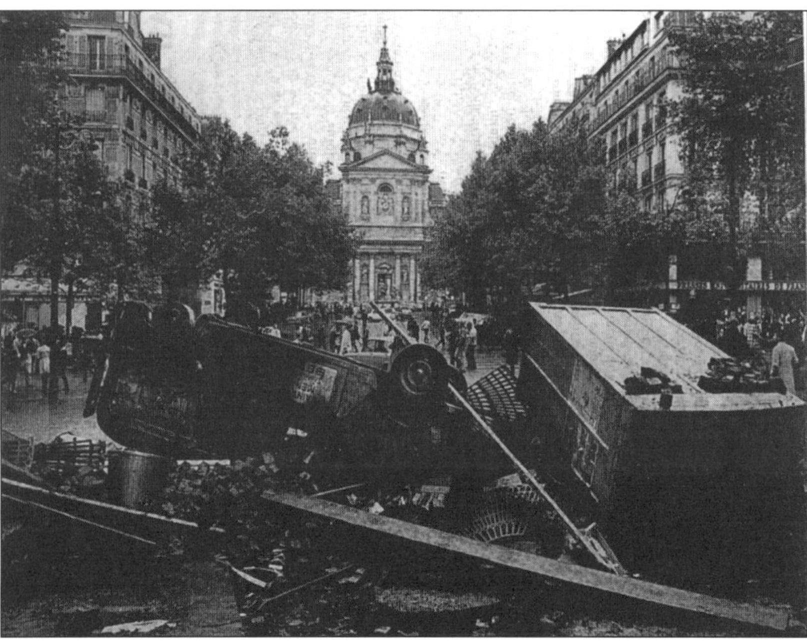

ALL THE KING'S MEN

The problem of language is at the heart of every struggle between those who wish to abolish alienation and those who wish to preserve it. It is present wherever these battles are fought. Language is the poisoned air we live in. In spite of all our jokers, words don't play; and in spite of Breton, they don't make love except in dreams. Words *work*, to the profit of the dominant organisation of life. Yet they aren't completely automated; tough luck for information theorists, words can't be reduced to pure information. They embody forces that can upset all calculations. Words co-exist with power in a similar relationship to that between poor and proletarians (in the classical or the modern sense). Employed *almost* all the time, screwed every second of this time for all the sense and nonsense which they can produce, they still remain in some respects radical outsiders.

Power only presents the forged identity card of words. It forces them to hold a permit, determines their place in the productive process (some certainly work overtime) and gives them their payslip. Remember Humpty-Dumpty on the meaning of words: "The question is which is to be master, that's all." And he, enlightened boss that he is, pays double-time to the ones he uses a lot. We should also understand the *insubordination of words*, from flight to open resistance, which is evident in all modern writing from Baudelaire to the dadaists and Joyce, as the symptom of an overall revolutionary crisis in society.

When it is controlled by power, language always designates something other than authentic lived experience. This fact leaves it open to a total contestation. The organisation of language has fallen into such a state of confusion that the mode of communication imposed by power is being exposed as trickery and imposture. The prophets of cybernetic power try in vain to make language dependent on the machines that they control so that 'information' would become the only possible communication. Even in this field, resistance has broken out. Electronic music can be seen as an attempt (evidently limited and ambiguous) to reverse the direction of domination by re-deploying machines to the profit of language. But the opposition is much more general and radical than this. It attacks all unilateral 'communication' whether it takes the old form of art or the modern form of mass media. It advocates a kind of communication that will be the ruin of all separated power. Where there is real communication there can't be any waste.

Power lives on stolen goods. It creates nothing, it recuperates. If power created the meanings of words there would no longer be any poetry but only 'useful information'. Opposition could never be expressed in language, and any refusal would have to place itself *outside*, like Lettrism. What is poetry but the revolutionary movement of language, inseparable from the revolutionary moments of history and the history of personal life?

The hold which power has over language derives from its hold over the totality. Only a language that has been deprived of any immediate reference to the totality of society could become the language of *news*. News is the poetry of power, the counter-poetry of law and order, the mediating falsification of what exists. Inversely, poetry must be understood as immediate communication taking place in reality and real modification of this reality. It is none other than liberated language: language which takes back its lost wealth and smashing signs, recovers words, music, shouts, gestures, painting, mathematics, actions, facts. Therefore, poetry depends on the highest level at which life, in a given socio-economic formation, can be lived *and changed*. It is unnecessary to add that this relationship between poetry and its material base is therefore not a one-way dependence but an interaction.

Rediscovering poetry may become indistinguishable from reinventing revolution, as may be seen from certain phases of the Mexican, Cuban and Congolese revolutions. In revolutionary periods the masses become poets of action. In non-revolutionary periods one might think that the circles of poetic adventure are the only places where revolution survives in its totality: a virtuality unrealised but close at hand, the shadow of an absent character. So that what we mean by poetic adventure is difficult, dangerous and always uncertain of success. In fact, it means all the things that are *almost impossible to do* in a particular time. What is certain is that the recognised, permitted and false poetry of the time is no longer a poetic adventure. At the time of its attack on the oppressive order of culture and everyday life, surrealism rightly defined its weapon as 'poetry which doesn't always need poems'. But today the SI is only interested in a poetry without any poems. And what we say about poetry has nothing to do with the retarded reactionaries of neo-versification, even if they do subscribe to the very least ancient of formal modernisms. The programme of the realisation of poetry means nothing less than the simultaneous creation of events and their language, inseparably.

All closed languages – those of informal groups of young people; those which developing avant-gardes elaborate for internal use; those esoteric poetic languages which once called themselves '*trobar clus*' or '*dolce stil nuovo*' – all these have as their objective, and their effect, the immediate transparency of a certain communication, mutual recognition, agreement. But such attempts have been the work of small groups isolated in many ways. The events that they have been able to prepare, the celebrations which they have been able to give themselves, have had to remain within the most narrow limits. One of the problems of revolution is that of federating these soviets, councils of communication, to install everywhere a direct communication which will no longer have to rely on the enemy's communication network (that is, power's language), and will thus be able to transform the world according to its desire.

It is no longer a question of putting poetry at the service of the revolution, but rather of putting the revolution at the service of poetry. This is the only way in which the revolution will not betray its own project. We shall not repeat the mistake of the surrealists, who put themselves at the service of the revolution at the precise moment when the revolution ceased to exist. Bound to the memory of a revolution that was partial and rapidly crushed, Surrealism soon became a reformism of the spectacle, a critique of a certain form of the established spectacle that was carried on inside the dominant organisation of this spectacle. The surrealists seemed to be unaware that every improvement or modernisation internal to the spectacle is translated by power into its own language.

Every revolution has been born in poverty, has begun by the impulse of poetry. This fact continues to escape theorists of revolution – indeed, it can't be understood by those who keep to the old conceptions of revolution and poetry – but has generally been sensed by counter-revolutionaries. Poetry frightens them; they do their best to get rid of it by means of all kinds of exorcism, from *auto-da-fé* to pure stylistic research. The moment of real poetry, which 'has all of time in front of it', always wants to rearrange to its own ends the whole of the world and all the future. As long as it lasts its demands can stand no compromise. It digs up all the unpaid debts of history. Fourier and Pancho Villa, Lautréamont and the dynamiters of Asturias – whose successors are now inventing new forms of strike – the sailors of Kronstadt and Kiel, and all the people in the world who are preparing to fight with us or without us for a long revolution, are also the troubadours of the new poetry.

Poetry is becoming more and more clearly the empty space or rather the anti-matter of consumer society, since it is not consumable: a consumable object must be of equal value to each of a passive mass of isolated consumers. Poetry is nothing when it is not quoted, it can only be *subverted*, thrown back into action. The study of the old poetry is nothing more than an academic exercise and shares the characteristics of all academic thought. The history of poetry is only a way of running away from the poetry of history, if we understand by this not the spectacular history of the bosses but rather the history of everyday life and its possible liberation; the history of each individual life and its realisation.

Let us leave no doubt about the role of the 'keepers' of the old poetry, the people who want to spread it around more and more thickly as the state (for quite different reasons) increases literacy. These people are only museum attendants. A large amount of poetry is usually 'kept' in the world. But nowhere are there places, moments, people to relive it, communicate it, use it. Given that this could only be done by subverting it: because the understanding of the old poetry had been changed by the loss of knowledge as well as by the acquisition of it; and because at every moment when old poetry can be effectively rediscovered, its confrontation with particular events gives it a largely new meaning. But above all, a situation where poetry is impossible could not repeat any of the poetic failures of the past (this failure being what is left behind, in the history of poetry, transformed into success and poetic monument). Such a situation leads naturally to the communication, and the possible sovereignty, of *its own poetry*.

While poetic archaeologists carefully restore selections of the old poetry and arrange LPs of specialists reciting it for the new illiterates created by the modern spectacle, information theorists propose to eliminate all the 'redundancies' of freedom and simply transmit *orders*. The thinkers of automation are explicitly aiming to automate thought by eliminating all the sources of error from life as well as from language. Yet they are still finding bones in their cheese! For example, translating machines, whose mission is to ensure the global standardisation of information, at the same time as preparing the information-theoretic revision of the old culture, are dependent on their pre-set programmes, which necessarily miss any new meaning taken on by a word as well as its past dialectical ambivalences. In this way the life of language – which is bound up with every advance in theoretical understanding: 'Ideas improve and the meanings of words change' – is cast out of the mechanised garden of official information; but this also means that free thought can develop with a secrecy which will be outside the reach of the information police. Information theorists and prophets of cybernetic control systems give themselves away even in their more insane formulations as the builders of the same brave new world which the dominant forces of contemporary society are working towards: the construction of the cybernetic state. They are the vassals of all the lords of the coming technological feudalism. There is no innocence in their clowning. They are the king's jesters.

The choice between informationism and poetry has nothing to do with the poetry of the past; just as no variant of what the classical revolutionary movement has turned into is of any relevance anywhere as part of a real alternative to contemporary life. The same judgement leads us to announce the total disappearance of poetry in the old forms in which it has been produced and consumed, and its return in forms that are unexpected but operational. It is time to stop writing poetic orders – time to start carrying them out.

IS, no. 8, 1963

ISOLATION

One non-revolutionary weekend is infinitely more bloody than a month of permanent revolution.

Graffiti, School of Oriental Languages, 1968.

In contemporary society, the entire body of technology – above all the means of so-called communication – is oriented towards the maximum of passive isolation of individuals, towards their control by a 'direct and permanent contact' *that only works in one direction*. Endless incitations to which it is impossible to reply are broadcast daily by every sort of *leader*. Some applications of this technique can be seen as hilariously funny consolation prizes for what is basically absent. Others are considerably less funny.

"If you are a TV fan, you are sure to be interested by this, the most extraordinary TV set ever made. It will go everywhere with you. Of an entirely new design, invented by the Hughes Aircraft Corporation of the USA, it is made to be worn on the head. It weighs 950g and is mounted on a pilot-style helmet. It has a tiny round screen made of plastic, looking something like a monacle, which is held four centimetres in front of the eye. Only one eye is used to look at the screen. With the other, the manufacturers claim, you can be looking elsewhere, or even write or be occupied with manual labour."

Journal de Dimanche, 29 July 1962

"The trouble at the coalmines has finally been settled and it seems that work will start again next Friday... Perhaps it's the feeling of having participated in the debate that explains the almost-unbroken calm that has reigned these 34 days in the miners' quarters and at the pitheads. Television and transistor radios were an enormous help in maintaining this direct and permanent contact between the miners and their delegates, and at the same time they forced everyone to go home at the decisive hours while, even a few days before, everyone used to go and meet at the union building."

Le Monde, 5 April 1963

"A new cure for lonely travellers at Chicago station. For a 'quarter', a wax-covered robot shakes you by the hand and says: 'Hello. How are you? It's been really nice seeing you. Hope you have a good time.'"

Marie-Claire, January 1963

"'I no longer have any friends. I'll never talk to anyone again.' This is the beginning of the confession, recorded on his own tape recorder, of a Polish worker who had just turned on the gas tap in his kitchen. 'I am almost unconscious. There is no longer any chance of saving me. The end is very close.' These were the last words of Joseph Czternastek."

AFP, London, 7 April 1962

IS, no. 9, 1964

"SHAKE IN YOUR SHOES BUREAUCRATS": THE SITUATIONISTS, 1965-1969

by Christopher Gray

By the mid-sixties, the situationist project had taken on its definitive form. The SI was to be a small, tightly-knit group of revolutionaries devoted to forging a critique of the *contemporary*, that is to say, consumer capitalism – and to publicising this critique in every form of scandal and agitation possible. All practical experiment with art went by the board. Everything depended on universal insurrection. Poetry could only be made by everyone.

During 1965-67, they put forward an analysis of life in the West more incisive than any made since the twenties. Lefebvre, the only thinker on the same level in France, was left looking distinctly pedestrian, as was Marcuse in the States. And both for the same reason. Because the SI refused to define themselves as detached observers. They knew that in the last analysis they were as proletarianised as everyone else, and because of this they were able to detect and identify with the unacknowledged and snowballing 'revolt of youth' of the early and mid-sixties in both the middle-class 'dropout' and its working class 'delinquent' forms. At the same time they were among the very few revolutionary groups both to understand the crucial importance of the *wildcat strikes* and to see that this whole new stage of industrial struggle was in no way incompatible with the psychological distress experienced by the younger generation.

They did a far batter job on the newspapers than *Private Eye*: repeatedly quoting the growing number of openly-acknowledged signs of utter world-weariness and bitter anger spreading throughout Europe and the States. And they used these explosions of genuine revolt as a stick with which to still further belabour 'revolutionary' intellectuals. Anyone who thought that revolution was only possible somewhere on the other side of the planet – which meant that *they* couldn't see anything wrong with contemporary society and its consumer goods; anyone who bemoaned the absence of a revolutionary movement in Europe without doing anything about it *themselves*. They were really incredibly rude, and rude in the worst possible taste, to the entire political and cultural avant-garde establishment. MR GEORGES LAPASSADE IS A CUNT, in huge letters, filled one page of the magazine. In return, French culture boycotted them completely. The censorship of the SI has probably been the most blatant case of cultural repression since before the war.

July 1965, the first copies of a cheaply-duplicated magazine called *Provo*, appeared on the streets in Amsterdam – and were promptly seized by the police, owing to the unusual precision of their recipe for homemade bombs. The torchlight meetings, the street demonstrations, the smoke-bombs, the white bicycles, the sabotage of state occasions, etc, that followed, marked the first eruption into public consciousness of precisely what the situationists had been heralding for years: an anarchic, festive

WORDS AND THEIR BOSSES

President Johnson, while addressing several thousand students who have just completed probationary periods in various government departments this summer, saluted them as 'revolutionary comrades'. "All my life", he said to them, "I have been a revolutionary, struggling against sectarianism, poverty and injustice."

AP, Washington, 5 August 1965

RENDEZ-VOUS, BUT WHERE? While at the Gare Saint-Lazare you are still forced either to hang around and wait for your friends, or to look for them and get lost; Orly airport has just constructed an unmistakable 'meeting place'. It is a gigantic metal ball hanging from the ceiling of the ground floor hall encircled by a neon sign proclaiming 'Meeting place' with no two ways about it.

Elle, 31 August 1962

attack on the *quality* of life, organised as a *political* movement. The Provos were the occasion of the situationists' first appearance in the French press – as the 'occult international', the theoretical driving force behind the Provos' political carnival. Exactly how much influence the SI had on the Provos is difficult to ascertain. In a loose sense, a good deal: Amsterdam had been one of the hubs of situationist activity a few years before and at least one of the Provo leaders, Constant the architect, was ex-SI. There wasn't, however, any constructive interaction between the two groups: the SI was as haughty with the Provos as with everyone else. All they had to say was that unless the Provo street lumpenproletariat shook off its own bureaucracy and star system and fused with the Dutch working class, the whole episode would end like a damp squib – which was precisely what did happen. Be that as it may, it was only after the Provos that situationist-type politics began to gain any real credibility.

The same year saw an even more violent corroboration of their theses: the Watts riots in the States. The SI's analysis of these riots – *The Decline and Fall of the 'Spectacular' Commodity Economy* – was translated and distributed in England and the States, even before it appeared in French. The text achieved some notoriety, though largely for its violence and incomprehensibility – the idea that there was a revolutionary crisis brewing in America and that the blacks would play any part in it being obviously out of the question. As for the enthusiastic analyses of violence, looting and arson, let alone the discovery of poetry within them (poetry..?), the good pacifist souls of the Anglo-American left simply threw up their hands and fled. During the summer of 1966, an embryonic English section was formed, translated Vaneigem's *Banalités de Base* as *The Totality for Kids*, ran a magazine, *Heatwave*, and began to make contact with other lunatic fringe groups in London and the States.

By this time the situationist critique of society was almost complete. The problem before them was one of publicising their position: of breaking the very real conspiracy of silence against them. Some publicity came from the fact that their main base in Denmark was blown up and burnt down – to the situationists' great delight – apparently by the extreme right wing, for the role they had played in fomenting a series of riots in the Danish town of Randers. However, it was the 'occupation' of the Strasbourg University in November 1966 that finally rocketed the SI to national headlines.

A small group of students from Strasbourg University approached the SI in early 1966. Over the summer they worked out their tactics.

This small group got itself elected, amidst the apathy of Strasbourg's 16,000 students, to the committee of the left-wing students' union. Once in this position of power they began to put union funds to good use. They founded a Society for the Rehabilitation of Karl Marx and Ravachol. They plastered the walls of the city with a Marxist comic-strip: 'The return of the Durruti column'. They proclaimed their intention to dissolve the union once and for all. Worst of all, they enlisted the aid of the notorious situationist international and ran off ten thousand copies of a lengthy pamphlet which poured shit on student life and loves (and a few other things). When this was handed out at the official ceremony marking the beginning of the academic year, only de Gaulle was unaffected. The press – local, national and international – had a field day. It took three weeks for the local party of order – from right-wing students to the official left, via Alsatian mill-owners – to eject these fanatics. The union was closed by a court order on 14 December. The judge's summing up was disarmingly lucid:

"The accused have never denied the charge of misusing the funds of the students' union. Indeed they openly admit to having made the union pay some £500 for the printing and distribution of 10,000 pamphlets, not to mention the cost of other literature inspired by Internationale Situationniste. *These publications express ideas and aspirations which, to put it mildly, have nothing to do with the aims of a students' union. One has only to read what the accused have written for it to be obvious that these five students, scarcely more than adolescents, lacking all experience of real life, their minds confused by ill-digested philosophical, social, political and economic theories, and perplexed by the drab monotony*

of their everyday life, make the empty, arrogant and pathetic claim to pass definitive judgements, sinking to outright abuse, on their fellow students, their teachers, God, religion, the clergy, the governments and political systems of the whole world. Rejecting all morality and restraint, these cynics do not hesitate to commend theft, the destruction of scholarship, the abolition of work, total subversion and a worldwide proletarian revolution with 'unlicensed pleasure' as its only goal. In view of their basically anarchist character, these theories and propaganda are eminently noxious. Their wide diffusion in both student circles and among the general public by the local, national and foreign press are a threat to the morality, the studies, the reputation and thus the very future of the students of the University of Strasbourg" (From the first English edition of *Ten Days that Shook the University*).

This was Europe's first university occupation and for weeks the scandal echoed through all the student unions in France. The pamphlet referred to, *On the Poverty of Student Life*, became a bestseller overnight and there can hardly have been a single left-wing student in France who didn't hear of the SI. During 1967 the pamphlet was translated into half-a-dozen European languages. The English version was reproduced several times in the States, both in the underground press and as a pamphlet. In France, the court cases dragged on for several months and the scandal was still further exacerbated by another batch of exclusions ('the Garnautins'), a nasty and protracted business this time, solely about the supposed authoritarian role played by Debord. Their new-found fame, however, remained untarnished. The SI had become synonymous with the utmost extremism. It bathed in revolutionary charisma.

The whole of that year, the SI gained greater and greater influence in French universities. They made personal contact with a fair number of students (via their official PO Box no., the way they made contact with anyone), but always insisted that the people they met developed on their own and formed autonomous and self-sufficient groups. Of all these students, the ones they became closest to were a group from Nanterre – a handful of anarchists destined, the following year, to become almost as notorious as the SI itself. The situationists' theoretical expression was completed by the publication of two full-length books, Raoul Vaneigem's *Traité de savoir-faire a l'usage des jeunes générations* and Guy Debord's *La Société du Spectacle*, treating what could be called the subjective and objective aspects of alienation respectively. Both books were almost entirely ignored by the French press until the following summer.

Yet for all this there was a growing desire for direct action within the group itself. Amongst many plans there was one particularly good one to cause a massive scandal in the heart of Paris by staining the Seine blood-red and dumping the bodies of a couple of hundred vaguely Vietnamese Asiatics in it, so they floated downstream past Notre Dame and l'Ile Saint-Louis. The corpses were a cinch. One of the medical schools in Paris bought dead Chinamen by the ton for dissection. The route taken by the refrigerated truck was known and quite sensible plans for highjacking it were worked out. The bodies were to be dropped into the Seine upstream in the suburbs. The fuck-up was the red industrial dye. The quantities necessary seemed enormous. The connection didn't come through and the thing petered out...

Much has been made, both in the newspapers at the time and in subsequent sociological studies, of the situationists' influence on May '68: on the first general wildcat strike in history and the wave of occupations that left France tottering on the brink of a revolutionary crisis more vertiginous than anything since the Spanish civil war. This influence can't be measured in any meaningful way. In the first place the SI never claimed to stand for more than the consciousness of a real social and historical process embodied by millions of people; nor to act as more than a catalyst in certain quite specific social areas. However, once that has been said, one can only add that the extent to which they had *pre-figured* everything that materialised in May was little short of clairvoyant.

More specifically: it should be remembered that the first spark that set off the whole gunpowder keg came from the handful of *enragés* – a group which had adopted the theses of the SI and who turned

= MAY 17 1968 / POLITBUREAU OF THE CHINESE COMMUNIST PARTY GATE OF CELESTIAL PEACE PEKING SHAKE IN YOUR SHOES BUREAUCRATS . THE INTERNATIONAL POWER OF THE WORKERS COUNCILS WILL SOON WIPE YOU OUT . HUMANITY WILL ONLY BE HAPPY THE DAY THAT THE LAST BUREAUCRAT IS STRUNG UP BY THE GUTS OF THE LAST CAPITALIST . LONG LIVE THE FACTORY OCCUPATIONS. LONG LIVE THE GREAT PROLETARIAN CHINESE REVOLUTION OF 1927 BETRAYED BY THE STALINISTS. LONG LIVE THE PROLETARIAT OF CANTON AND ELSEWHERE WHO TOOK UP ARMS AGAINST THE SO-CALLED POPULAR ARMY . LONG LIVE THE WORKERS AND STUDENTS OF CHINA WHO ATTACKED THE SO-CALLED CULTURAL REVOLUTION AND THE BUREAUCRATIC MAOIST ORDER . LONG LIVE REVOLUTIONARY MARXISM . DOWN WITH THE STATE .
OCCUPATION COMMITTEE OF THE AUTONOMOUS AND POPULAR SORBONNE

the University of Nanterre upside down in carly 1968. Several of them were disciplined by university authorities along with other radicals and this action precipitated the immediate crisis at the university level. The *22nd March Movement* had been thoroughly impregnated with situationist ideas by the *enragés*, although they had walked out of it at its inception because of its mish-mash composition and its refusal to expel certain known Stalinists. Situationist ideas had also spread far among many students, 'artists' and politicos in the Latin Quarter and throughout the entire French university system. (After it was all over, Vaneigem's *Traité* turned out to be the most ripped-off book in France.)

As the crisis developed, the SI and the *enragés* played a decisive part. The *enragé*, Riesel, and others, were elected to the Sorbonne Occupation Committee and were the first to communicate the call for self-management and the creation of the workers' councils after the first factories were occupied by French workers. But they were unable to prevent the steady encroachment of the various bureaucratic leftist sects and the endless verbalisation so beloved of students, so they left in disgust.

On 17 May they founded the *Council for the Maintenance of the Occupations* (CMDO), which occupied the National Pedagogical Institute on rue d'Ulm, and then, from the end of May, the basement of a 'School of Decorative Arts' next door. The CMDO dissolved itself on 15 June with the nationwide ebbing of the occupations. About forty people made up the permanent base of the CMDO, who were joined for a while by other revolutionaries and strikers coming from various industries, from abroad or from the provinces, and returning there. The CMDO was more or less constantly made up of about ten situationists and *enragés* (among them Debord, Khayati, Reisel and Vaneigem), and as many respectively from the workers, high school students or 'students', and other councillists without specific social functions. Throughout its existence, it was a successful experiment in direct democracy, guaranteed by an equal participation of everyone in debates, decisions and their execution. It was essentially an uninterrupted general assembly deliberating day and night. No faction or private meetings ever existed outside the common debate.

A unit spontaneously created in the conditions of a revolutionary moment, the CMDO was obviously less of a council than a councillist organisation, thus functioning

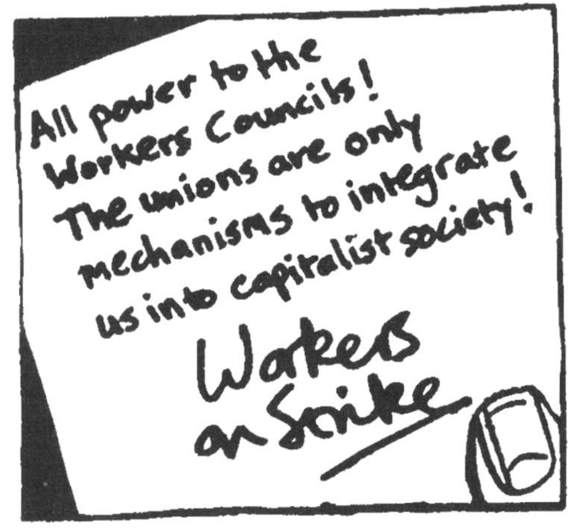

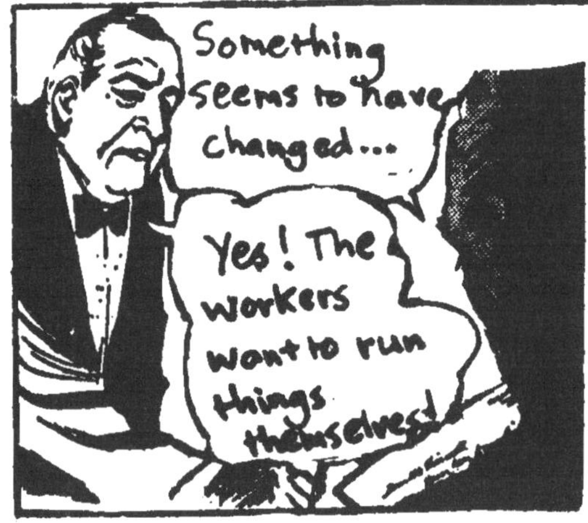

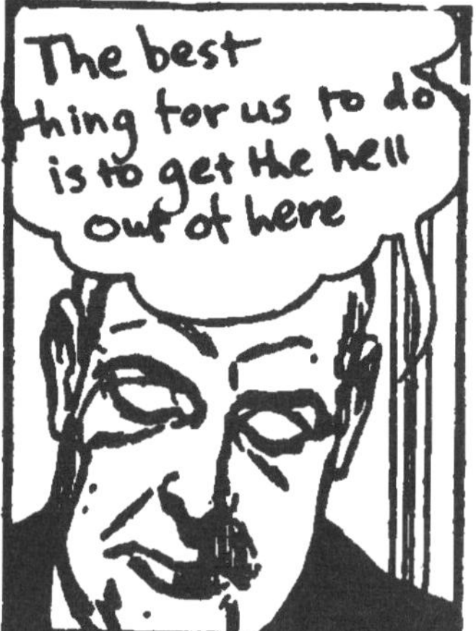

Premier comics realisé par le Conseil pour le maintien des occupations.

on the model of soviet democracy. As an improvised response to that precise moment, the CMDO could neither present itself as a permanent councillist organisation nor, as such, attempt to transform itself into an organisation of that kind. Nonetheless, general agreement on the major situationist theses reinforced its cohesion. Three committees had organised themselves within the general assembly to make possible its practical activity. The printing committee took charge of the writing and printing of the CMDO's publications, both using the machines to which it had access and in collaboration with certain occupied printshops whose workers gladly put back into operation the excellent equipment at their disposal. The liaison committee, with ten cars available, took care of contacts with occupied factories and the delivery of material for distribution. The requisitions committee, which excelled during the most difficult period, made sure that paper, petrol, food and money were never lacking. There was no permanent committee to ensure the rapid writing of the texts, whose content was determined by everyone, but on each occasion several members were designated, who then submitted the result to the assembly.

The CMDO printed a series of very curt, simple posters and a series of leaflets and throwaways – amongst which were an *Address to all Workers* and a reprinting of the *Minimum Definition of a Revolutionary Organisation*. The major texts had printings of between 150,000 and 200,000 copies, and responsibility was taken for translation into English, German, Spanish, Italian, Danish and Arabic. They also published several appropriate songs and about forty comic-strips, which seem to have been popular (at any rate, several of the occupied factories produced their own), though the massive use of graffiti was a more successful medium, indeed the first new form of expression since the twenties. The spray can, far more than the street poster, offers the writer the one way he can be certain of being read by everyone.

The CMDO recognised that what had initially been a student revolt now contained, because of the factory occupations, the possibilities for a social revolution. As such, it attempted to show what prevented the May movement from becoming revolutionary. In its interventions it denounced the recuperators of the parties, Stalinist unions and the confusion of the 'groupuscules' (Trotskyists, Maoists and anarchists who formed 'action committees' of militants united only on the most immediate particulars – the banal demands of 'reform the university' and 'end police repression') who sought to impose their 'non'-leadership on the movement. But more importantly, the CMDO posed the issue of self-management concretely as an immediate possibility. Revolution was the only demand to be made by the French proletariat.

QUE PEUT
LE MOUVEMENT
REVOLUTIONNAIRE
MAINTENANT?
TOUT
QUE DEVIENT-IL
ENTRE LES MAINS DES PARTIS
ET DES SYNDICATS?
RIEN
QUE VEUT-IL? LA REALISATION
DE LA SOCIETE SANS CLASSE
PAR LE POUVOIR
DES CONSEILS OUVRIERS

conseil pour le maintien des occupations

What can the revolutionary movement do today? Everything. What is it turning into in the hands of the parties and the unions? Nothing. What does it want? The realisation of a classless society through the power of the workers' councils.

Conseil pour le maintien des occupations, Paris, May-June 1968

The occupations were the reappearance, out of the blue, of the proletariat as a historic class – suddenly enlarged to include almost everyone working for someone else – inevitably bent on the real abolition of the class system and of wage labour. The occupations were a rediscovery of history – personal and social history at one and the same time, a rediscovery of the sense that 'history' can lie in the hands of ordinary people, of the sense of irreversible time – above all, of the sense that 'things just can't go on in the same old way'. The alien life everyone had been living eight days before just seemed ridiculous. The occupations were a *total attack* on every form of alienation, on every form of ideology, on the whole straitjacket into which real life has been crammed. Everything radiated the desire to unify: to make one. Inevitably, property rights were trampled underfoot. Everything belonged to everybody. *Frankly confessed desire* to meet people, to be completely honest with them, to enjoy a real community, were fostered by occupied buildings whose sole purpose was to make people meet, fostered by fighting side-by-side in the streets. The telephones, among the few public services still functioning, the number of messengers and of people just generally on the road throughout Paris and all over the country, prefigured something of what real 'communications' could be. The occupations, to say the least of it, were a rejection of all that's understood by work today. They were exuberance, they were playfulness, they were the real dance of men and time. Authority was rejected in all its forms. So was specialisation. So was hierarchical rip-off. So was the State. So were the political parties. So were the trade unions. So were sociologists. So were professors. So were moralists. So were doctors. 'Quick', advised perhaps the best of all the graffiti – and everyone that the occupations had awoken to themselves felt nothing but embarrassment and contempt for the way of life they had been leading and for all those, from superstars to town planners, who had done their best to keep them bogged down in it. It was an end to bullshit: in particular all the CP bullshit from Castro to Sartre. Real internationalism sprang up overnight. Workers and intellectuals from all over Europe came to fight. The importance of the role played by women throughout the whole of May is a clear indication of the extent of the revolutionary crisis. Free love began to become something real. The occupations for all their chaos were an attack on the commodity form (even if this was still understood crudely and 'sociologically' as an attack on the 'consumer society'). Art was also put down pretty heavily, though few people actually realised they had reached the stage where the abolition of art had become the next logical thing to do. The best anyone came up with was the abstract and somewhat vague slogan, 'All power to the imagination'. But there wasn't any idea of how this power could be put into effect: how everything could be reinvented. Once it ran out of power, it ran out of imagination. Utter *detestation* of recuperators, though felt by everyone, failed to reach a level of theoretico-practical consciousness sufficient to liquidate them: neo-artists and neo-political road managers, neo-spectators of the very movement that had them up against the wall. If this active criticism of the spectacle of non-life failed to become its revolutionary supersession, it was only because the May insurrection's 'spontaneous orientation towards the workers' councils' was in advance of almost all concrete preparations for it, amongst which the theoretical and organisational consciousness which would have allowed it to express itself as power: as the only power...

'The dawn which in a single moment lights up the whole shape of the new world' – that was what we saw that May in France. The red and black flags of workers' democracy flew together in the wind. The axe is laid to the root of the tree. And if we, to however small an extent, have emblazoned our name on the reawakening of this movement, it is not to preserve any single moment of it nor to attain any particular celebrity. Now we are sure of a satisfactory conclusion to all we have done: the SI will be superseded.

IS, no. 12, 1969

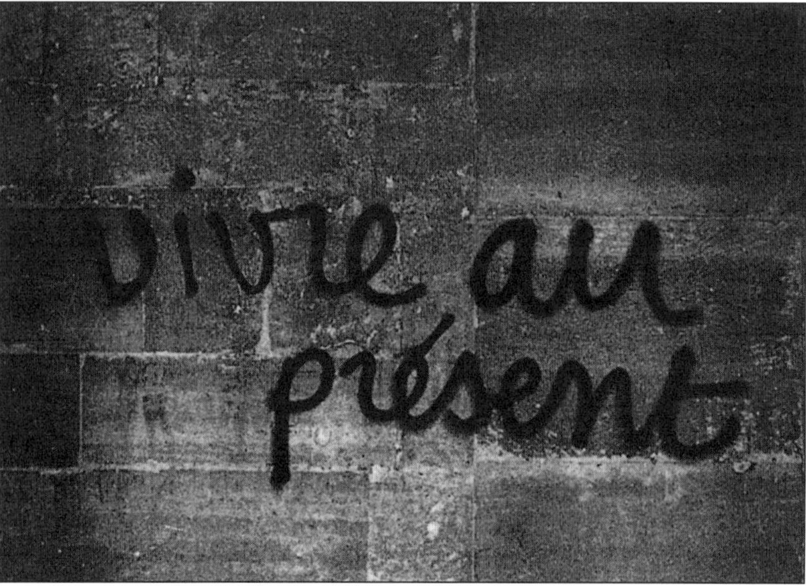

WATTS 1965: THE DECLINE AND FALL OF THE 'SPECTACULAR' COMMODITY ECONOMY

From 13-18 August 1965, the blacks of Los Angeles revolted. An incident involving traffic police and pedestrians developed into two days of spontaneous riots. The forces of order, despite repeated reinforcement, were unable to gain control of the streets. By the third day, the blacks had armed themselves by pillaging such arms shops as were accessible, and were so enabled to open fire on police helicopters. Thousands of soldiers – the whole military weight of an infantry division, supported by tanks – had to be thrown into the struggle before the Watts area could be surrounded, after which it took several days and much street fighting for it to be brought under control. The rioters didn't hesitate to plunder and burn the shops of the area. The official figures testify to thirty-two dead, including twenty-seven blacks, plus 800 wounded and 3,000 arrested.

Reactions on all sides were invested with clarity: the revolutionary act always discloses the reality of existing problems, lending an unaccustomed and unconscious truth to the various postures of its opponents. Police chief William Parker, for example, refused all mediation proposed by the main black organisations, asserting correctly that the rioters had no leader. Evidently, as the blacks were without a leader, this was the moment of truth for both parties. What did Roy Wilkins, general secretary of the NAACP, want at that moment? He declared the riots should be put down "with all the force necessary". And the Cardinal of Los Angeles, McIntyre, who protested loudly, had not protested against the violence of the repression, which one would have supposed the subtle thing to do, at the moment of the *aggiornamento* of the Roman church. Instead, he protested in the most urgent tone about "a premeditated revolt against the rights of one's neighbour; respect for the law and the maintenance of order", calling upon Catholics to oppose the plundering and the apparently unjustified violence. All the theorists and 'spokesmen' of the international Left (or, rather of its nothingness) deplored the irresponsibility and disorder, the pillaging, and above all the fact that *arms and alcohol* were the first targets for plunder; finally, that 2,000 fires had been started by the Watts gasoline throwers to light up their battle and their ball. But who was there to defend the rioters of Los Angeles in the terms they deserve? Well, we shall. Let us leave the economists to grieve over the twenty-seven million dollars lost, and the town planners over one of their most beautiful supermarkets gone up in smoke, and McIntyre over his slain deputy sheriff. Let the sociologists weep over the absurdity and the intoxication of this rebellion. The job of a revolutionary journal is not only to justify the Los Angeles insurgents, but to help uncover their just reasons. To explain theoretically the truth for which such practical action expresses the search.

In Algiers in July 1965, following

Boumedienne's *coup d'état*, the situationists published an *Address* to the Algerians and to revolutionaries all over the world, which interpreted conditions in Algeria and in the rest of the world *as a whole*. Among their examples, they evoked the American blacks, who, if they could "affirm themselves significantly" would unmask the contradictions of the most advanced of capitalist systems. Five weeks later this significance found an expression on the street. Theoretical criticism of modern society in its advanced forms, and criticism in actions of the same society, co-exist at this moment: still separated, but both advancing towards the same reality, both talking of the same thing. These two critiques are mutually explanatory, each being incomprehensible without the other. Our theory of 'survival' and the 'spectacle' is illuminated and verified by these actions so unintelligible to the American false consciousness. One day these actions will in turn be illuminated by this theory.

Up to this time, the black 'civil rights' demonstrations had been kept by their leaders within the limits of a legal system that overlooked the most appalling violence on the part of the police and the racialists. In Alabama the previous March, for instance, at the time of the Montgomery March and, as if this scandal was not sufficient, a discreet agreement between the Federal government, Governor Wallace and Pastor King had led the Selma marchers of 10 March to stand back at the first request, in dignity and prayer. Thus, the confrontation expected by the crowd had been reduced to the charade of a merely potential confrontation. In that moment, non-violence reached the pitiful limit of its courage. First you expose yourself to the enemies' blows, then force your moral grandeur to the point of sparing him the trouble of using more force. But the basic fact is that the civil rights movement, by remaining within the law, only posed legal problems. It is logical to make an appeal to the law legally. What is not logical is to appeal legally against a patent illegality as if this contradiction would disappear if pointed out. For it is clear that the superficial and outrageously visible illegality – from which the blacks still suffer in many American states – has its roots in a socio-economic contradiction which existing laws simply cannot touch, and which no future juridicial law will be able to get rid of in face of more basic cultural laws of the society. And it is against these that the blacks are at last daring to raise their voices and asking the right to live. In reality, the American black wants the total subversion of that society – or nothing.

The problem of this necessity for subversion arises of its own accord the moment blacks start using subversive means. The changeover to such methods happens on the level of their daily life, appearing at one and the same time as the most accidental and the most objectively justified development. This issue is no longer the status of the American black, but the status of America, even if this happens to find its first expression among the black. This was not a *racial* conflict. The rioters left alone certain whites who were in their path, attacking only the white policemen. Similarly, black solidarity did not extend to black shopkeepers, not even to black car drivers. Even Luther King, in Paris last October, had to admit that the limits of his competence had been overshot: "They were not race riots", he said, "but class ones".

The Los Angeles rebellion was a rebellion against commodities and of worker consumers *hierarchically* subordinated to commodity values. The blacks of Los Angeles – like the young delinquents of all advanced countries, but more radically, because at the level of a class globally deprived of a future, it is a sector of the proletariat unable to believe in a significant chance of integration and promotion – take modern capitalist propaganda *literally*, with its displays of affluence. They want to possess *immediately* all the objects shown and made abstractly accessible. They want to *make use* of them. That is why they reject values of exchange, the *commodity-reality* that is its mould, its purpose and its final goal, which has *pre-selected* everything. Through theft and gift they retrieve a use that at once gives the lie to the oppressive rationality of commodities, disclosing their relations and invention to be arbitrary and unnecessary. The plunder of the Watts sector was the most simple possible realisation of the hybrid principle: "To each according to his (false) needs" – needs determined and produced by the economic system, which the act of pillaging rejects.

But the fact that the vaunting abundance is taken at its face value and discovered *in the immediate* instead of being eternally pursued in the course of alienated labour and in the face of increasing but unmet social needs – this fact means that real needs are expressed in carnival, playful affirmation and the *potlach* of destruction. The man who destroys commodities shows his human superiority of commodities. He frees himself from the arbitrary forms that cloak his real needs. The flames of Watts consumed the system of consumption! The theft of large refrigerators by people with no electricity, or with their electricity cut off, gives the best possible metaphor for the life of affluence transformed into a truth *in play*. Once it is no longer bought, the commodity lies open to criticism and modification, and this under whichever of its forms it may appear. Only so long as it is paid for with money, as a status symbol of survival, can it be worshipped fetishistically. Pillage is the natural response to the affluent society: the affluence, however, is by no means *natural* or human – it is simply abundance of goods. Pillage, moreover, which instantly destroys commodities as such, discloses the *ultima ratio* of commodities, namely, the army, the police and the other specialised detachments which have the monopoly of armed force within the state. What is a policeman? He is the active servant of commodities, the man in complete submission to commodities, whose job is to ensure that a given product of human labour remains a commodity with the magical property of having to be paid for instead of becoming a mere refrigerator or rifle – a mute, passive, insensible thing, itself in submission to the first comer to make use of it. Over and above the indignity of depending on a policeman, the blacks reject the indignity of depending on commodities. The Watts youth, having no future in market terms, grasped another *quality* of the present, and the truth of that present was so irresistible that it drew on the whole population, women, children and even sociologists who happened to find themselves on the scene. A young, black sociologist of the district, Bobbi Hollon, had this to say to the *Herald Tribune* in October. "Before, people were ashamed to say they came from Watts. They'd mumble it. Now they say it with pride. Boys who always went around with their shirts open to the waist and who'd have cut you into strips in half a second, used to apply here every morning. They organised the distribution of food. Of course it's no good pretending the food wasn't plundered… All that Christian blah has been used too long against the blacks. These people could plunder for ten years and they wouldn't get back half the money that has been stolen from them all these years… Myself, I'm just a little black girl." Bobbi Hollon, who has sworn never to wash from her sandals the blood that splashed on them during the rioting, adds: "All the world looks to Watts now."

How do men make history, starting from the conditions pre-established to persuade them not to take a hand in it? The Los Angeles blacks are better paid than any others in the US, but it is also here that they are furthest behind the high point of affluence which is California. Hollywood, the pole of the worldwide spectacle, is in their immediate vicinity. They are promised that, with patience, they will join in America's prosperity, but they realise that this prosperity is not a static sphere, but

DETROIT

Anti-white feeling ran high on 12th Street in the heart of the city's major Negro ghetto, but elsewhere – and especially in integrated neighbourhoods – Negro looters smiled and waved at white policemen and newsmen.

Along one section of Grand River Avenue, where Negroes and Southern whites live in adjoining neighbourhoods, stores were raided by integrated bands of looters. At Packer's, a block-long food and clothes center, a Negro looter boosted a white looter through a window.

Scores of other Negroes and whites looted and chatted side by side in the store, loading shopping carts, boxes and bags with booty.

Negroes, who on Monday were carting off almost everything in sight, milled about the streets yesterday afternoon waving and smiling at the heavily-integrated paratroop units.

It was clear, too, that the looting cut across class, as well as racial lines. One well-dressed Negro filled up the trunk of a new Pontiac convertible with shoes, shirts and suits. Nearby, an emaciated woman pushed a shopping cart heaped high with smoked hams and canned goods.

Some Negroes obviously considered the riot a summertime frolic. At 3am, two Negro couples perched on a fence just off John Lodge Freeway, alternately kissing and watching firemen battle a major blaze.

Once, the couples broke their embrace to shout a warning to firemen. A drunken middle-aged Negro man had staggered from a building and was firing a shotgun into the still night air. Police arrived within minutes and placed the man in handcuffs.

"God damn it, shoot me!" the man shouted at the policemen.

The New York Times, Thursday 17 July 1967.

NEWARK

Nearby, several teenagers danced and laughed in the street as two of them held aloft sticks with yellow wigs on them. "We've scalped the white man!" they shouted. Governor Hughes, touring the shattered city, said bitterly, "It's like laughing at a funeral."

It was a wild and violent funeral of sorts as the Governor and Mayor, and other officials, sought yesterday to restore law and order.

Governor Hughes said after his morning inspection tour that he had found the "holiday atmosphere" among the looters most repelling.

The New York Times, Saturday 15 July 1967.

rather a ladder without end. The higher they climb, the further they get from the top, because they don't have a fair start, because they are less qualified and thus more numerous among the unemployed, and finally because the hierarchy which crushes them is not one based simply on buying power as a pure economic fact. An essential inferiority is imposed on them in every area of daily life by the customs and prejudices of a society in which all human power is based on buying power. So long as the human riches of the American black are despised and treated as criminal, monetary riches will never make him acceptable to the alienated society of America. Individual wealth may make a rich black, but the blacks as a whole *must represent poverty* in a society of hierarchised wealth. Every witness noted this cry, which proclaims the fundamental meaning of the rising: "This is the black revolution, and we want the world to know it!" *Freedom now!* is the password of all historical revolutions, but here for the first time it is not poverty but material abundance which must be controlled according to new laws. The control of abundance is not just changing the way it is shared out, but redefining *its every orientation*, superficially and profoundly alike. This is the first skirmish of an enormous struggle, infinite in its implications.

The blacks are not isolated in their struggle because a *new proletarian consciousness* – the consciousness of not being the master of one's activity, of one's life, in the slightest degree – is taking form in America among strata whose refusal of modern capitalism resembles that of the blacks. Indeed, the first phase of the black struggle has been the signal to a movement of opposition which is spreading. In December 1964, the students of Berkeley, frustrated in their participation in the civil rights movement, ended up calling a strike to oppose the system of California's 'multiversity', and by extension the social system of the US, in which they are allotted such a passive role. Immediately, drinking and drug orgies were uncovered among the students – the same supposed activities for which the blacks have long been castigated. This generation of students has since invented a new form of struggle against the dominant spectacle – the teach-in – a form taken up by the Edinburgh students on 20 October apropos of the Rhodesian crisis. This clearly imperfect and primitive type of opposition represents the stage of discussion which refuses to be limited in time (academically), and in this its logical outcome is a progression to practical activity. Also in October, thousands of demonstrators appeared in the streets of Berkeley and New York, their cries echoing those of the Watts rioters: "Get out of our district and out of Vietnam!" The whites, becoming more radical, have stepped outside the law. 'Courses' are given on how to defraud the recruiting boards, draft cards are burned and the act televised. In the affluent society, disgust for affluence and *for its price* is finding expression.

The spectacle is being spat on by an advanced sector whose autonomous activity denies its values. The classical proletariat, to the extent to which it had been provisionally integrated into the capitalist system, had itself failed to *integrate* the blacks (several Los Angeles unions refused blacks until 1950). Now, the blacks are the rallying point for all those who refuse the logic of integration into that system – integration into capitalism being, of course, the *ne plus ultra* of all integration promised. And comfort will never be comfortable enough for those who seek what is not on the market – or rather, that which the market eliminates. The level reached by the technology of the most privileged becomes an insult – and one more easily expressed than that most basic insult, which is reification. The Los Angeles rebellion is the first in history able to justify itself by the argument that there was no air-conditioning during a heatwave.

The American black has his own particular spectacle, his press, magazines, coloured film stars. And if the blacks realise this, if they spew out this spectacle for its phoneyness, as an expression of their unworthiness, it is because they see to it to be a *minority* spectacle – nothing but the appendage of a general spectacle. They recognise that this parade of their consumption-to-be-desired is a colony of the white one, and thus they see through the lie of this total economico-cultural spectacle more quickly. By wanting to participate really and immediately in affluence – and this is an official value of every American –

they demand the equalitarian *realisation* of the American spectacle of everyday life. They demand that the half-heavenly, half-terrestrial values of this spectacle be put to the test. But it is of the essence of the spectacle that it cannot be made real either immediately or equally; and this, *not even for the whites*. (In fact, the function of the black in terms of the spectacle is to serve as the perfect prod: in the race for riches, such underprivilege is an incitement to ambition.) In taking the capitalist spectacle at its face value, the blacks are already rejecting the spectacle itself. The spectacle is a drug for slaves. It is not supposed to be taken literally, but followed at just a few paces distance. If it were not for this albeit tiny distance, it would become total mystification. The fact is that in the US today, the whites are enslaved to commodities while the blacks negate them. The blacks ask for *more than the whites* – that is the core of an insoluble problem, or rather one only soluble through the dissolution of the white social system. This is why those whites who want to escape their own servitude must needs rally to the black cause. Not in a solidarity based on colour, obviously, but in a global rejection of commodities and, in the last analysis, of the state. The economic and social backwardness of the blacks allows them to see what the white consumer is, and their justified contempt for the white is nothing but contempt for any passive consumer. Whites who cast off their role have no chance unless they link their struggle more and more to the blacks' struggle, uncovering his real and coherent reasons and supporting them until the end. If such an accord were to be ruptured at a radical point in the battle, the result would be the formation of a black nationalism and a confrontation between the two splinters exactly after the fashion of the prevailing system. A phase of mutual extermination is the other possible outcome of the present situation, once resignation is overcome.

The attempts to build a black nationalism, separatist and pro-African as they are, are dreams giving no answer to the reality of oppression. The American black has no fatherland. He is in *his own country* and he is *alienated*: so is the rest of the population, but the blacks differ insofar as they are aware of it. In this sense, they are not the most backward sector of their society, but the most advanced. They are the negation at work, "the bad aspect producing the movement which makes history by setting the struggle in motion" (Marx, *The Poverty of Philosophy.*) Africa has nothing to do with it.

The American blacks are the product of modern industry, just as are electronics, advertising or the cyclotron. And they carry within them its contradictions. These are men whom the spectacle-paradise must integrate and repulse simultaneously, so that the antagonism between the spectacle and the real activity of men surrenders completely to their enunciations. The spectacle is *universal* in the same way as the commodities. But as the world of commodities is based in class conflict, commodities are themselves hierarchic. The necessity of commodities – and hence of the spectacle whose job it is to *inform* about the commodities – to be at once universal and hierarchic, leads to a universal hierarchisation. But as this hierarchisation must remain *unavowed*, it is expressed in the form of unacknowledgeable hierarchic value judgements, in a world of *reasonless rationalisation*. It is this process which creates *racialisms* everywhere. The English Labour government has just restrained coloured immigration, while the industrially-advanced countries of Europe are once again becoming racialist as they import their sub-proletariat from the Mediterranean area, so exerting a colonial exploitation within their borders. And if Russia continues to be anti-semitic, it is because she is still a society of hierarchy and commodities, in which labour must be bought and sold as a commodity.

Together, commodities and hierarchies are constantly renewing their alliance, which extends its influence by modifying its form. It is seen just as easily in the relations between trade unionist and worker as between two car owners with artificially distinguished models. This is the original sin of commodity rationality, the sickness of bourgeois reason, whose legacy is bureaucracy. But the repulsive absurdity of certain hierarchies and the fact that the whole world strength of commodities is directed blindly and automatically towards their protection, leads us to see – the moment we engage on a negating praxis – that every hierarchy is absurd.

The rational world produced by the industrial revolution has rationally liberated individuals from their local and national limitations, and related them on a world scale; but denies reason by separating them once more, according to a hidden logic which finds its expression in mad ideas and grotesque value systems. Man, estranged from his world, is everywhere surrounded by strangers. The barbarian is no longer at the ends of the earth, he is on the spot, made into a *barbarian* by this very same forced participation in hierarchised consumption. The humanism cloaking all this is opposed to man, and the negation of his activity and his desires. It is the humanism of commodities, expressing the benevolence of the parasite, merchandise, towards the men off whom it feeds. For those who reduce men to objects, objects seem to acquire human qualities, and manifestations of real human activity appear as unconscious *animal behaviour*. Thus the chief humanist of Los Angeles, William Parker, can say: "They started behaving like a bunch of monkeys in a zoo."

When the state of emergency was declared by the California authorities, the insurance companies recalled that they do not cover risks at that level: they guarantee nothing beyond survival. Overall, the American blacks can rest assured that, if they keep quiet, their *survival* is guaranteed; and capitalism has become sufficiently centralised and entrenched in the state to distribute 'welfare' to the poorest. But simply because they are *behind* in the process of intensification of socially organised survival, the blacks present problems of *life* and what they demand is not to survive but to live. The blacks have nothing to insure of their own; they have to destroy all the forms of security and private insurance known up to now. They appear as what they really are: the irreconcilable enemies – not of the vast majority of Americans – but of the alienated way of life of all modern society. The most advanced country industrially only shows us the road that will be everywhere followed unless the system is overthrown.

Certain black nationalist extremists, in showing why they could never accept less than a separate state, have advanced the argument that American society, even if it someday concedes total civic and economic equality, will never get around to accepting mixed marriages. *It is therefore this American society which must disappear*, not only in America but everywhere in the world. The end of all racial prejudice (like the end of so many other prejudices such as sexual ones related to inhibitions) can only lie beyond 'marriage' itself; that is, beyond *the bourgeois family* (which is questioned by the American blacks). This is the rule as much in Russia as in the United States, as a model of hierarchical relations and of the stability of an *inherited power* (be it money or socio-bureaucratic status). It is now often said that American youth, after thirty years of silence, is rising again as a force of opposition and that the black revolt is their Spanish civil war. This time, its 'Lincoln Battalions' must understand the full significance of the struggle in which they engage, supporting it up to the end of its

On sale as a suitable Christmas present for a child: 'The Conway Stewart Riot Control Set'.

The illustration below is taken from the box. The set comprises "eight colouring cards with 48 pop-out characters, two vehicles and one barricade" and "approximately 36-in. of street scene".

A spokesman for Conway Stewart says they thought it would be quite a good theme to have: "It's the sort of thing that goes."

What about the man on the ground and the one with the truncheon? "He's not 'hitting' him, is he?" said the spokesman.

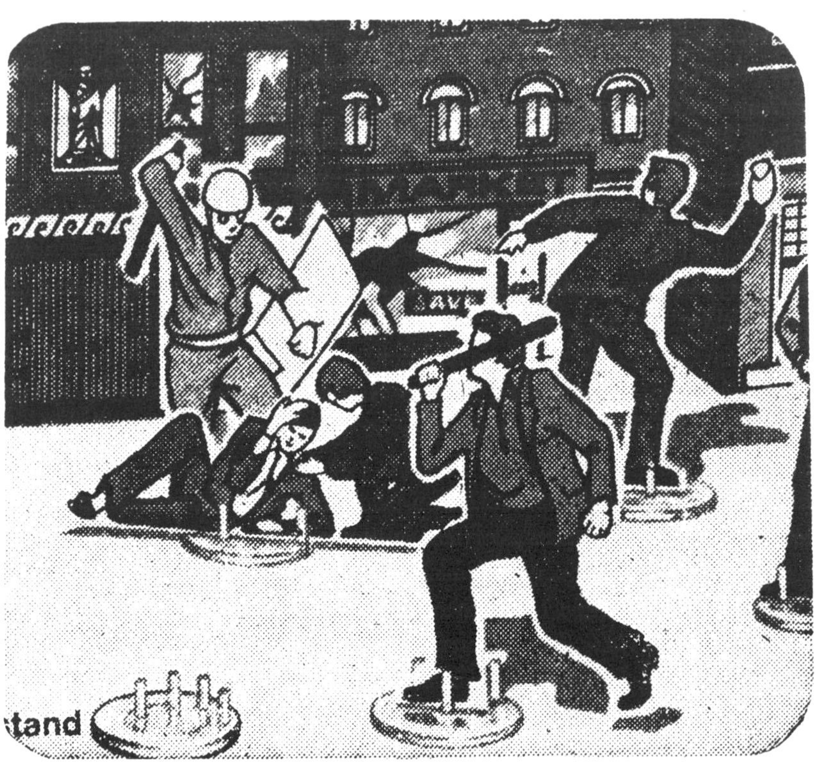

universal implications. The ‘excesses’ of Los Angeles are no more a political error in the Black Revolt than the armed resistance of the POUM in Barcelona, May 1937, was a betrayer of the anti-Franquist war. A rebellion against the spectacle is situated on the level of the *totality*, because – even were it only to appear in a single district, Watts – it is a protest by men against the inhuman life; because it begins at the level of the *real single individual*, and because community, from which the individual in revolt is separated, is the *true social nature* of man, human, nature: the positive supersession of the spectacle.

Martin/Strijbosch/Vaneigem/Viénet, IS no. 9 1964.

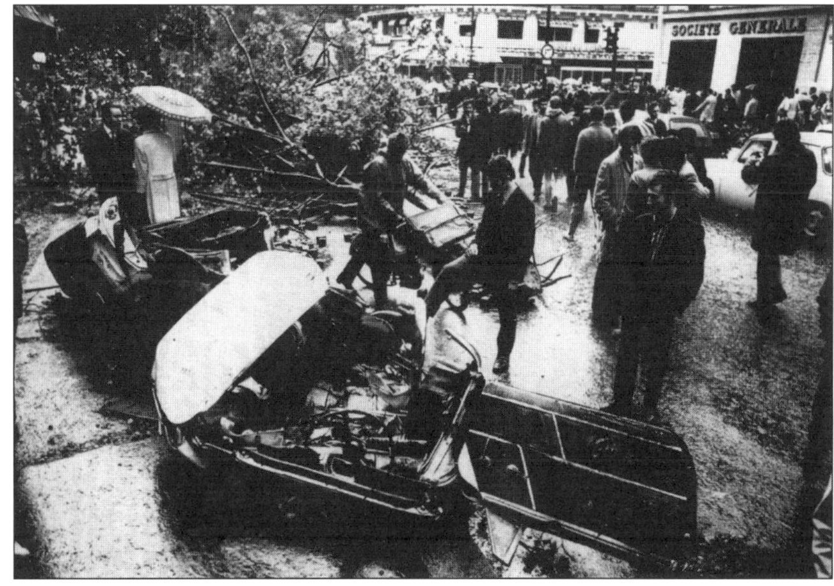

THE DECOR AND THE SPECTATORS OF SUICIDE

AMERICANS CHANGE THEIR FACES

New York, Thursday – Chain stores are meeting a rush of orders for a newly-invented realistic face-fitting rubber mask, thin and easy to wear. A New York drug store reports that it is selling – for a dollar each – more than 100 a day – many to businessmen and well-dressed women. A New York psychiatrist, Dr JL Moreno, commenting that many people are "dissatisfied with their personalities", said: "Wearing a mask enables them to become anonymous and to play at being someone else – someone more glamorous, perhaps."

– AP

Suicide has now practically reached epidemic proportions in the United States. In 1965 it took tenth place among the causes of death in the country, and *third place* among those of young people. Setting up 'anti-suicide centres', one of them operating on a nationwide level, is now being seriously considered.

Recently, in France, a certain Bernard Durin killed himself – apparently without reason. He was 37 years' old and had been a model employee for the last fifteen of them. Everyone who knew him agreed that "he had everything one needs to be happy". He had a "ten-year-old daughter, Agnès, who got on well at school. A charming wife. A good job at IBM. A salary of F2,500 a month. An attractively-furnished modern apartment. A 404. A television, a washing machine, a refrigerator and even an aquarium".

In an article in *France-Soir* (24 December 1964), Charles Caron wrote: "The shop where Durin worked was situated in a multi-storey, glass-fronted building. His section consisted largely of small metal offices. Shelves stretched out of sight. Metal shelves. Metal filing cabinets. It was there that the spare parts Durin sorted out and packaged up were kept. No windows. Neon light. His timetable was irregular. The shop was open from seven in the morning until twelve at night. His shift was changed every fortnight. Sometimes he got up at five-thirty in the morning and finished at four in the afternoon. Sometimes he finished at one in the morning. Durin was a model employee. No one worked harder. Someone suggested he take a postal course in English. He did so. He studied in the evening. He studied on Saturday and Sunday... When he left the shop in Vincennes, Durin drove back to his home in Bondy in his 404. He drove in the queues of traffic you all know. He waited in the traffic jams. He saw the lights of the tower blocks of Bondy. The straight lines. The concrete. The shopping centre in the middle. He lived in apartment number 1153, 13 rue Léon-Blum, FG3. That was his life: electronics, skyscraper housing estates, cars, refrigerators and televisions. It was also his death."

For several years now, at least in the States, it hasn't been uncommon to see excited crowds watching someone who has been driven desperate threaten to hurl themselves down from a window-ledge or a roof. Whether the public has become blasé, or whether it is attracted by more professional spectacles, it doesn't intend to pay any further attention to these 'unofficial stars' unless they got on with it, and jump. So far as we know, it was on 16 April 1964, in Albany, New York State, that, for the first time this new attitude came out into the open. While Richard Reinemann, aged 19, prevaricated for the best part of two hours on a twelfth-storey ledge, a crowd of some four thousand people watching him

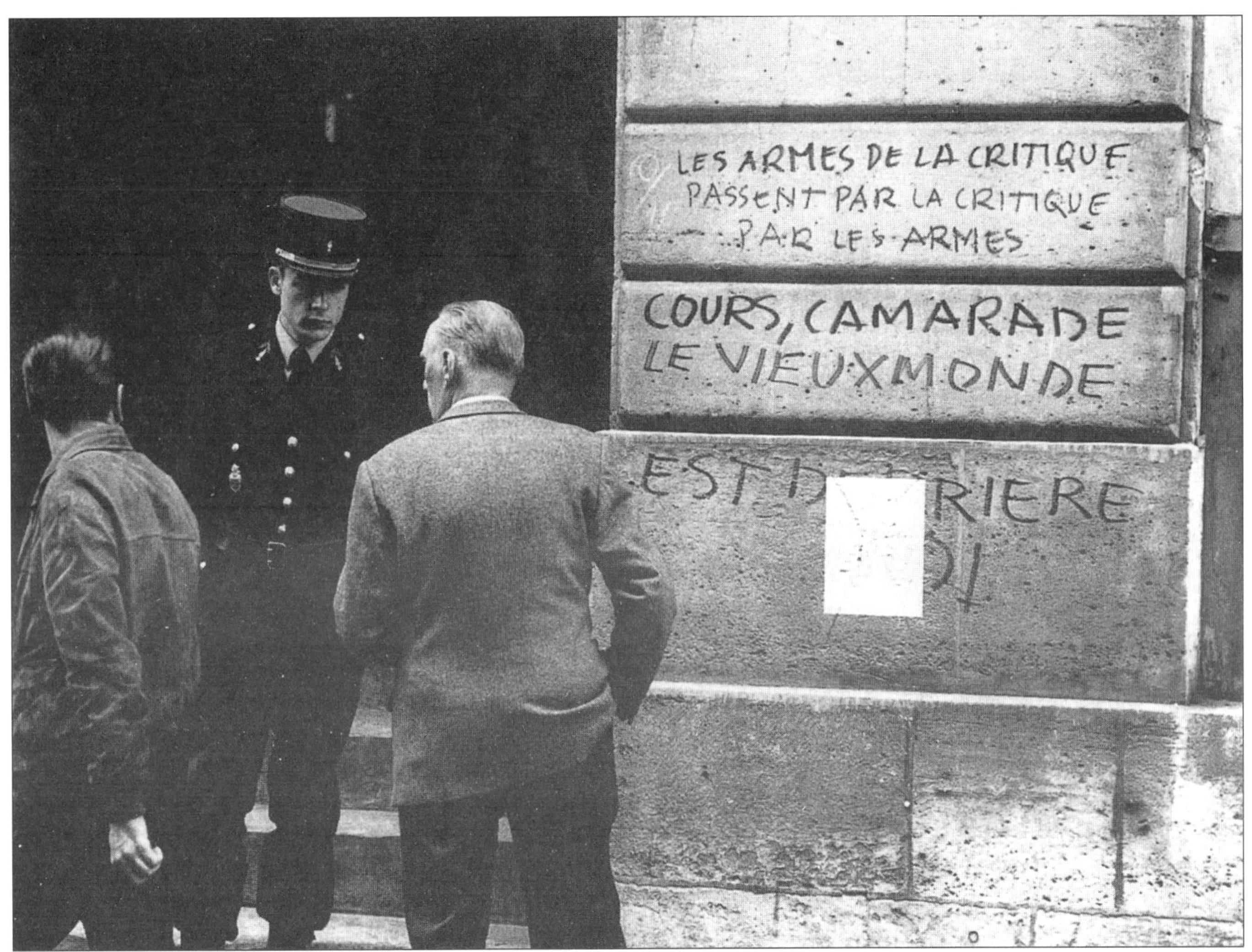

chanted "Jump". A female passerby explained: "I don't want to have to wait all night. I've already missed my favourite TV programme.

IS no. 10, 1966

THE SITUATIONISTS AND THE NEW FORMS OF STRUGGLE AGAINST POLITICS AND ART

For higher industrial productivity, get workers and their bosses acting in plays together, recommend psychodrama experts at their most recent congress in Paris.

Headline France-Soir, 3 September 1964

To date we have seen subversive activity almost exclusively in terms of forms and categories inherited from revolutionary struggles, most of which took place in the last century. I would like to suggest that we find new weapons that can dispense with any reference to the past. I'm not saying we should simply abandon those forms we have used to fight on the traditional grounds of the supersession of philosophy, the realisation of art and the abolition of politics. What I am saying is that we should complete the work of the magazine; find its complement in areas where the magazine has failed to have any effect.

Countless workers know perfectly well that they have no control over the use of their lives. They know it, but they don't say so in the language of nineteenth century socialism.

What we have to do is to relate theoretical criticism of this society to the more practical forms of opposition appearing in its midst. Merely by subverting the spectacle's own propositions, we can produce, straight away, more than enough reasons to justify any revolt, either today or tomorrow.

I would suggest:

1 THE SUBVERSION OF PHOTO-COMICS

Also of so-called pornographic photos. The latter could be made very powerful indeed simply by adding some real dialogue. Subversive *bubbles* begin to form inside everyone looking at these photos: instead of leaving these bubbles to dissolve and disappear again, this operation will make them break out all over the surface of things. In fact, *the whole of commercial advertising* could be subverted simply by adding speech bubbles; in particular, the posters along the underground corridors, some of which fall into pretty extraordinary sequences in any case.

2 GUERRILLA IN THE MASS MEDIA

An extremely important form of struggle, even before the stage of urban guerrilla properly speaking. The way has been paved by those Argentinians who seized the control deck of one of those giant neon signs that can produce whole series of changing pictures and slogans and broadcast their own recommendations to society at large. Anyone who was thinking of having a crack at radio or TV studios had better get a move on as it won't be too long before they're actually guarded by the army. More modestly, if anyone into ham radio can, for next to nothing, jam, if not broadcast on a local level. The small size of the equipment concerned allowing one extreme mobility and other expedients to escape detection. A few years ago, a small group of people kicked out of the Danish CP had their own pirate radio station for a while. Fake numbers of various periodicals could add to the general confusion of the enemy. This list of examples is vague and limited for reasons that should be obvious.

The illegality of this type of action cuts it out for any organisation that hasn't chosen to go underground. Otherwise it means the formation of a separate *specific organisation* within the main one; and this is impossible without watertight compartmentalisation, thus hierarchy etc: without, in a word, being on the primrose path to terrorism. Propaganda by the deed, however, is a very different matter and would seem to be far more to the point. Our ideas are in everyone's mind – we all know that – and any small group of people can improvise and improve upon experiments already made by others. This type of non-concerted action cannot hope to cause any major upheaval, but it could play quite a considerable role in speeding up the consciousness growing throughout society. In any case, there's no need to get so hung up about the word illegal. Most cases of this type of action aren't actually illegal anyway. But fear of this sort of action will make newspaper editors paranoid about their typesetters, directors of broadcasting paranoid about their technicians, etc, at least until a more up-to-date, more specific, repressive legislation has been worked out.

3 SITUATIONIST COMICS

Comics are the only truly popular literature of the twentieth century. Those permanently damaged by their years at school seem to have difficulty stopping themselves writing PhDs on the subject. However, they'll get little joy out of reading and collecting ours. Presumably they'll buy them just for the pleasure of burning them. This approach – as against pop art, which breaks comics down into pieces – is designed to restore to comics their lifeblood and their grandeur.

4 SITUATIONIST FILMS

The cinema, the most modern and clearly the most flexible form of expression in our time, has remained static for nearly three-quarters of a century. It may well be the 'seventh art' so dear to *cinéastes* and film clubs, but, so far as we are concerned, the cycle has been completed (Ince, Stroheim, the only *Age d'or, Citizen Kane, Mr Arkadin* and the lettrist films), even if there are a few masterpieces still to be unearthed in film archives or on the shelves of foreign distributors. We should take over the first lispings of this new language; in particular its most sophisticated, its most modern examples, which have escaped artistic ideology even more successfully than American grade 'B' movies: newsreels, trailers and, above all, ads.

In the service of the commodity and the spectacle, to say the least of it, but free technically, commercial advertising on TV and in the cinema has laid the foundations of what Eisenstein had glimpsed when he talked of filming *The Critique of Political Economy* or *The German Ideology*.

I am sure I could film *The Decline and Fall of the Spectacular Commodity Economy* in such a way that any worker in Watts could understand it, even if he hadn't a clue as to the meaning of the title. And this working in a new medium would indefinitely help to sharpen up our handling of the same problems in prose. This could be checked out by, for example, making the film *Incitation to Murder and Debauchery* before writing *Correctives to the Consciousness of a Class which will be the Last One*, its equivalent in the magazine. The cinema lends itself particularly well to the study of the present as a historic problem, to the dismantling of the process of reification. Certainly, historic reality can only be apprehended, known and filmed in the course of a complicated process of mediations which allow consciousness to recognise one moment in another, its goal and its action in destiny, its destiny in its goal and its action, and its own essence in this necessity. A mediation which would be difficult if the empiric existence of facts themselves was not already a mediated existence which only takes on the appearance of immediacy insofar as, and because of, a) consciousness of mediation is absent, and b) facts have been uprooted from their determining circumstances and placed in an artificial isolation, ill-related in terms of montage in the traditional cinema, which ground to a halt with so-called objective forms, with the refurbishing of politico-moral concepts, on the rare occasions it managed to avoid academic type

The Mayor of the Chilean town of Punta Arenas has announced that Santa Claus will be granted a safe-conduct to pass through military checkpoints during the country's emergency curfew.

The Guardian

SITUATIONIST PROPAGANDA IN SPAIN (1964)

I can't think of anything better than sleeping with an Asturian miner. They're real men!

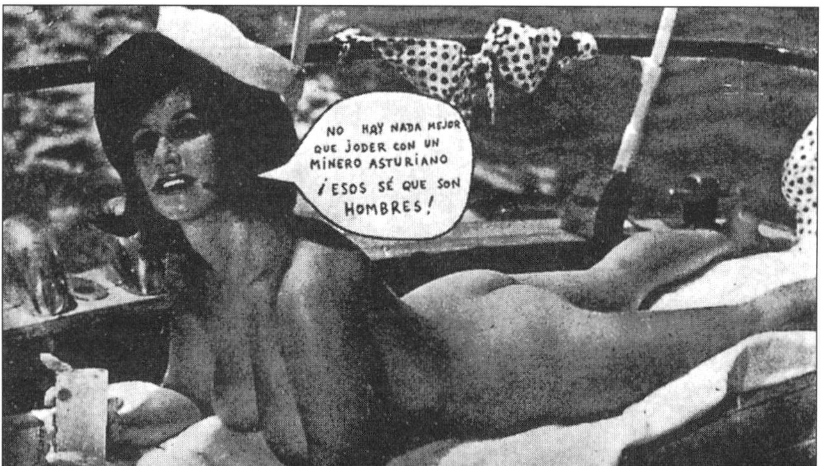

The emancipation of the proletariat will be the work of the proletariat itself!

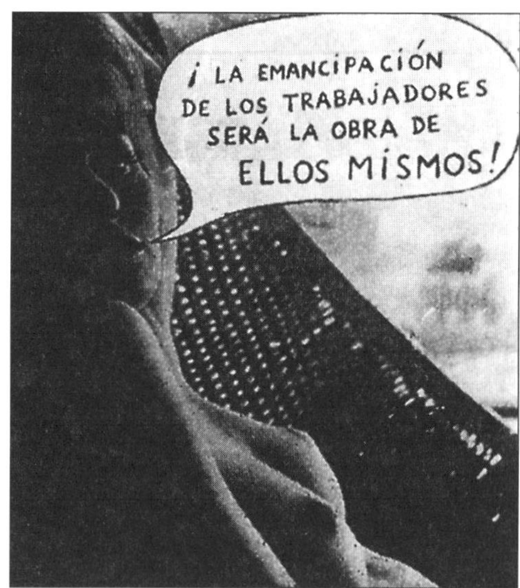

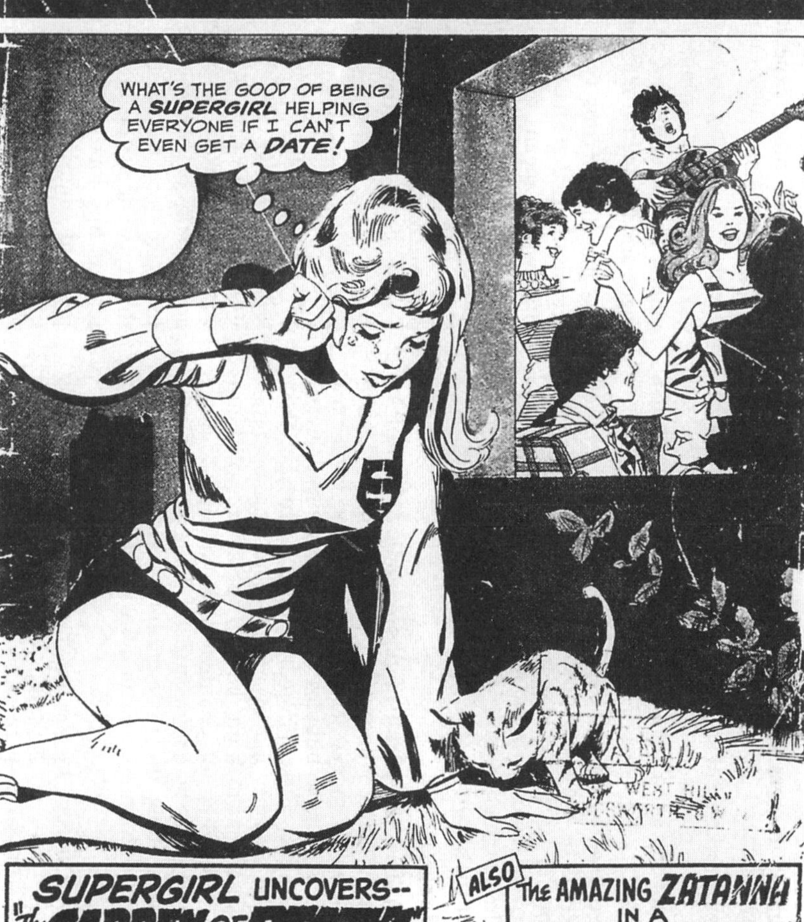

narrative with all its bullshit. That little lot, for a start, would be better off as a film than as prose. Not that Godard – the best known of the pro-Chinese Swiss – would understand much of it either way... though he might try and recuperate it, a word or a phrase taken from it, like commercial advertising. He'll never be able to do more than make a noise about the latest novelties he has picked up, the images or star words of the time (Bonnot, worker Marx, made in the USA, Pierrot le Fou, Debord, poetry, etc). He really is the child of Mao and Coca-Cola.

The cinema allows one to express anything, just as much as a book, an article, a leaflet or a poster. Which is why we should stipulate that from now on every situationist should be as good at making a film as at writing an article. Nothing is too good for the blacks of Watts.

René Viénet, IS no. 11 1967

MINIMUM DEFINITION OF A REVOLUTIONARY ORGANISATION

I

The only possible purpose of a revolutionary organisation is the abolition of all existing classes in such a way that no new division of society is produced. Thus we see an organisation as being revolutionary if it pursues *effectively*, drawing on the experience of the proletarian revolutions of this century, the international and absolute power of the workers' councils.

II

A revolutionary organisation either develops a critique of life as a whole or it is worthless. By critique of life we mean a critique of all the geographic zones where diverse forms of socio-economic power are established, plus a critique of every aspect of life.

III

The Alpha and Omega of a revolutionary programme is the total decolonisation of everyday life. Its goal is not the self-management of the world as it is by the masses; its goal is the permanent transformation of the world. This entails a radical critique of political economy: the supersession of the commodity and of wage labour.

IV

A revolutionary organisation rejects any reproduction within itself of the hierarchical structure of contemporary society. The only limit of participation in its total democracy is the recognition and self-approbation of each of its members of the coherence of its critique. This coherence resides in the critical theory itself and in the relation between this theory and practical activity. It radically criticises all ideology as separate power of ideas and as ideas of separate power. It is at once the negation of any survival of religion and of the prevailing social spectacle, which, from news media to mass culture, monopolises communication between people around their passive reception of the images of their own alienated activity. It erodes all 'revolutionary ideology' by showing it to be the most important symptom of the failure of the revolutionary project, the private property of new power specialists, the imposture of a new representation which erects itself above our real proletarianised life.

adopted by the Seventh Conference of the SI, July 1966.

Monkey skins, duck feathers, palm leaves and artificial flowers stolen from graveyards seem to be the distinguishing features of the mulelist uniform, but individual idiosyncrasy isn't frowned upon. Pan scrubs, typewriter ribbons and Christmas tree decorations are also extremely fashionable...

At this moment, one of the 'simbas' on guard sees two Europeans taking the air on a second floor balcony. He shouts in French, intoxicated with his own power:

— Didn't you know that you were invited too? Come on now, come down or we'll shoot. Brothers, this is the revolution!

The two whites comply. Everyone is watching them: the chit-chat, the attempt to socialise has vanished into thin air. All that's left is a feeling of malaise that creeps over one insiduously, like depression.

— They play, someone whispers to me sadly, they play the whole time, even when they kill you.

'Eight days with the strange rebels of the Congo', France-Soir, 4 August 1964.

LE PROLÉTARIAT COMME SUJET ET COMME REPRÉSENTATION

LA SOCIETE DU SPECTACLE
par Guy Debord

(Buchet-Chastel)

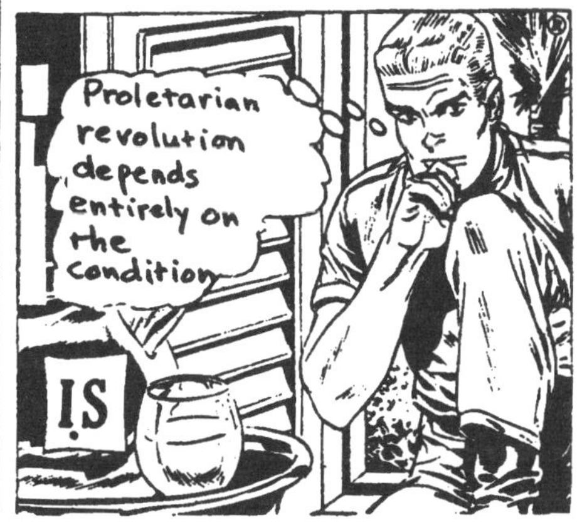

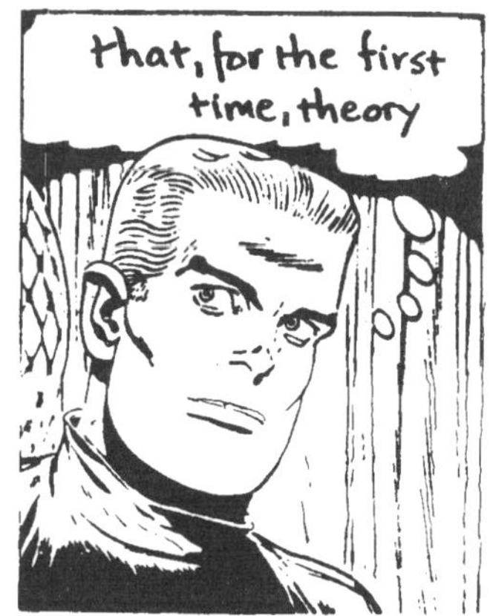

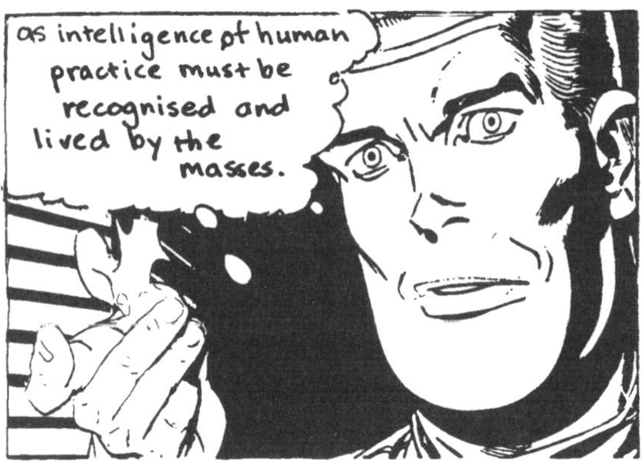

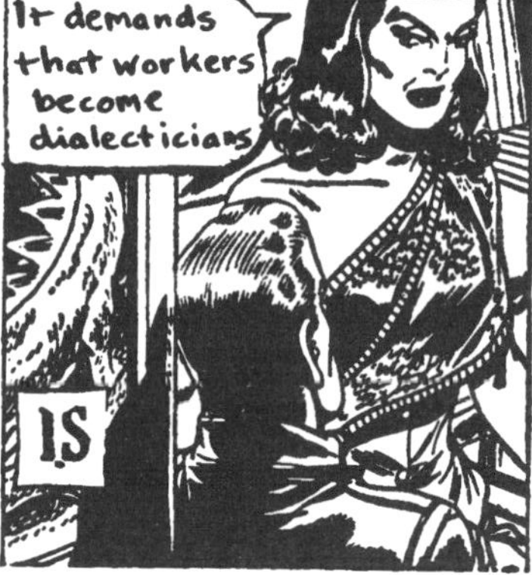

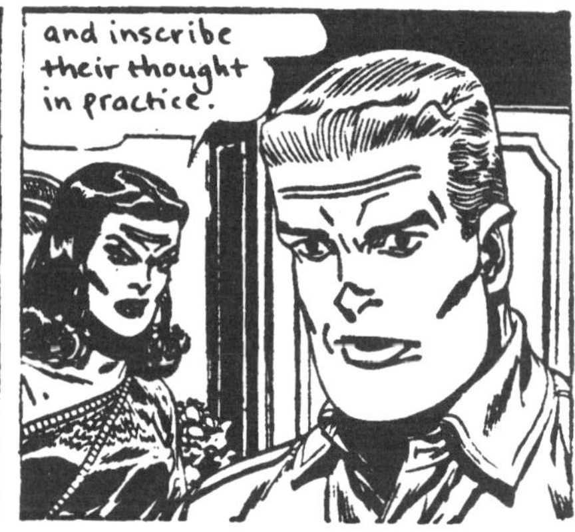

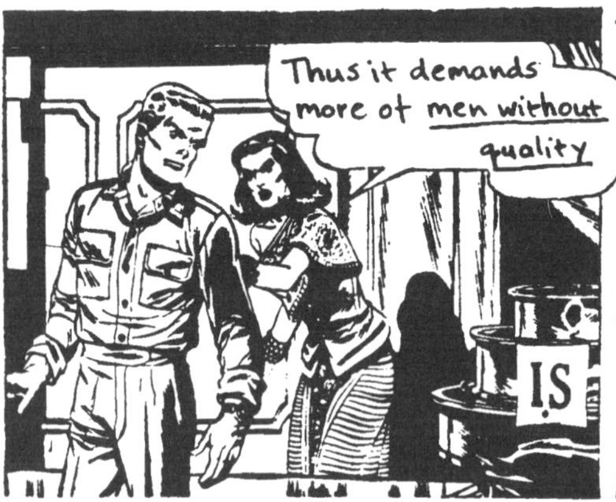

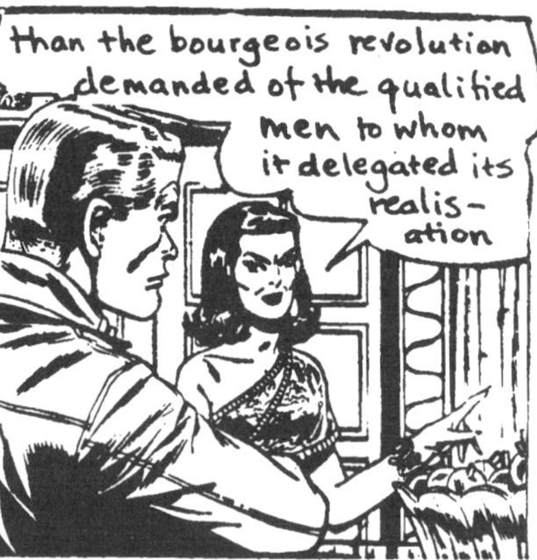

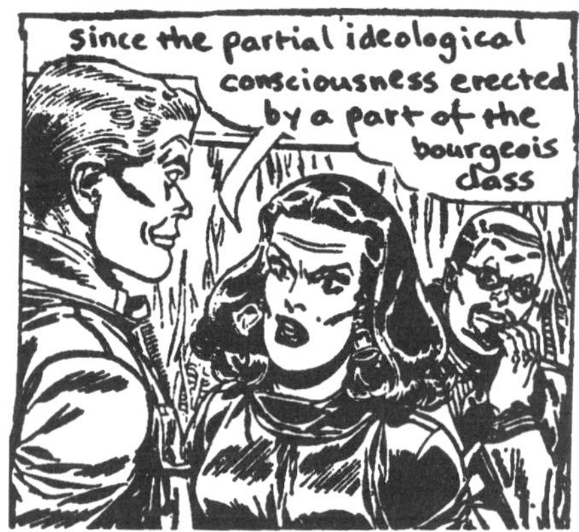

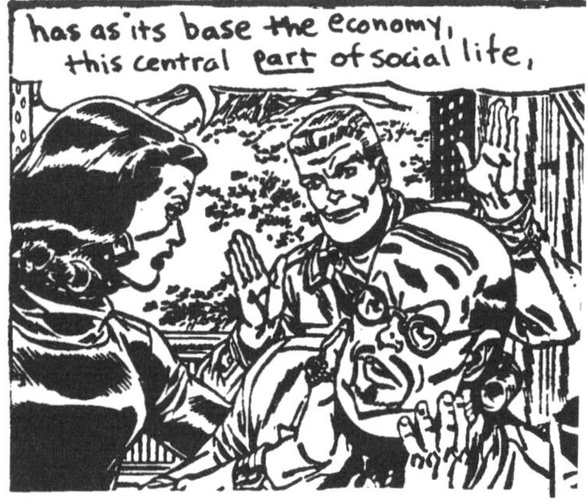

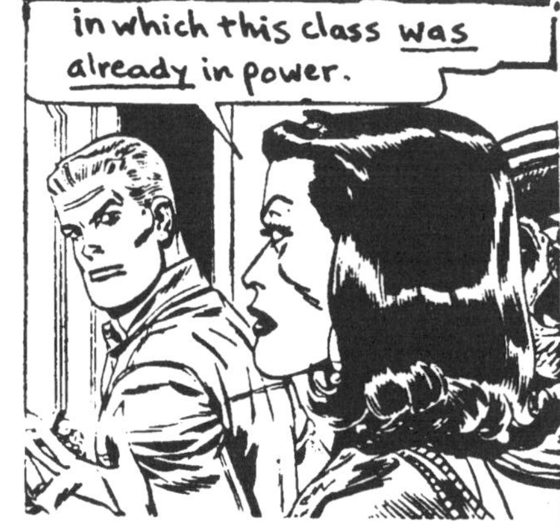

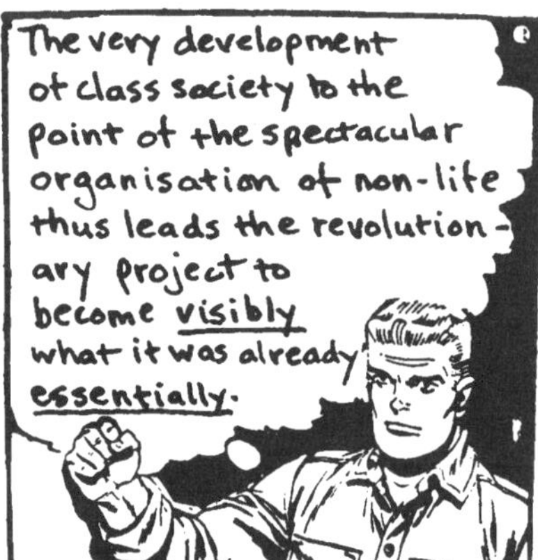

THE PROLETARIAT AS SUBJECT AND AS REPRESENTATION

The equal right of all to the goods and joys of this world, the destruction of all authority, the negation of all moral restraint – there, if one goes to the heart of the matter, is the profound reason for the insurrection of 18 March and the charter of the fearsome association that provided it with an army.

Parliamentary inquest on the insurrection of 18 March

The real movement that expresses the existing conditions rules over society from the moment of the bourgeoisie's victory in the economy, and visibly after the political translation of this victory. The development of productive forces shattered the old relations of production and all static order turns to dust. Whatever was absolute becomes historical.

By being thrown into history, by having to participate in the labour and struggles which make up history, men find themselves forced to view their relationships in a lucid manner. This history has no object distinct from what it realises by itself, even though the last unconscious metaphysical vision of the historical epoch could view the productive progression through which history has unfolded as the very object of history. The *subject* of history can only be the living producing himself, becoming master and possessor of his world which is history, and existing as *consciousness of his game*.

The class struggles of the long *revolutionary epoch* introduced by the rise of the bourgeoisie, develop in the same current as the *thought of history*, the dialectic, the thought which no longer lingers to look for the meaning of what is, but rises to a knowledge of the dissolution of all that is, and in its movement dissolves all separation.

Hegel no longer had to *interpret* the world, but the *transformation* of the world. By *only interpreting* the transformation, Hegel is only the *philosophical* completion of philosophy. He wants to understand a world *which makes itself*. This historical thought is so far only the consciousness which always arrives too late, and which pronounces the justification after the fact. Thus it has gone beyond separation only in *thought*. The paradox which consists of making the meaning of all reality depend on its historical completion, and at the same time of revealing this meaning as it makes itself into the completion of history, flows from the simple fact that the thinker of the bourgeois revolutions of the seventeenth and eighteenth centuries sought in his philosophy only a *reconciliation* with the results of these revolutions. "Even as a philosophy of the bourgeois revolution, it does not express the entire process of this revolution but only its final conclusion. In this sense, it is not a philosophy of the revolution, but of the restoration" (Karl Korsch, *Theses on Hegel and Revolution*). Hegel did, for the last time, the work of the philosopher, 'the glorification of what exists'; but what existed for him could already be nothing less than

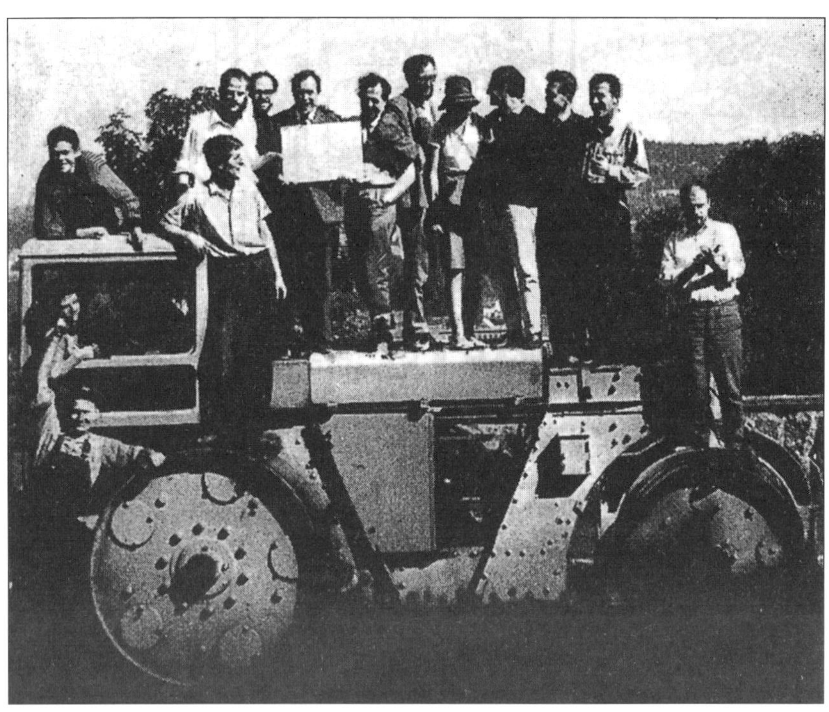

After the 5th Conference of the IS, at Goteborg in 1961, the situationists fraternise with Swedish workers.

the totality of historical movement. The external position of thought having in fact been preserved, it could be masked only by its identification with an earlier project of Spirit, absolute hero who did what he wanted and wanted what he did, and whose accomplishment coincides with the present. Thus philosophy, which dies in the thought of history, can no longer glorify its world only by denying it, since in order to speak it must presuppose that this total history to which it has reduced everything is already complete and that the only tribunal where the judgement of truth could be given is closed.

When the proletariat shows by its own existence through acts that this thought of history is not forgotten, the denial of the *conclusion* is at the same time the confirmation of the method.

The thought of history can only be saved by becoming practical thought; and the practice of the proletariat as a revolutionary class cannot be less than historical consciousness operating on the totality of its world. All the theoretical currents of the *revolutionary* workers' movement grew out of a critical confrontation with Hegelian thought – Stirner and Bakunin as well as Marx.

The inseparable character of Marx's theory and the Hegelian method is itself inseparable from the revolutionary character of this theory, namely from its truth. In respect to the latter, this first relationship has been generally ignored, misunderstood, or, worse yet, denounced as the weakness of what erroneously became a Marxist *doctrine*. Bernstein, in his *Theoretical Socialism and Social-Democratic Practice*, perfectly reveals the connection between the dialectical method and historical *partisanship* by deploring the unscientific forecasts of the 1847 *Manifesto* on the imminence of proletarian revolution in Germany: "This historical auto-suggestion, so erroneous that any political visionary could hardly have found better, would be incomprehensible in a Marx, who at that time had already seriously studied economics, if one could not see in this the product of a leftover of the antithetical Hegelian dialectic from which Marx, no less than Engels, could never completely free himself. In those times of general effervescence, this was all the more fatal to him."

The *reversal* which Marx brings about for a 'salvage through transfer' of the thought of bourgeois revolutions does not trivially consist in putting the materialist development of productive forces in the place of the trajectory of the Hegelian Spirit moving towards its encounter with itself in time, its becoming objective being identical to its alienation, and its historical wounds leaving no scars. History become real no longer has a *goal*. Marx has ruined the *separate* position of Hegel confronted with what its does. On the other hand, it is the contemplation of the economy's movement in the dominant thought of the present society which is the *non-reversed* heritage of the *non-dialectical* part of Hegel's efforts towards a circular system. It is an approval which has lost the dimension of the concept and which no longer needs a Hegelianism to justify itself, because the movement which it seeks to praise is no more than a sector without a world view, whose mechanical development effectively dominates the whole. Marx's project is the project of a conscious history. The quantitative which arises in the blind development of merely economic productive forces must be transformed into a qualitative historical appropriation. The *critique of political economy* is the first act of this *end of prehistory*: "Of all the instruments of production, the greatest productive power is the revolutionary class itself."

What closely links Marx's theory with scientific thought is the rational understanding of the forces which really operate in society. But Marx's theory is fundamentally *beyond* scientific thought, where scientific thought is only preserved inasmuch as it is superseded. The question is to understand *struggle*, and not the *laws*. "We know only one science: the science of history" (*The German Ideology*).

The bourgeois epoch, which wants to give a scientific foundation to history, overlooks the fact that this existing science had itself rather to be historically based in the economy. Inversely, history radically depends on economic knowledge only to the extent that it remains *economic history*. The degree to which the role of history in the economy (the global process which modifies its own basic scientific premises) could be overlooked by the viewpoint of scientific observation is shown by the vanity of those socialist calculations which thought they had established the exact periodicity of crises. Since the constant intervention of the state succeeded in compensating for the effect of tendencies towards crisis, the same type of reasoning sees in this equilibrium a definitive economic harmony. The project of overcoming the economy, the project of taking possession of history, even if it must know – and bring back to itself – the science of society, cannot itself be *scientific*. In this latter movement which thinks it can dominate present history by means of scientific knowledge, the revolutionary point of view remains.

The utopian currents of socialism, although themselves historically grounded in the critique of the existing social organisation, can rightly be called utopian to the extent that they reject history – namely the real struggle taking place – as well as the movement of time beyond the immutable perfection of their picture of a happy society; but not because they reject science. On the contrary, utopian thinkers are completely dominated by the scientific thought of earlier centuries. They sought the completion of this general rational system: they did not in any way consider themselves disarmed prophets, since they believed in the social power of scientific proof and even, in the case of Saint-Simonism, in the seizure of power by science. How, asked Sombart, "did they want to seize through struggle what must be *proved*?" Nevertheless, the scientific conception of the utopians did not extend to the knowledge that some social groups have interests in the existing situation, the forces to maintain it, and also the forms of false consciousness corresponding to such positions. This conception remained well within the historical reality of the development of science itself, which was largely oriented by the *social demand* that came from such factors which selected not only what could be admitted, but also what could be researched. The utopian socialists, remaining prisoners of the *mode of exposition of scientific truth*, conceived this truth in terms of its pure abstract image, in the same way as it had been imposed at a much earlier stage of society. As Sorel observed, it is on the model of *astronomy* that the utopians thought they would discover and demonstrate the laws of society. The harmony envisaged by them, hostile to history, flows from an attempt to apply to society the science least dependent on history. This harmony tries to make itself visible with the experimental innocence of Newtonianism, and the happy destiny constantly postulated "plays in their social science a role analogous to that which inertia holds in rational mechanics" (*Matériaux pour une théorie du prolétariat*).

The deterministic-scientific side in the thought of Marx was precisely the gap through which the process of 'ideologisation' penetrated into the theoretical heritage left to the workers' movement when he was still alive. The coming of the historical subject is still pushed off until later, and it is economics, the historical science par excellence, which tends increasingly to guarantee the necessity of its own future negation. But what is pushed out of the field of theoretical vision in this manner is the revolutionary practice which is the only truth of this negation. What becomes important is patiently to study economic development, and continue to accept suffering with a Hegelian tranquillity, so that the result remains a 'graveyard of good intentions'. One discovers that now, according to the science of revolutions, *consciousness always* comes too soon, and has to be taught. "History has shown that we, and all who thought as we did, were wrong. History has clearly shown that the state of economic development on the continent at that time was far from being ripe...", Engels was to say in 1895. Throughout his life, Marx had maintained a unitary point of view in his theory, but the *statement* of the theory was carried out on the *terrain* of the dominant thought by becoming precise in the form of critiques of particular disciplines, principally the critique of the fundamental science of bourgeois society, political economy. It is this mutilation, later accepted as definitive, which has constituted 'Marxism'.

The shortcoming of Marx's theory is naturally the shortcoming of the revolutionary struggle of the proletariat of his time. The working class did not set off the permanent revolution in the Germany of 1848; the Commune was defeated in isolation. Revolutionary theory thus cannot yet achieve its own total existence. Marx's being reduced to defending and clarifying it within the separation of scholarly work, in the British Museum, implied a loss in the theory itself. It is precisely the scientific justifications drawn about the future development of the working class, and the organisational practice combined with these justifications, which were to become the obstacles to proletarian consciousness at a more advanced stage.

All the theoretical insufficiency of the *scientific* defence of proletarian revolution can be traced, in terms of content as well as form of statement, to an identification of the proletariat with the bourgeoisie.

The tendency to base a proof of the scientific validity of proletarian power on *repeated* experiments in the past obscures Marx's historical thought, from the *Manifesto* on, forcing Marx to advocate a *linear* image of the development of modes of production brought on by class struggles which end, each time, "with a revolutionary transformation of the entire society or with a mutual destruction of the classes in struggle". But in the visible reality of history, as Marx observed elsewhere, the 'Asiatic mode of production' preserved its immobility in spite of all class confrontations, just as the serf uprisings never defeated the landlords, nor the slave revolts of Antiquity the free men. The linear schema loses sight of the fact that *the bourgeoisie is the only revolutionary class that ever won*; at the same time it is the only class for which the development of the economy was the cause and the consequence of its taking hold of society. The same simplification led Marx to neglect the economic role of the state in the management of a class society. If the rising bourgeoisie seemed to liberate the economy from the state, this only took place to the extent that the former state was the instrument of class oppression in a *static economy*. The bourgeoisie developed its autonomous economic power in the mediaeval period of the weakening of the state, at the moment of feudal fragmentation of balanced powers. But the modern state, which through Mercantilism began to support the development of the bourgeoisie, and which finally became *its state* at the time of '*laisser faire, laisser passer*', was to reveal later that it was endowed with a central power in the calculated management of the *economic process*. Marx was nevertheless able to describe, in *Bonapartism*, the outline of the modern statist bureaucracy, the fusion of capital and state, the formation of a "national power of capital over labour, a public force organised for social enslavement", in which the bourgeoisie renounces all historical life which is not its reduction to the economic history of things, and would like to "be condemned to the same political nothingness as other classes". Here, the socio-political foundations of the modern spectacle are already established, negatively defining the proletariat as *the only pretender to historical life*.

The only two classes which effectively correspond to Marx's theory, the two pure classes towards which the entire analysis of *Capital* leads, the bourgeoisie and the proletariat, are also the only two revolutionary classes in history, but in very different conditions. The bourgeois revolution is completed; the proletarian revolution is a project born on the foundation of the preceding revolution but differing from it qualitatively. By neglecting the *originality* of the historical role of the bourgeoisie, one masks the concrete originality of the proletarian project, which can attain nothing if not by carrying its own colours and by knowing the 'immensity of its tasks'. The bourgeoisie came to power because it is the class of the development economy. The proletariat cannot itself be the power except by becoming the *class of consciousness*. The growth of productive forces cannot guarantee such a power, even by the detour of the increasing dispossession which it creates. A Jacobin seizure of power cannot be its instrument. No *ideology* can serve the proletariat to disguise its partial goals because it cannot preserve any partial reality which is effectively its own.

If Marx, in a given period of his participation in the proletariat's struggle, expected too much from scientific forecasting, to the point of creating the intellectual foundation for the illusions of economism, it is known that he did not personally succumb to those illusions. In a well-known letter of 7 December 1867, accompanying an article where he himself criticised *Capital*, an article which Engels had to pass off to the press as the work of an adversary, Marx clearly exposed the limits of his own science: "...The *subjective* tendency of the author (which was perhaps imposed on him by his political position and his past), namely the manner in which he views and presents to others the ultimate results of the real movement, the real social process, has no relation to his own actual analysis." Thus Marx, by denouncing the 'tendentious conclusions' of his own objective analysis, and by the irony of the 'perhaps' with reference to the extra-scientific choices imposed on him, at the same time shows the methodological key of the fusion of the two aspects.

The fusion of knowledge and action must be realised in the historical struggle itself, so that each of these terms places the guarantee of its truth in the other. The formation of the proletarian class into a subject means the organisation of revolutionary struggles and the organisation of society at the *revolutionary moment*: it is then that the *practical conditions of consciousness* must exist, conditions in which the theory of praxis is confirmed by becoming practical theory. However, this central question of organisation was the question least developed by revolutionary theory at the time when the workers' movement was founded, namely when this theory still had the *unitary* character which came from the thought of history. (Theory had undertaken precisely this task in order to develop a unitary historical *practice*.) On the contrary, this question is the locus of *inconsistency* for this theory, allowing its recapture by statist and hierarchic methods of application borrowed from the bourgeois revolution. The forms of organisation of the workers' movement developed on the basis of this renunciation of theory have in turn tended to prevent the maintenance of a unitary theory, disintegrating it into varied specialised and partial disciplines. This ideological estrangement from theory can then no longer recognise the practice verification of the unitary historical thought which it had betrayed when such verification emerges in the spontaneous struggle of the workers; it can only help in repressing the manifestation and the memory of it. Yet these historical forms which appeared in the struggle are precisely the practical milieu which the theory needed to be true. They are requirements of the theory which have not been formulated theoretically. The *soviet* was not a theoretical discovery, while its existence in practice was already the highest theoretical truth of the International Workingmen's Association.

The first successes of the struggle of the International led it to free itself from the confused influences of the dominant ideology which survived in it. But the defeat and repression which it soon encountered

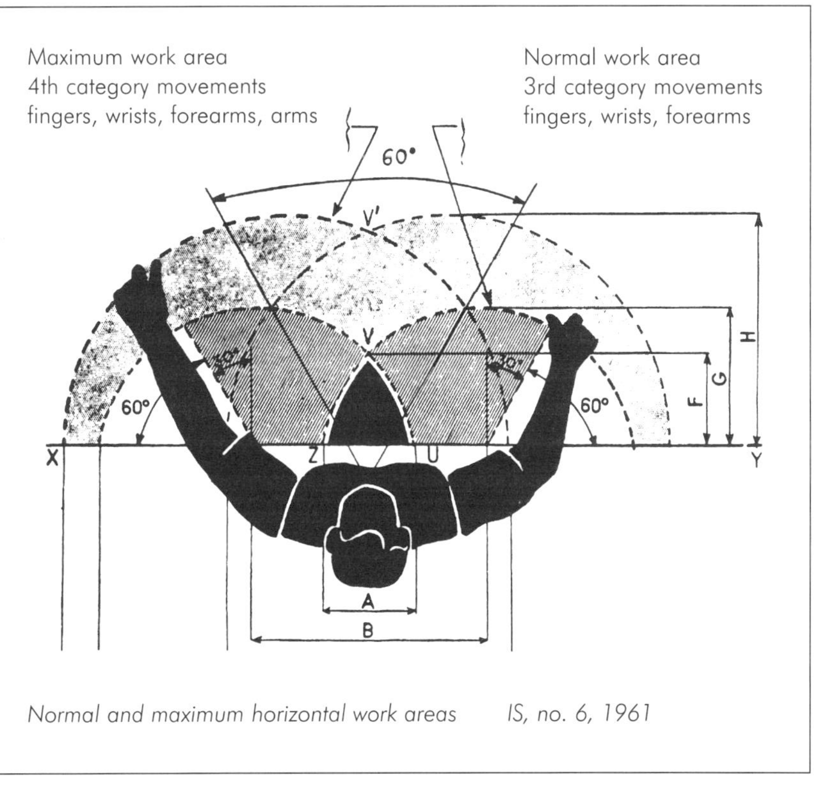

Normal and maximum horizontal work areas *IS, no. 6, 1961*

brought to the foreground a conflict between the two conceptions of the proletarian revolution. Both of these conceptions contained an *authoritarian* dimension through which the conscious self-emancipation of the working class is abandoned. In effect, the quarrel which became irreconcilable between Marxists and Bakuninists was two-edged, referring at once to power in the revolutionary society and to the organisation of the present movement, and when the positions of the adversaries passes from one aspect to the other, they reversed themselves. Bakunin fought the illusion of abolishing classes by the authoritarian use of state power, foreseeing the reconstitution of a dominant bureaucratic class and the dictatorship of the most knowledgeable, or those who would be reputed to be such. Marx, who thought that a maturing process inseparable from economic contradictions, and democratic education of the workers, would reduce the role of the proletarian state to a simple phase of legitimating the new social relations imposing themselves objectively, denounced Bakunin and his followers for the authoritarianism of a conspiratorial élite which deliberately placed itself above the International and formulated the extravagant plan of imposing on society the irresponsible dictatorship of those who are most revolutionary or those who would designate themselves to be such. Bakunin, in fact, recruited followers on the basis of such a perspective: "Invisible pilots in the centre of the popular storm, we must direct it, not with a visible power, but with the collective dictatorship of all the *allies*. A dictatorship without badge, title or official right, yet all the more powerful because it will have none of the appearances of power." Thus two *ideologies* of the workers' revolution opposed each other, each containing a partially true critique, but losing the unity of the thought of history, and instituting themselves into ideological *authorities*. Powerful organisations, like German Social Democracy and the Iberian Anarchist Federation, faithfully served one or the other of these ideologies, and everywhere the result greatly differed from what had been desired.

The fact of looking at the goal of proletarian revolution as *immediately present* marks at the same time the greatness and weakness of the real anarchist struggle (since in its individualist variants, the pretentions of anarchists remain laughable). Collectivist anarchism retains only the conclusion of the historical thought of modern class struggles, and its absolute demand for this conclusion is also rendered as a deliberate contempt for method. Thus its critique of the *political struggle* has remained abstract, while its choice of economic struggle is affirmed only as a function of the illusion of a definitive solution brought about by one single blow on this battleground, on the day of the general strike or the insurrection. The anarchists *have an ideal to realise*. Anarchism is still an *ideological* negation of the state and of classes, that is to say of the social conditions of separate ideology. It is *the ideology of pure liberty* which equates everything and sets aside all idea of historical evil. This viewpoint, which fuses all partial desires, has given anarchism the merit of representing the rejection of existing conditions in favour of the whole of life, and not around a privileged critical specialisation. But this fusion being considered in the absolute, according to individual caprice, before its actual realisation, has also condemned anarchism to an incoherence too easily demonstrated. Anarchism has merely to repeat, and to put at stake the same simple, total conclusion in every single struggle, because this first conclusion was from the beginning identified with the entire outcome of the movement. Thus Bakunin could write in 1873, when he left the *Fédération Jurassienne*: "During the past nine years, more ideas have been developed within the International than would be needed to save the world, if ideas alone could save it, and I challenge anyone to invent a new one. It is no longer the time for ideas, but for facts and acts." There is no doubt that this conception preserves, from the historical thought of the proletariat, this certainty that ideas must become practical, but it leaves the historical terrain by assuming that the adequate forms for this transition to practice have already been found and will never change.

The anarchists, who distinguish themselves explicitly from the rest of the workers' movement by their ideological conviction, reproduce this separation of competences among themselves. They provide a favourable ground for the informal domination over every anarchist organisation by propagandists and defenders of their own ideology, specialists who are generally more mediocre the more their intellectual activity strives to repeat certain definitive truths. Ideological respect for unanimity of decision has on the whole been favourable to the uncontrolled authority, within the organisation itself, of *specialists in freedom*; and revolutionary anarchism expects the same type of unanimity from the liberated population, obtained by the same means. Furthermore, the refusal to take into account the opposition of conditions between a minority grouped in the present struggle and the society of free individuals, has nourished a permanent separation among anarchists at the moment of common decision, as shown by an infinity of anarchist insurrections in Spain, limited and destroyed on a local level.

The illusion entertained more or less explicitly by genuine anarchism is the permanent imminence of a revolution which, by being instantaneously accomplished, will prove the truth of the ideology and the mode of practical organisation derived from the ideology. Anarchism in fact led, in 1936, to a social revolution and the most advanced foreshadowing in all time of a proletarian power. In this context, it must be noted that the signal for a general insurrection had been imposed by the *pronunciatiamento* of the army. On the other hand, to the extent that this revolution was not achieved during the first days (because of the existence of Franco's power in half the country, strongly supported from abroad, while the rest of the international proletarian movement was already defeated, and because of survivals of bourgeois forces or other statist worker parties within the camp of the Republic) the organised anarchist movement showed that it was incapable of extending the semi-victories of the revolution, or even of just defending them. Its known leaders became ministers and hostages of the bourgeois state which destroyed the revolution only to lose the civil war.

The 'orthodox Marxism' of the Second International is the scientific ideology of the socialist revolution: it identifies its whole truth with objective processes in the economy and with the progress of a recognition of this necessity by the working class educated by the organisation. This ideology rediscovers the confidence in pedagogical demonstration which had characterised utopian socialism, but mixes it with a *contemplative* reference to the course of history. This attitude has lost as much of the Hegelian dimension of a total history as it has of the immobile image of totality present in the utopian critique (most highly developed by Fourier). This scientific attitude can do no more than revive a symmetry of ethical choices; it is from this attitude that the nonsense of Hilfering springs when he states that recognising the necessity of socialism gives "no indication of the practical attitude to be adopted. For it is one thing to recognise a necessity, and it is quite another thing to put oneself at the service of this necessity" (*Finanzkapital*). Those who failed to recognise that, for Marx and the revolutionary proletariat, the unitary thought of history *was in no way distinct from the practical attitude to be adopted*, regularly had to become victims of the practice they simultaneously adopted.

The ideology of the social-democratic organisation gave power to *professors* who educated the working class, and the form of organisation adopted was the form most suitable for this passive apprenticeship. The participation of socialists of the Second International in political and economic struggles was admittedly concrete but profoundly *uncritical*. It was conducted in the name of *revolutionary illusion* by means of an obviously *reformist practice*. Thus the revolutionary ideology was to be shattered by the very success of those who held it. The separation of deputies and journalists in the movement drew toward a bourgeois way of life those bourgeois intellectuals who had already been recruited from the struggles of industrial workers, and who were themselves workers, into brokers of labour power who sold labour as a commodity, for a just price. If their activity was itself conveniently unable to *support* economically this reformism which it tolerated politically in the legalistic agitation of the social-democrats. Such incompatibility was guaranteed by their science; but history constantly gave the lie to it.

Bernstein, the social-democrat furthest from political ideology and most openly

Where are you? In Paris, in Marseille, in Lille, in Nantes, in Toulouse? It doesn't matter: it's the same home, equally well-furnished and decorated. Whose home is it? A white collar worker's? A bricklayer's? A magistrate's? A skilled technician's? There's no perceptible difference... A bright, gay and uniform lifestyle is sweeping all before it, and it is common to all social classes. I am just a reporter, not a political analyst, but I would like to remind you that during the last century a gulf separated the middle from the working classes... Today the wages of a skilled worker and those of a professor are drawing closer and closer together; and both could be found living in the same high-rise estate. Is this a good thing, or a bad one? You must decide for yourself, but the fact is that this process of levelling out is not coming from the top or from the bottom, but from the middle.

Elle, 10 May 1963

attached to the methodology of bourgeois science, had the honesty to want to demonstrate the reality of this contradiction. The English workers' reformist movement had also demonstrated it, by doing without revolutionary ideology. However, the contradiction was definitively demonstrated only by historical development itself. Though full of illusions in other respects, Bernstein had denied that a crisis in capitalist production would miraculously force the hand of socialists who wanted to inherit the revolution only by this legitimate rite. The moment of profound social upheaval which arose with the first world war, though fertile with the awakening of consciousness, twice demonstrated that the social-democratic hierarchy had not educated in a revolutionary manner, and had in no way made the German workers into *theoreticians*. The first time, when the vast majority of the party rallied to the imperialist war, and then, in defeat, when it squashed the Spartacist revolutionaries. The ex-worker Ebert still believed in sin, since he admitted that he hated revolution "like sin". And the same leader showed himself a good forerunner of the *socialist representation* which shortly afterwards opposed itself to the Russian proletariat as its absolute enemy, moreover formulating exactly the same programme of this new alienation: "Socialist means working a lot."

Lenin, as a Marxist thinker, was no more than a *faithful* and consistent *Kautskyist* who applied the *revolutionary ideology* of this 'orthodox Marxism' to Russian conditions, conditions which did not allow the reformist practice carried on by the Second International. In the Russian context, the *external* direction of the proletariat, acting by means of a disciplined clandestine party subordinated to intellectuals who had become 'professional revolutionaries', forms a profession which will not negotiate with any leading profession of capitalist society (the Czarist political regime being in any case unable to offer such an opening, which is based on an advanced stage of bourgeois power). It therefore becomes the *profession of the absolute management* of society.

The authoritarian ideological radicalism of the Bolsheviks extended itself all over the world with the war and the collapse of the social-democratic international in the face of the war. The bloody end of the democratic illusions of the workers' movement transformed the entire world into a Russia, and Bolshevism, reigning over the first revolutionary breach brought on by this epoch of crisis, offered to proletarians of all lands its hierarchic and ideological model, so that they could 'speak Russian' to their ruling classes. Lenin did not reproach the Marxism of the Second International for being a revolutionary *ideology*, but for ceasing to be one.

The same historical moment when Bolshevism triumphed *for itself* in Russian and when social-democracy fought victoriously *for the old world* marks the complete birth of the state of affairs which is at the heart of the modern spectacle's domination: *working class representation* radically opposed itself to the working class.

"In all previous revolutions", wrote Rosa Luxembourg in *Rote Fahne* of 21 December 1918, "the combatants faced each other directly: class against class, programme against programme. In the present revolution, the troops protecting the old order do not intervene under the insignia of the ruling class, but under the flag of a 'social-democracy party'. If the central question of revolution had been posed openly and honestly — capitalism or socialism? – the great mass of the proletariat would today have no doubts or hesitations". Thus, a few days before its destruction, the radical current of the German proletariat discovered the secret of the new conditions which had been created by the preceding process (towards which working class representation had greatly contributed): the spectacular organisation of defence of the existing order, the social reign of appearances where no 'central question' can any longer be posed 'openly and honestly'. The revolutionary representation of the proletariat had at this stage become both the main factor and the central result of the general falsification of society.

The organisation of the proletariat on the Bolshevik model, born out of Russian backwardness and the resignation from revolutionary struggle of the workers' movement in advanced countries, found in the backwardness of Russia all the conditions which carried this form of organisation toward the counter-revolutionary reversal which is unconsciously held at its source. The repeated retreat of the mass of the European workers' movement in the face of the *Hic Rhodus, hic salta* of the 1918-1920 period, a retreat which included the violent destruction of its radical minority, favoured the completion of the Bolshevik development and let this deceitful result present itself to the world as the only proletarian solution.The seizure of a state monopoly of representation and the defence of the workers' power, which justified the Bolshevik party, made the party *become what it was*, the party of the proprietors of the proletariat, essentially eliminating the earlier forms of property.

For twenty years the varied tendencies of Russian social-democracy had envisaged all the conditions for the liquidation of Czarism in a theoretical debate that was never satisfactory. They had pointed to the weakness of the bourgeoisie, the weight of the peasant majority and the decisive role of a concentrated and combative but hardly numerous proletariat. These conditions finally found their solution in practice, but because of a factor which had not been present in the hypotheses of the theoreticians: the revolutionary bureaucracy which directed the proletariat seized state power and gave society a new class domination. Strictly bourgeois revolution had been impossible; the "democratic dictatorship of workers and peasants" had no meaning. The proletarian power of the Soviets could not maintain itself simultaneously against the class of small landowners, the national and international White reaction, and its own representation externalised and alienated in the form of a workers' party of absolute masters of the state, the economy, expression and soon of thought. The theory of permanent revolution of Trotsky and Parvus, which Lenin adopted in April 1917, was the only theory which became true for countries where the social development of the bourgeoisie was retarded, but this theory became true only after the introduction of the unknown factor: the class power of the bureaucracy. The concentration of dictatorship in the hands of the supreme representation of ideology was defended most consistently by Lenin in the numerous confrontations of the Bolshevik directorate. Lenin was right every time against his adversaries in that he supported the solution implied by earlier choices of absolute minority power. The democracy which was kept from peasants *by means of the state* would have to be kept from workers as well, which led to keeping it from communist leaders of unions, and from the entire party, and even from the leading party hierarchs. At the 10th Congress, when the Kronstadt Soviet had been defeated by arms and buried under calumny, Lenin pronounced the following conclusion against the leftist bureaucrats organised in a 'Workers' Opposition', the logic of which Stalin would later extend to a perfect division of the world: "here or there with a rifle, but not with the opposition... We've had enough opposition."

After Kronstadt, at the time of the 'new economic policy', the bureaucracy, remaining sole proprietor of a *state capitalism*, first of all assured its power internally by means of a temporary alliance with the peasantry. Externally, it defended its power by using workers regimented into the bureaucratic parties of the Third International as supports for Russian diplomacy, thus sabotaging the entire revolutionary movement and supporting bourgeois governments whose aid it needed in international politics (the power of the Kuomintang in China in 1925-27, the Popular Front in Spain and in France, etc). But the bureaucratic society was to continue its own consolidation by exerting terror on the peasantry in order to realise the most brutal primitive capitalist accumulation in history. The industrialisation of the Stalinist epoch reveals the reality behind the *bureaucracy*: it is the continuation of the power of the economy, the salvaging of the essential of the commodity society, namely preserving commodity labour. It is proof of the independent economy, which dominates society to the point of recreating for its own ends the class domination necessary to it. In other words, the bourgeoisie has created an autonomous power which, so long as its autonomy lasts, can even do without a bourgeoisie. The totalitarian bureaucracy is not "the last owning class in history" in the sense of Bruno Rizzi; it is only a *substitute ruling class* for the commodity economy. Ineffective capitalist private property is replaced by a simplified sub-product, one which is less diversified and is concentrated into the collective property of the bureaucratic class. This underdeveloped form of ruling class is also the expression of economic underdevelopment, and it has no other perspective than to overcome the retardation of this development in certain regions of the world. It was the workers' party organised according to the bourgeois model of separation which provided the hierarchical-statist cadre for this supplementary edition of the ruling class. Anton Ciliga observed in one of Stalin's prisons that "technical questions of organisation turned out to be social questions" (*Lenin and the Revolution*).

Revolutionary ideology, the *coherence of the separate*, of which Leninism represents the greatest voluntaristic effort, managing a reality which rejects it, *returns to its truth in incoherence* with Stalinism. At that point, ideology is no longer a weapon but a goal. The lie which is no longer challenged becomes lunacy. Reality as well as the goal dissolve in the totalitarian ideological proclamation: all it says is all there is. It is a local primitivism of the spectacle, whose role is nevertheless essential in the development of the world spectacle. The ideology which is materialised in this context has not economically transformed the world, as capitalism has, having reached the stage of abundance; it has merely transformed *perception* in a police manner.

The totalitarian-ideological class in power is the power of an upside-down world. The stronger it is, the more it claims not to exist, and its force serves above all to affirm its non-existence. It is modest only on this point, because its official non-existence must also coincide with the *nec plus ultra* of historical development which is simultaneously due to its infallible command. Spread everywhere, the bureaucracy must be the *class invisible* to consciousness; as a result, all social life becomes insane. The social organisation of absolute falsehood flows from this fundamental contradiction.

Stalinism was a reign of terror within the bureaucratic class itself. The terrorism at the base of the power of the class must also strike this class because it possesses no juridicial guarantee, no recognised existence as owning class, which it could extend to every one of its members. Its real property is hidden; the bureaucracy only became proprietor by way of false consciousness. False consciousness preserves its absolute power only by means of absolute terror, where all real motives are finally lost. The members of the bureaucratic class in power have a right of ownership over society only collectively, as participants in a fundamental lie. They have to play the role of a proletariat leading a socialist society; they have to be actors loyal to a script of ideological disloyalty. But effective participation in this lying existence must see itself recognised as truthful participation. No bureaucrat can support his right to power individually, since proving that he's a socialist proletarian would mean presenting himself as the opposite of a bureaucrat, and proving that he's a bureaucrat is impossible since the official truth of the bureaucracy is that it does not exist. Thus, every bureaucrat depends absolutely on the *central guarantee* of the ideology which recognises the collective participation in its 'socialist power' *of all the bureaucrats it does not annihilate*. If all the bureaucrats taken together decide everything, the cohesion of their own class can only be assured by the concentration of their terrorist power in a single person. In this person resides the only practical truth of falsehood *in power*: the indisputable permanence of its constantly adjusted frontier. Stalin decides without appeal who is finally to be a possessing bureaucrat; in other words, who should be named 'proletarian in power' or 'traitor in the pay of the Mikado or Wall Street'. The bureaucratic atoms find the common essence of their right only in the person of Stalin. Stalin is the world sovereign who in this manner knows himself as the absolute person for the consciousness of which there is no higher spirit. "The sovereign of the world has actual consciousness of what he is – the universal power of efficacy – in the destructive violence which he exerts against the self of his subjects who contrast him." Just as he is the power that defines the sphere of domination, he is "*the power that ravages this sphere*".

When ideology, having become absolute through the possession of absolute power, changes from partial knowledge into totalitarianised falsehood, the thought of history is so perfectly annihilated that history itself can no longer exist at the level of the most empirical knowledge. The totalitarian bureaucratic society lives in a perpetual present where everything that happened exists for it only as a place accessible to its police. The project already formulated by Napoleon of "directing the energy of memory from the throne" has found its total concretisation in a permanent manipulation of the past, not only of implications but of facts as well. But the price paid for this emancipation from all historical reality is the loss of all rational reference that is indispensable to the *historical* society, capitalism.

It is known how much the scientific application of insane ideology has cost the Russian economy, if only through the imposture of Lysenko. The contradiction of the totalitarian bureaucracy administering an industrialised society, caught between its need for rationality and its rejection of the rational, is one of its main deficiencies with regard to normal capitalist development. In the same way that the bureaucracy cannot resolve the question of agriculture the way capitalism had done, it is ultimately inferior to capitalism in industrial production, planned from the top and based on unreality and generalised falsehood.

Between the two world wars, the revolutionary workers' movement was annihilated by the joint action of the Stalinist bureaucracy and of fascist totalitarianism which had borrowed its form of organisation from the totalitarian party tried out in Russia. Fascism was an extremist defence of the bourgeois economy threatened by crisis and proletarian subversion. Fascism is a *state of siege* in capitalist society, by means of which this society saves itself and gives itself emergency rationalisation by making the state intervene massively in its management. But this rationalisation is itself burdened by the immense irrationality of its means. Fascism rallies to the defence of the main points of a bourgeois ideology that has become conservative (the family, property, the moral order, the nation), reuniting the petty bourgeoisie and the unemployed routed by crisis or deceived by the impotence of socialist revolution. However, fascism is not itself fundamentally ideological. It presents itself as it is: a violent resurrection of *myth* which demands participation in a community defined by archaic pseudo-values: race, blood, the leader. Fascism is *technically-equipped archaism*. Its decomposed *ersatz* of myth is revived in the spectacular context of the most modern means of conditioning and illusion. Thus it is one of the factors in the formulation of the modern spectacle, and its role in the destruction of the old workers' movement makes it one of the founding forces of present-day society. However, since fascism is also *the most costly* form of preserving the capitalist order, generally it had to leave the front of the stage to the great roles played by

PIGEONS GO TO WORK IN A FACTORY

There is a new staff of inspectors keeping a beady eye on things down at the ball-bearing factory.

Products rolling off the assembly line are being checked by educated pigeons.

And their bosses claim that they are just as good as any human at making sure the finished article is up to scratch.

The pigeons' eyesight is so good that they can spot the slightest blemishes in the steel balls, which are produced at a Moscow factory.

They have been trained to peck a special plate when one bearing looks different from the others, even if it has only a fingerprint on it.

A reject sign lights up, the bearing is taken away, and the pigeon gets its 'pay' – a few millet seeds.

The Russians say the birds can be trained to peck out the rogue balls in three to five weeks.

They can inspect between 3,000 and 4,000 bearings an hour, claims an article in Soviet Weekly.

And they never try to get extra wages by pecking out of turn.

Trained

Any attempt to bring feathered inspectors into this country is unlikely to get off the ground.

An executive with one of Britain's largest ball-bearing manufacturers said, "It really sounds like one for the birds.

"I shall be interested to read the Russian report, but in Britain we rely on electronic inspection and the trained human eye.

"I would much rather depend on a competent human inspector than a bird any day.

"I know there are a lot of pigeons flying around, but it has never occurred to us to train any for this kind of work."

But support for the Russian idea came from pigeon expert Dr Ronald Morton, of the National Environmental Research Council.

He said, "Scientifically it is quite possible.

"Pigeons, like other birds, have remarkable eyesight and they are easily domesticated.

"The Russians have simply put them to work for economic ends.

"The pecking, of course, is a conditioned reflex, and the Russians have been very keen on conditioned reflexes ever since Pavlov and his dogs."

The Daily Mirror, 14 January 1974

capitalist states; it is eliminated by stronger and more rational forms of the same order.

When the Russian bureaucracy finally does away with the remains of bourgeois property which hampered its rule over the economy, when it develops this property for its own use, and when it is recognised externally among the great powers, it wants to enjoy its world calmly and to suppress the arbitrary element that it exerted over itself. It denounces Stalinism of its origin. But such a denunciation remains Stalinist, arbitrary, unexplained or continually corrected, because *the ideological lie at its origin can never be revealed*. Thus the bureaucracy can liberalise neither culturally nor politically because its existence as a class depends on its ideological monopoly which, whatever its weight, is its only title to property. The ideology has no doubt lost the passion of its positive affirmation, but what still survives of indifferent triviality still has the repressive function of prohibiting the slightest competition, of holding the totality of thought captive. Thus the bureaucracy is bound to an ideology which is no longer believed by anyone. What used to be terrorist has become laughable, but this laughing matter itself can only as a last resort preserve itself by holding on to the terrorism it would like to be rid of. Thus precisely at the moment when the bureaucracy wants to demonstrate its superiority in the sphere of capitalism, it confesses itself a *poor relative* of capitalism. Just as its actual history contradicts its right and its vulgarly maintained ignorance contradicts its scientific pretensions, so its project of becoming a rival to the bourgeoisie in the production of a commodity abundance is hampered. This project is hampered by the fact that such an abundance carries its *implicit ideology* within itself, and is usually accompanied by an indefinitely extended freedom in spectacular false choices, a pseudo-freedom which remains irreconcilable with the bureaucratic ideology.

At the present moment of its development, the bureaucracy's title of ideological property is already collapsing internationally. The power which established itself nationally as a fundamentally internationalist model must admit that it can no longer pretend to uphold its cohesion, based on lies, beyond every national frontier. The unequal economic development of some bureaucracies with competing interests who succeeded in possessing their 'socialism' outside a single country has led to the public and total confrontation between the Russian lie and the Chinese lie. From this point on, every bureaucracy in power, or every totalitarian state party which is a candidate to the power left behind by the Stalinist period in some national working classes, must follow its own path. The global decomposition of the alliance of bureaucratic mystification is further aggravated by manifestations of internal negation which began to be visible to the world with the East Berlin workers' revolt, opposing the bureaucrats with the demand for a "government of steel workers", manifestations which have already once led all the way to the power of workers' councils in Hungary. However, the global decomposition of the bureaucratic alliance is in the last analysis the least favourable factor for the present development of capitalist society. The bourgeoisie is in the process of losing the adversary which objectively supported it by providing an illusory unification of all negation of the existing order. This division of spectacular labour comes to an end when the pseudo-revolutionary role in turn divides. The spectacular element of the collapse of the workers' movement will itself collapse.

The Leninist illusion has no contemporary base outside of the various Trotskyist tendencies. Here the identification of the proletarian project with a hierarchic organisation of ideology steadfastly survives the experience of all its results. The distance which separates Trotskyism from revolutionary critique of the present society also permits the respectable distance which it keeps towards positions which were already false when they were used in a real combat. Trotsky remained basically in solidarity with the high bureaucracy until 1927, seeking to capture it so as to undertake a genuinely Bolshevik action externally. (It is known that in order to hide Lenin's famous 'testament' he went as far as slanderously disavowing his supporter Max Eastman, who had made it public.) Trotsky was condemned by his basic perspective, because at the moment when the bureaucracy recognises itself in its result as a counter-revolutionary class internally, it must also choose to be effectively counter-revolutionary externally in the name of the revolution, *just as it is at home*. Trotsky's subsequent struggle for a Fourth International contains the same inconsistency. All his life he refused to recognise the power of a separate class in the bureaucracy, because during the second Russian revolution he became an unconditional supporter of the Bolshevik form of organisation. When Lukacs, in 1923, showed that this form was the long-sought mediation between theory and practice, in which the proletarians are no longer 'spectators' of the events which happen in their organisation, but consciously choose and live these events, he described as actual merits of the Bolshevik party everything that the Bolshevik party was not. Except for his profound theoretical work, Lukacs was still an ideologue speaking in the name of the power most grossly external to the proletarian movement, believing and making believe that he found himself, with his entire personality, within this power as if it were *his own*. At the same time, the rest of the story made it obvious just how this power disowns and suppresses its stooges. Lukacs, repudiating himself without end, made visible with the clarity of a caricature exactly what he had identified with: with the *opposite* of himself and what he had supported in *History and Class Consciousness*. Lukacs is the best proof of the fundamental rule that judges all the intellectuals of this century; what they *respect* exactly measures their own *despicable* reality. However, Lenin had hardly called for this type of illusion about his activity. In his view "a political party cannot examine its members to see if there are contradictions between their philosophy and the party programme". The real party whose imaginary portrait Lukacs had presented was coherent only for one precise and partial task: to seize power.

The neo-Leninist illusion of present-day Trotskyism, constantly exposed by the reality of modern bourgeois as well as bureaucratic capitalist societies, naturally finds a favoured field of application in 'underdeveloped' countries that are formally independent. Here the illusion of some variant of state and bureaucratic socialism is consciously manipulated by local ruling classes as *the simple ideology of economic development*. The hybrid composition of these classes is more or less clearly related to a level on the bourgeois-bureaucratic spectrum. Their games with the two poles of existing, capitalist power on an international scale, and their ideological compromises (notably with Islam), which express the hybrid reality of their social base, succeed in removing from this final sub-product of ideological socialism everything serious except their police character. A bureaucracy is able to form by stiffening a national struggle with an agrarian peasant revolt; from that point on, as in China, it tends to apply the Stalinist model of industrialisation in societies less developed than Russia in 1917. A bureaucracy able to industrialise the nation can set itself up from the petty bourgeoisie, or out of army cadres who seize power, as in Egypt. On certain points, as in Algeria at the beginning of its war of independence, the bureaucracy, which sets itself up as a para-statist leadership during the struggle, seeks the balancing point of a compromise in order to fuse with a weak national bourgeoisie. Finally, in the former colonies of black Africa which remain openly tied to the American and European bourgeoisie, a bourgeoisie constitutes itself (usually on the basis of the power of the traditional tribal chiefs), *by seizing the state*. These countries, where foreign imperialism remains the real master of the economy, enter a stage where the *compradores* have received an indigenous state as compensation for their sale of indigenous products, a state which is independent with regard to the local masses but not with regard to imperialism. This is an artificial bourgeoisie which is not able to accumulate, but which simply *wastes* the share of surplus value from local labour that reaches it, as well as the foreign subsidies from the states or monopolies which protect it. Because of the obvious incapacity of these bourgeois classes to fulfil the normal economic function of a bourgeoisie, each of them faces a subversion based on the bureaucratic model, more or less adapted to local peculiarities, and eager to seize their heritage. But the very success of a bureaucracy in its fundamental project of industrialisation necessarily contains the perspective of its historical defeat: by accumulating capital it accumulates a

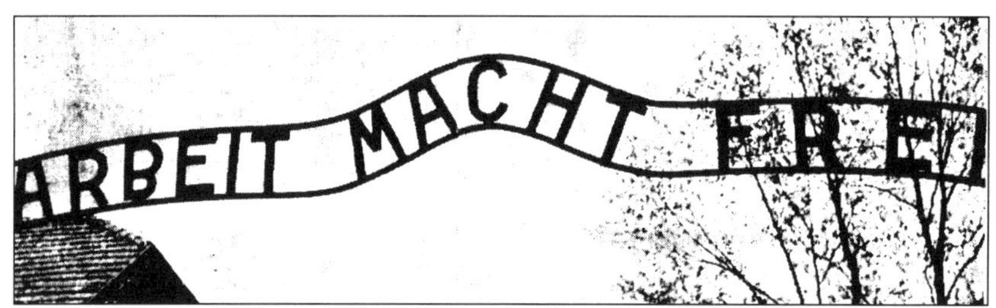

"Work makes free" – entrance to Auschwitz.

proletariat and thus creates its own negation in a country where it did not yet exist.

In this complex and terrible development which has swept the epoch of class struggles towards new conditions, the proletariat of industrial countries has completely lost the affirmation of its autonomous perspective and also, in the last analysis, *its illusions*, but not its being. It has not been suppressed. It remains irreducibly in existence within the intensified alienation of modern capitalism: it is the immense majority of workers who have lost all power over the use of their lives and who, *once they know this*, redefine themselves as the proletariat, the negation at work in this society. The proletariat is objectively reinforced by the progressive disappearance of the peasantry and by the extension of the logic of factory labour to a large sector of 'services' and intellectual professions. The proletariat is *subjectively* still far removed from its practical class consciousness, not only among white collar workers but also among wage workers who have as yet discovered only the impotence and mystification of the old politics. Nevertheless, when the proletariat discovers that its own externalised power helps constantly to reinforce capitalist society, not only in the form of its labour but also in the form of unions, parties, or the state power it had built to emancipate itself, it also discovers from concrete historical experience that it is the class totally opposed to all frozen externalisation and all specialisation of power. It carries the *revolution that can leave nothing external to it*, the demand for the permanent domination of the present over the past, and the total critique of separation. It is this that must find its suitable form in action. No quantitative amelioration of its misery, no illusion of hierarchic integration is a lasting cure for its dissatisfaction, because the proletariat cannot truly recognise itself in a particular wrong it suffered nor in *the righting of a particular wrong*. It cannot recognise itself in the righting of a large number of wrongs either, but only in the *absolute wrong* of being relegated to the margin of life.

From the new signs of negation which multiply in the economically most advanced countries, signs which are misunderstood and falsified by spectacular arrangement, one can already draw the conclusion that a new epoch has begun. After the first attempt at workers' subversion, *it is now capitalist abundance that has failed*. When anti-union struggles of Western workers are repressed first of all by unions, and when rebellious undercurrents of youth launch their first amorphous protest which directly implies a rejection of the old specialised politics, of art and of daily life, we see the two sides of a new spontaneous struggle which begins under a *criminal* guise. These are the portents of a second proletarian assault against the class society. When the lost children of this still immobile army reappear on this battleground, having become other and yet remaining the same, they follow a new 'General Ludd' who, this time, throws them into the destruction of the *machines of permitted consumption*.

"The political form, at last discovered, in which the economic emancipation of labour could be realised" has in this century acquired a clear outline in the revolutionary workers' councils which concentrate in themselves all the functions of decision and execution, and federate with each other by means of delegates responsible to the base and revocable at any moment. Their actual existence has as yet only been a brief sketch, immediately fought and defeated by different forces of defence of class society, among which one must often count their own false consciousness. Pannekoek rightly insisted on the fact that the choice of a power of workers' councils "poses problems" rather than bringing a solution. But this power is precisely where the problems of the proletarian revolution can find their real solution. This is where the objective conditions of historical consciousness are reunited. This is where direct, *active* communication is realised, where specialisation, hierarchy and separation end, where the existing conditions are transformed "into conditions of unity". Here, the proletarian subject can emerge from his struggle against contemplation; his consciousness is equal to the practical organisation it assumes, because this consciousness is itself inseparable from coherent intervention in history.

In the power of the councils, which must internally replace all other power, the proletarian movement is its own product and this product is the producer himself. He is to himself his own goal. Only there is the spectacular negation of life negated in its turn.

The appearance of the councils was the highest reality of the proletarian movement in the first quarter of this century, a reality which was not seen or was travestied, because it disappeared with the rest of the movement which was denied and eliminated by the entire historical experience of the time. In this new movement of proletarian critique, this result returns as the only undefeated point of the defeated movement. The historical consciousness which knows that this is the only milieu where it can exist can now recognise it, no longer at the periphery of what is ebbing, but at the centre of what is rising.

A revolutionary organisation existing before the power of the councils (it will find its own form through struggle), for all these historical reasons, already knows that it *does not represent* the working class. It must only recognise itself as a radical separation from *the world of separation*.

Revolutionary organisation is the coherent expression of the theory of praxis entering into non-unilateral communication with practical struggles, in the process of becoming practical theory. Its own practice is the spread of communication and of coherence in these struggles. At the revolutionary moment when social separation dissolves, this organisation must recognise its own dissolution as a separate organisation.

Revolutionary organisation can be nothing less than a unitary critique of society, that is to say a critique which does not compromise with any form of separate power anywhere in the world, and a critique proclaimed globally against all the aspects of alienated social life. In the struggle of the revolutionary organisation against the class society, weapons are nothing but the *essence* of the combatants themselves: the revolutionary organisation cannot reproduce within itself the conditions of rupture and hierarchy which are those of the dominant society. It must struggle permanently against its deformation in the ruling spectacle. The only limit to participation in the total democracy of the revolutionary organisation is the recognition and actual self-appropriation of the coherence of its critique by all its members, a coherence which must be proved in the critical theory as such and in the relation between the theory and practical activity.

Ever-increasing capitalist alienation at all levels makes it increasingly difficult for workers to recognise and name their own misery, thus confronting them with the alternative of rejecting *the totality of their misery, or nothing*. From this, revolutionary organisation must learn that it can no longer *combat alienation in alienated forms*.

Proletarian revolution depends entirely on the condition that, for the first time, theory as intelligence of human practice must be recognised and lived by the masses. It demands workers to become dialecticians and to inscribe their thought into practice. Thus it demands more of *men without quality* than the bourgeois revolution demanded of qualified men to which it delegated its realisation, since the partial ideological consciousness erected by a *part* of the bourgeois class has as its base the economy, this central *part* of social life in which this class *was already* in power. The very development of class society to the point of the spectacular organisation of non-life thus leads the revolutionary project to become *visibly* what it was already *essentially*.

Revolutionary theory is now the enemy of all revolutionary ideology *and knows it*.

From *The Society of the Spectacle* by Guy Debord, 1967

Soon to be picturesque ruins.

Graffiti, Nanterre, 1968

NIHILISM

Rozanov's definition of nihilism is the best: "The show is over. The audience get up to leave their seats. Time to collect their coats and go home. They turn round... No more coats and no more home."

Nihilism is born of the collapse of myth. During those periods when the contradiction between mythical explanation – Heaven, Redemption, the Will of Allah – and everyday life becomes patent, *all* values are sucked into the vortex and destroyed. Once myth no longer justifies the ways of Power to men, the real possibilities of social action and experiment appear. Myth excuses social repression, but it also reinforces it. Its explosion frees an energy and creativity too long syphoned away from authentic experience into religious transcendence and abstraction.

During the interregnum between the end of classical philosophy and the instauration of the Church, every previous form of social order was suddenly called into question. A thousand lifestyles were improvised, from those of the sects and heresies to those of a Caligula or a Nero. Once the unity of myth is challenged, the whole pattern of social existence breaks up. The same thing took place with the disintegration of feudal society and Christian myth. Nothing was sure any longer and everything had become possible. Every kind of experiment and research. Gilles de Rais tortured nearly a thousand children to death; the revolutionary peasants of 1525 were out to build Heaven on Earth. 1789 precipitated the same total collapse. This time there was a major difference: in spite of the political reaction, the reconstruction of a *coherent* myth had become utterly impossible.

Christianity neutered the explosive nihilism of certain gnostic sects, and improvised a new order from the remains. But the establishment of the bourgeois world made any new *recuperation* of nihilistic energy onto the plane of myth impossible. The bourgeois project had been precisely the destruction of a transcendent 'other world', the enforcement of the rule of *this* world and its market values. In place of a myth, the bourgeoisie can only produce ideologies. And because ideology is essentially a *partial, technical* rationality, it can never integrate the total negation of the nihilist. In the conspicuous absence of God, the reality of exchange can never be concealed, for the *complete* illusion of myth has gone. As a last-ditch effort, Power has produced the *spectacle* of nihilism – on the principle that the more we contemplate, as spectators, the degradation of all values, the less likely we are to get on with a little real destruction.

For the last century and a half the most striking contribution to art and life has been the fruit of free experiment with the possibilities of a bankrupt civilisation. The erotic reason of de Sade; Kierkegaard's sarcasm, Nietzsche's lashing irony; Ahab's blasphemy, Mallarmé's deadpan; Carroll's fantasy; Dada's negativism – these are the forces which have reached out to confront people with some of the dankness and acridity of decaying values. And, with it, the desire for a reversal of perspective, a need to discover the alternative forms of life – the area Melville called "that wild, whaling life where individual notabilities make up all totalities". But to create that world, the nihilist must *act*.

PARADOX

I The great propagators of nihilism lacked an essential weapon: the sense of historical reality, the sense of the reality of decay, erosion and fragmentation.

II Those who have *made* history in the period of bourgeois decline have lacked a sense of the *total* decomposition of social forms which nihilism announces. Marx failed to analyse Romanticism and the artistic phenomenon in general. Lenin was wilfully blind to the importance of everyday life and its degeneration, of the futurists, of Mayakovsky and the dadaists.

What we need now is the conjunction of nihilism and historical consciousness (Marx smashing something better than the street lights in Kentish Town; Mallarmé with fire in his belly). As long as the two fail to join forces, we shall have to endure the present empire of political and artistic hacks, all preaching the fragmentary, all working assiduously for the Big Sleep, and justifying themselves in the name of one order or another: the family, morality, culture, the space-race, the future of margarine... Everyone is going to pass through nihilism. It is the bath of fire. The best arguments against 'moral seriousness' are the faces on the hoardings. The end of all values is the Nothing-Box. All that is left of the past or the future is the demand for the present – for a present *which has still to be constructed*. Today, *the destructive and the constructive moments of history* are slowly coming together. When the two meet, *that* will be total revolution. And revolution is the only wealth left in the affluent society.

A nihilist is someone who takes the distinction between living and surviving seriously. If living is impossible, why survive? Once you are in that void, everything breaks up. The horrors. Past and future explode; the present is ground zero. And from ground zero there are only two ways out, two kinds of nihilism: *active* and *passive*.

The passive nihilist compromises with his own lucidity about the collapse of all values. He makes one final nihilistic gesture: he throws dice to decide his 'cause', and becomes its devoted slave, for Art's sake, and for the sake of a little bread... Nothing is true, so a few gestures become hip. Joe Soap intellectuals, pata-physicians, crypto-fascists, aesthetes of the *acte gratuit*, mercenaries, Kim Philbies, pop-artists, psychedelic impresarios – bandwagon after bandwagon works out its own version of the *credo quia absurdum est*. You don't believe in it, but you do it anyway; you get used to it and you even get to like it in the end. Passive nihilism is an overture to conformism.

After all, nihilism can never be more than a transition, a shifting, ill-defined sphere, a period of wavering between two extremes, one leading to submission and subservience, the other to permanent revolt. Between the two poles stretches a no-man's-land, the wasteland of the suicide and the solitary killer, of the criminal described so aptly by Bettina as the crime of the state. Jack the Ripper is essentially inaccessible. The mechanisms of hierarchical power cannot touch him; he cannot be touched by revolutionary will. He gravitates around that zero-point beyond which destruction, instead of reinforcing the destruction wrought by power, beats it at its own game, excites it to such violence that the machine of the *Penal Colony*, stabbing wildly, shatters into pieces and flies apart. Maldorer takes the disintegration of contemporary social organisation to its logical conclusion: to the stage of its self-destruction. At this point the individual's absolute rejection of society corresponds to society's absolute rejection of the individual. Isn't this the still point of the turning world, the place where all perspectives are interchangeable, the exact point where movement, dialectics and time no longer exist? Noon and eternity of the great refusal. Before it, the pogroms; beyond it, the new innocence. The blood of Jews or the blood of cops.

The active nihilist does not intend to

Revolutionary theory can only be based on a critique of everyday life in capitalist society; it must broadcast a different conception of happiness. The left and the right are in agreement as to the nature of poverty: shortage of food. They are also in agreement as to the nature of happiness. This is the root of the mystification that has wrecked the workers' movement in the highly-industrialised countries. Revolutionary propaganda must offer everyone the possibility of a radical change in their way of life, a change that they will experience right away. In Europe this task entails a far more specific conception of what true wealth would be – only in this way can the poverty of cars and television sets become truly intolerable to the exploited. Revolutionary intellectuals must cast aside the last shreds of their disintegrating culture and try themselves to live in a revolutionary way. So doing they will finally be brought face-to-face with the problems of the popular avant-garde...

IS no. 2, 1958

We must go further, dissociate ourselves from both modern culture and from its negation. We are not working for the spectacle of the end of the world, but for the end of the world of spectacle.

IS no. 3, 1959

simply watch things fall apart. He intends to speed up the process. Sabotage is a natural response to the chaos ruling the world. *Active nihilism is pre-revolutionary; passive nihilism is counter-revolutionary*. And most people oscillate between the two. Like the red soldier described by some Soviet author – Victor Chlovsky perhaps – who never charged without shouting, "Long live the Tsar!". But circumstances inevitably end by drawing a line, and people suddenly find themselves, once and for all, on one side or the other of the barricades.

You always learn to dance for yourself on the off-beat of the official world. And you must follow your demands to their logical conclusion, not accept a compromise at the first setback. Consumer society's frantic need to manufacture new needs adroitly cashes in on the way-out, the bizarre and the shocking. Black humour and real agony turn up on Madison Avenue. Flirtation with non-conformism is an integral part of prevailing values. Awareness of the decay of values has its role to play in sales strategy. There's money in decomposition. More and more pure *rubbish* is marketed. The figurine salt-cellar of Kennedy, complete with 'bullet holes' through which to pour the salt, for sale in the supermarket, should be enough to convince anybody, if there is anybody who still needs convincing, how easily a joke which once would have delighted Ravachol or Peter the Painter, now merely helps to keep the market going.

Consciousness of decay reached its most explosive expression in Dada. Dada really did contain the seeds by which nihilism could have been surpassed; but it just left them to rot, along with all the rest. The whole ambiguity of Surrealism, on the other hand, lies in the fact that it was an accurate critique made at the wrong moment. While its critique of the supersession aborted by Dada was perfectly justified, when it in its turn tried to surpass Dada, it did so without beginning again with Dada's initial nihilism, without basing itself on Dada-anti-Dada, without seeing Dada historically. History was the nightmare from which the surrealists never awoke. They were defenceless before the Communist Party; they were out of their depth with the Spanish civil war. For all their yapping they slunk after the official left like faithful dogs.

Certain features of romanticism had already proved, without awaking the slightest interest on the part of either Marx or Engels, that art – the pulse of culture and society – is the first index of the decay and disintegration of values. A century later, while Lenin thought that the whole issue was beside the point, the dadaist could see the artistic abscess as a symptom of a cancer whose poison was spread throughout society as a whole. *Unpleasant* art only expresses the repression of pleasure demanded by the state. It is this the1916 dadaists proved so cogently. To go beyond this analysis could mean only one thing: to take up arms. The neo-dadaist larvae pullulating in the shit-heap of present-day consumption seem to have found more profitable employment.

The dadaists, working to cure themselves and their civilisation of its discontents – working, in the last analysis, far more coherently than Freud himself – built the first laboratory to revitalise everyday life. Their activity was far more radical than their theory. "The point was to work completely in the dark. We didn't know where we were going." The Dada group was a funnel sucking in all the trivia and pure rubbish cluttering up the world. Reappearing at the other end, everything was transformed. Though people and things stayed the same, they took on totally new meanings. The beginning of Dada was the rediscovery of lived experience and its possible delights – its end was the reversal of all perspectives, the invention of a new universe. Subversion, the tactics of radical change, overthrew the rigid structure of the old world. Amidst this upheaval the *poetry made by everyone* revealed its concrete sense – something very different from the literary mentality to which the surrealists surrendered so pitifully.

The initial weakness of Dada lay in its extraordinary humility. Every morning, Tzara, clown with the gravity of a Pope, is said to have repeated Descartes' statement: "I'm not even interested in knowing whether anyone ever existed before I did." Yet this same Tzara was to end up a Stalinist, sneering at men like Ravachol, Bonnot and Mahkno's peasant army. If Dada broke up because it could not supersede itself, then the blame lies on the dadaists themselves for having failed to search for the real historic occasions when such supersession becomes

The basic characteristic of the spectacle today is the way it calls attention to its own disintegration.

IS no. 2, 1959

possible: the moments when the masses arise and seize their destiny in their own hands.

The first compromise is always terrible in its effects. Through Surrealism to neo-Dada, its repercussions gradually infect and finally poison Surrealism's initial vigour. Consider the surrealists' ambivalent attitude towards the past. While they were right to recognise the subversive genius of a de Sade, a Fourier or a Lautréamont, all they could subsequently do was write so much – and so well – about them as to win for their heroes the honour of a few timid footnotes in progressive school textbooks. A literary celebrity much like the celebrity the neo-dadaists win for their forebears in the spectacle of our present decomposition.

IS no. 11, 1967

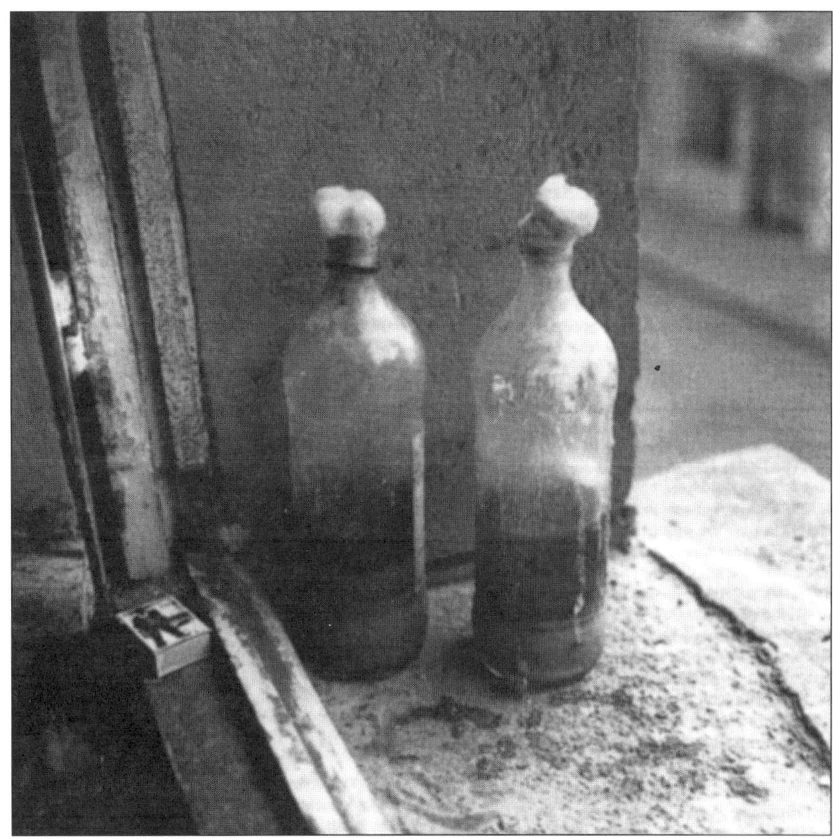

A warning to those who build ruins: after the town planners will come the last troglodytes of the slums and the ghettoes. They will know how to build. The privileged ones from the dormitory towns will only know how to destroy. Much can be expected from the meeting of these two forces: it will define the revolution.

IS no. 6, 1961

SELF-REALISATION, COMMUNICATION AND PARTICIPATION

The repressive unity of power is threefold: coercion, seduction and mediation. This is no more than the inversion and perversion of an equally threefold unitary project. The new society, as it develops underground, chaotically, is moving towards a total honesty – a transparency – between individuals: an honesty promoting the participation of each individual in the self-realisation of everyone else. Creativity, love and play stand in the same relation to true life as the need to eat and the need to find shelter stand in relation to survival. Attempts to realise oneself can only be based on creativity. Attempts to communicate can only be based on love. Attempts to participate can only be based on play. Separated from one another these three projects merely strengthen the repressive unity of power. Radical subjectivity is the presence – which can be seen in almost everyone – of the same desire to create a truly passionate life. The erotic is the spontaneous coherence fusing attempts to enrich lived experience.

The construction of everyday life fuses reason and passion. The plain confusion to which life has always been subject comes from the mystification covering up the utter triviality of merely continuing to exist. Will to live entails practical organisation. Individual desire for a rich, multi-dimensional life cannot be totally divorced from a collective project. The oppression exercised by human government is essentially threefold: coercion, alienating mediation and magical seduction. The will to live also draws its vitality and its coherence from the unity of a threefold project: self-realisation, communication and participation.

If human history was neither reduced to, nor dissociated from, the history of human survival, the dialectic of this threefold project (in conjunction with the dialectic of the productive forces) would prove sufficient explanation for most things men have done to themselves and to one another. Every riot, every revolution, reveals a passionate quest for exuberant life, for total honesty between people, for a collective form of transformation of the world. Today one can see throughout the whole of history three fundamental passions related to life in the same way that the need to eat and find shelter are related to survival. The desire to create, the desire to love and the desire to play interact with the need to eat and find shelter, just as the will to live never ceases to play havoc with the necessity of surviving. Obviously, the importance of the part played by each element changes from one time to another, but today their whole importance lies in the extent to which they can be unified.

Today, with the welfare state, the question of survival has become a part of the whole problem of life. As we hope to have shown, life economy has gradually absorbed survival economy and in this context the dissociation of the three projects, and of the passions underlying them, appears more and more clearly as a consequence of a fundamentally erroneous distinction between life and survival. However, since the whole of existence is torn between two perspectives – that of separation of power and that of revolution, of unity – and is therefore essentially ambiguous, I am forced to discuss each project at once separately and together.

The project of self-realisation is born of the passion of creativity, in a moment when subjectivity wells up and wants to reign universally. The project of communication is born of the passion of love, whenever people discover in one another the self-same will to conquest. The project of participation is born of the passion of playing, whenever group activity facilitates the self-realisation of each individual.

Isolated, the three passions become perverted. Dissociated, the three projects become falsified. The will to self-realisation is turned into the will to power; sacrificed to status and role-playing, it reigns in a world of restrictions and illusions. The will to communication becomes objective dishonesty, based on relationships between objects, it provides the field of operations for semiology, the science of fucked-up communications. The will to participation organises the loneliness of everyone in the lonely crowd; it creates the tyranny of the illusory community.

Isolated, each passion is integrated in a metaphysical vision which makes it absolute and, as such, leaves it completely out of touch. Intellectuals can be funny when they try: they pull the plug out and then announce that the electricity doesn't work. Not in the least abashed, they proceed to inform us that we're really in the dark and that's all there is to it. Wherever everything is separated from everything else, everything really is impossible. Cartesian analysis can produce only the jerry-built. The armies of Order can only recruit the crippled.

THE PROJECT OF SELF-REALISATION

Assurance of security leaves unused a large supply of energy formerly expended in the struggle for survival. The will to power tries to recuperate, for the reinforcement of hierarchical slavery, this free-floating energy which could be used for the blossoming of individual life. Universal oppression forces almost everyone to withdraw strategically towards what they feel to be their only uncontaminated possession: their subjectivity. The revolution of everyday life must create practical forms for the countless attacks on the outside world launched daily by subjectivity.

The historic phase of privative appropriation stopped man being the demiurge he was forced to create in an ideal form, and thus to confirm his own real failure. At heart everyone wants to be God. To date we have merely prevented ourselves being so. I have shown how hierarchical social organisation builds up the world by breaking men down; how the perfection of its structure and machinery makes its function like a giant computer whose programmers are also programmed; how, lastly, the cybernetic state is the coldest of all cost monsters.

In these conditions, the struggle for enough to eat, for comfort, for stable employment and for security are, on the social front, so many aggressive raids which slowly but surely are becoming rearguard actions, despite their very real importance. The struggle for survival took up and still takes up an amount of energy and creativity which revolutionary society will inherit like a pack of ravening wolves. Despite false conflicts and illusory activities, a constantly-stimulated creative energy is no longer being absorbed fast enough by consumer society. What will happen to this vitality suddenly at a loose end, to this surplus virility which neither coercion nor lies can really continue to handle? No longer recuperated by artistic and cultural consumption – by the ideological spectacle – creativity will turn spontaneously against the very safeguards of survival itself.

Rebels have only their survival to lose. And there are only two ways in which they can lose it: either by living or by dying. And since survival is no more than dying very slowly, there is a temptation, containing a very great deal of genuine feeling, to speed the whole thing up and to die a damn sight faster. To 'live' negatively the negation of survival. Or, on the other hand, to try and survive an anti-survivor, focussing all one's energy on breaking through to real life. To make survival no more than the basis of a systematic quest for happiness.

Self-realisation is impossible in this world. Half-demented rebellion remains, for all its ferocity, a prisoner of the authoritarian dilemma: survival or death. This half-rebellion, this savage creativity, so easily broken in by the order of things, is the *will to power*.

The will to power is the project of self-realisation falsified – divorced from any attempt to communicate with, or to participate in, the life of others. It is the passion of creating and of creating oneself, caught in the hierarchical system, condemned to turn the treadmill of repression and appearances. Accepting being put down because you can put others down in your turn. The hero is he who sacrifices himself to the power of his role and his rifle. And when, finally, he's burnt out, he follows Voltaire's advice and cultivates his garden. Meantime his mediocrity has become a model for thc common run of mortals.

The hero, the ruler, the superstar, the millionaire, the expert… How many times have they sold out all they hold most dear? How many sacrifices have they made to force a few people, or a few million people, people they rightly regard as complete idiots, to have their photograph on the wall, to have their name remembered, to be stared at in the street?

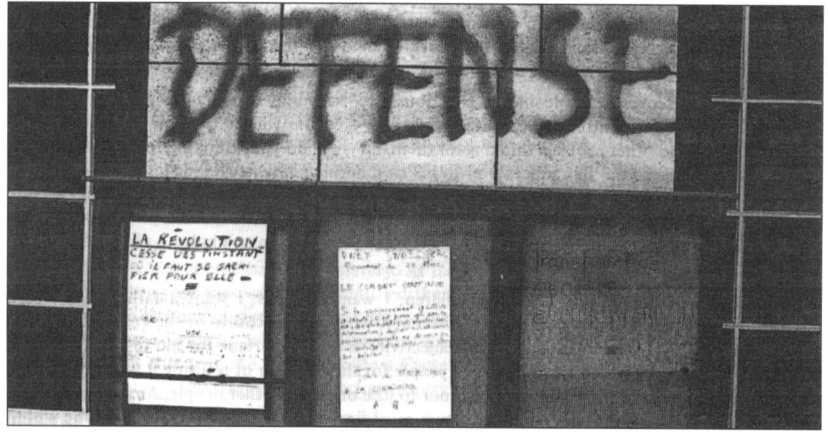

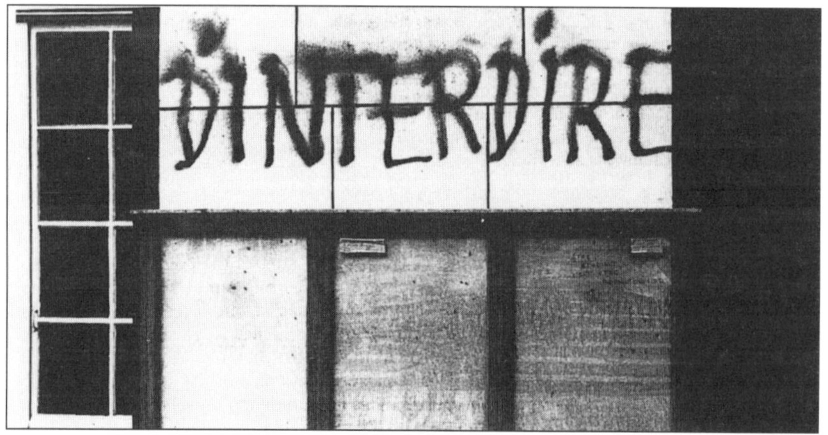

Yet, for all its bullshit, the will to power does contain traces of an authentic will to live. Think of the *virtu* of the *condottiere*, of the Titans of the Renaissance. But the *condottiers* are dead and buried. All that's left is industrial magnets, gangsters and hired guns, dealers in art and artillery. The adventurer and the explorer are comic-strip characters. And it's with these people that Zarathustra dreamt of peopling the heights of Sils-Maria; it's in these abortions he thought he could see the lineaments of a future race. Nietzsche is, in fact, the last master, crucified by his own illusions. His death was a reply, with more *brio*, and in slightly better taste, of the black comedy of Golgotha. It explains the disappearance of the feudal lords just as the death of Christ explained the disappearance of God. Nietzsche may have had a refined sensibility but the stench of Christianity didn't stop him breathing it in by the lungful. And he pretends not to understand that Christianity, however much contempt it may have poured on the will to power, is in fact its best means of protection, its most faithful bodyguard, since it stands in the way of the appearance of masters who no longer need slaves to be masters. Nietzsche blessed a world in which the will to live is condemned never to be more than the will to power. His last letters were signed 'Dionysus the Crucified'. He too was looking for someone to assume responsibility for his broken zest. You don't mess with the witch-doctor of Bethlehem.

Nazism is Nietzschean logic called to order by history. The question was: what can become of those who wish to live like a lord in a society from which all true rulers have disappeared? And the answer: a super-slave. Nietzsche's concept of the superman, however threadbare it may have been, is worlds apart from what we know of the domestics who ran the Third Reich. Fascism only knows one superman: the state.

The state superman is the strength of the weak. This is why the desires of an isolated individual can always fit in with a role played impeccably in the official spectacle. The will to power is an exhibitionist will. The isolated individual detests other people, feels contempt for the masses of which he is a perfect specimen himself. He is, in fact, the most contemptible man of all. Showing off, amidst the crassest sort of illusory community, is his 'dynamism'; the rat-race, his 'love of danger'.

The manager, the leader, tough guy, the mobster know little joy. Ability to endure is their main qualification. Their morale is that of pioneers, of spies, of scouts, of the shock troops of conformity. "No animal would have done what I have done…" What is the gangster trip? A will to appear, since one cannot be; a way of escaping the emptiness of one's own existence by running greater and greater risks. But only servants are proud of their sacrifices. Here the part rules the whole: sometimes the artificial being of the role, sometimes the directness of the animal. And the animal does what the men cannot do. The heroes who march past, colours flying — the Red Army, the SS, the US Marines — these are the same people who burnt and cut living flesh at Budapest, at Warsaw, at Algiers. Army discipline is based on the uprightness of the rank and file. Cops know when to snarl and when to fawn.

The will to power is a compensation for slavery. At the same time, it is a hatred of slavery. The most striking 'personalities' of the past never identified themselves with a Cause. They just used Causes to further their own personal hunger for power. But as great Causes began to break up and disappear, so did the ambitious individuals concerned. However, the game goes on. People rely on Causes because they haven't been able to make their own life a Cause sufficient unto itself. Through the Cause and the sacrifice it entails they stagger along, backwards, trying to find their own will to live.

Sometimes desire for freedom and for play breaks out among law and order's conscripts. I am thinking of Salvatore Giuliano, before he was recuperated by the landowners, of Billy the Kid, of various gangsters momentarily close to the anarchist territories. Legionnaires and mercenaries have defected their desire to play to its logical conclusion: blowing their whole scene sky-high, and jumping into the dark.

I also have teenage gangs in mind. The very childishness of their will to power has often kept their will to live almost contaminated. Obviously the delinquent is threatened with recuperation. Firstly, as a consumer, because he wants things he cannot afford to buy; then, as he gets older, as a producer. But, within the gang, playing remains of such great importance that truly revolutionary consciousness can never be far away. If the violence inherent in the teenage gangs stopped squandering itself in exhibitionistic and generally half-baked brawls and rave-ups, and only saw how much real poetry was to be found in a riot, then their game-playing, as it became increasingly riotous, would almost certainly set off a chain reaction: a qualitative flash. Almost everyone is fed up with their life. Almost everyone is sick of being pushed around. Almost everyone is sick of the lies they come out with all day long. All that's needed is a spark – plus tactics. Should delinquents arrive at revolutionary consciousness simply through understanding what they already are, and by wanting to be more so, then it's quite possible that they could prove the key factor in a general social retake on reality. This could be vitally important. Actually, all that's really necessary is the *federation* of their gangs.

So far, the heart of life has been sought anywhere but in the heart of man. Creativity has always been pushed to one side. It has been suburban; and, in fact, urbanism reflects very accurately the misadventures of the axis around which life has been organised for thousands of years. The first cities grew up around a stronghold or sacred spot, a temple or a church, a point where heaven and earth converged. Industrial towns, with their mean, dark streets, surround a factory or industrial plant; administrative centres preside over empty, rectilinear avenues. Finally, the most recent examples of town planning simply have no centre at all. It's becoming increasingly obvious: the reference point they propose is always somewhere else. These are labyrinths in which you are not allowed only to lose yourself. No games. No meetings. No living. A desert of plate-glass. A grid of roads. High-rise apartment blocks. Oppression is no longer centralised because oppression is everywhere. The positive aspects of this: everyone begins to see, in conditions of almost total isolation, that first and foremost it is themselves that they have to save, themselves that they have to choose as the centre, their own subjectivity out of which they have to build a world that everyone else will recognise as their native land.

One can only rediscover other people by consciously rediscovering *oneself*. For as long as individual creativity is not at the centre of social life, man's only freedom will be freedom to destroy and be destroyed. If you do other people's thinking for them, they will do your thinking for you. And he who thinks for you judges you, he reduces you to his own norm and, whatever his intentions may be, he will end by making you stupid – for stupidity doesn't come from a lack of intelligence, as stupid people imagine it does, it comes from renouncing, from abandoning one's own true self. So if anyone asks you what you are doing, asks you to explain yourself, treat him as a judge – that is to say, as an enemy.

"I want someone to succeed me; I want children; I want disciples; I want a father; I don't want myself." A few words from those high on Christianity, whether the Roman or the Peking brand. Only unhappiness and neurosis can follow. My subjectivity is too important for me to take my lack of inhibition to the point of either asking other people for their help or of refusing it when it is offered. The point is neither to lose oneself in oneself nor to lose oneself in other people. Anyone who realises that his problems are ultimately social in nature must first of all find himself. Otherwise he will find nothing in other people apart from his own absence.

Nothing is more difficult or more painful to approach than the question of one's own self-regeneration. In the heart of each human being there is a hidden room, a *camera obscura*, to which only the mind and dreams can find the door. A magic circle in which the world and the self are reconciled, where every childish wish comes true. The passions flower there, brilliant, poisonous blossoms clinging to and thriving on air, thin air. I create my universe for myself and, like some fantastic tyrannical God, people it with beings who will never live for anyone else. One of my favourite James Thurber stories is the one where Walter Mitty dreams that he is a swashbuckling captain, then an eminent surgeon, then a cold-blooded killer, and finally a war hero. All this as he drives his old Buick downtown to buy some dog biscuits.

The real importance of subjectivity can easily be measured by the general embarrassment with which it is approached. Everyone wants to pass it off as their mind 'wandering', as 'introversion', as 'being stoned'. Everyone censors their own daydreams. But isn't it the phantoms and visions of the mind that have dealt the most deadly blows at mortality, authority, language and our collective hypnotic sleep? Isn't a fertile imagination the source of all creativity, the alembic distilling the quick of life: the bridgehead driven into the old world and across which the coming invasions will pour?

Anyone who can be open-minded about their interior life will begin to see a different world outside themselves – values change, things lose their glamour and become plain instruments. In the magic of the imaginary, things exist only to be picked up and toyed with, caressed, broken apart and put together again in any way one sees fit. Once the prime importance of subjectivity is accepted, the spell cast upon things is broken. Starting from other people, one's self-pursuit is fruitless, one repeats the same futile gestures time after time. Starting from oneself, on the contrary, gestures are not repeated but taken back into oneself, corrected and realised in a more highly-evolved form.

Day-dreaming could become the most powerful dynamo in the world. Modern technological expertise, just as it makes everything considered 'Utopian' in the past a purely practical undertaking today, also does away with the purely fairytale nature of dreams. All my wishes can come true – from the moment that modern technology is put to their service.

And even deprived of these techniques, can subjectivity ever stray far from the truth? It is possible for me to objectify all that I have dreamt of being. Everyone, at least once in his life, has pulled off the same sort of thing as Lassailly or Nechaev. Laissally, passing himself off as the author of an unwritten book, ends up by becoming a real writer, author of the *Roueries de Trialph*. Nechaev, touching Bakunin for money in the name of a non-existent terrorist organisation, finally does get a real group of nihilists going. One day I must be as I have wanted to seem. The particular spectacular role I have so long wanted to be will be genuine. Thus subjectivity subverts roles and spectacular lies to its own ends. It reinvests appearance in reality.

Subjective imagination is not purely spiritual: it is always seeking its practical realisation. There can be no doubt that the artistic spectacle – above all, in its narrative forms – plays on subjectivity's quest for its own self-realisation, but solely by capitivating it, by making it function in terms of passive identification. Debord's propaganda film *Critique de la Séparation* stresses the point. "Normally, the things that happen to us, things which really do involve us and demand our attention, leave us no more than bored and distant spectators. However, almost any situation, once it has been transposed artistically, awakens our attention: we want to take part in it, to change it. This paradox must be turned upside down – put back on its feet." The forces of the artistic spectacle must be dissolved and their equipment pass into the arsenal of individual dreams. Once armed in this way, there will no longer be any question of treating them as fantasies. This is the only way in which the problem of making art real can be seen.

RADICAL SUBJECTIVITY

Each subjectivity is different from every other one, but they all obey the same will to self-realisation. The problem is one of setting their variety in a common direction, of creating a united front of subjectivity. Any attempt to build a new life is subject to two conditions: firstly, that the realisation of each individual subjectivity will either take place in a collective form or it will not take place at all; and, secondly, that, "To tell the truth, the only reason anyone fights is for what they love. Fighting for everyone else is only the consequence" (Saint-Just).

My subjectivity feeds on events. The most varied events: a riot, a sexual fiasco, a meeting, a memory, a rotten tooth. Reality, as it evolves, sweeps me with it. I am struck by everything and, though not everything strikes me in the same way, I am always struck by the same basic contradiction: although I can always see how beautiful anything could be if only I could change it, in practically every case there is nothing I can really do. Everything is changed into something else in my imagination, then the dead weight of things changes it back into what it was in the first place. A bridge between imagination and reality must be built. Only a truly radical perspective can give everyone the right to make anything out of anything. A radical perspective grasps men by their roots and the roots of men lie in their subjectivity – this unique zone they possess in common.

You can't make it on your own. You can't live your own life to the full in isolation. But can any individual – any individual who has got anything at all straight about himself and the world – fail to see a will identical to his own among everyone he knows: the same journey leaving from the same place.

All forms of hierarchical power differ from one another and yet all betray a fundamental identity in oneself by transforming the world, the will to live every sensation, every experience, every possibility to the full. This can be seen in everyone, at different stages of consciousness and determination. Its real power depends on the degree of collective unity it can attain without losing its variety. Consciousness of this necessity unity comes from what one could call a *reflex of identity* – the diametrically opposite movement to that of identification. Through identification we lose our uniqueness in the variety of roles; through the reflex of identity we strengthen our wealth of individual possibilities in the unity of federated subjectivities.

Radical subjectivity can only be based on the reflex of identity. One's own quest searches for itself everywhere in others. "While I was on a mission in the state of Tchou", says Confucius, "I saw some piglets suckling their dead mother. After a short while they shuddered and went away. They had sensed that she could no longer see them and that *she wasn't like them any more*. What they loved in their mother wasn't her body, but whatever it was that made her body live." Likewise, what I am looking for in other people is the richest part of myself hidden within them. Can the reflex of identity spread naturally? One can only hope so. Certainly it's high time for it.

No one has ever questioned the interest men take in being fed, sheltered, cared for, protected from hardship and disaster. The imperfections of technology – transformed at a very early date into social imperfections – have postponed the satisfaction of this universal desire. Today, planned economy allows one to foresee the final solution of the problems of survival. Now that the needs of survival are well on the way to being satisfied, at least in the hyper-industrialised countries, it is becoming painfully obvious, to say the least of it, that there are also human passions which must be satisfied, that the satisfaction of these passions is of vital importance to everyone and, furthermore, that failure to do so will undermine, if not destroy, all our acquisitions in terms of material survival. As the problems of survival are slowly but surely resolved they begin to clash more and more brutally with the problems of life which have been, just as slowly and just as surely, sacrificed to the needs of survival. The chickens are all coming home to roost: henceforward, socialist-type planning is opposed to the true harmonisation of life in common.

Radical subjectivity is the common front of rediscovered identity. Those who can't see themselves in other people are condemned for ever to be strangers to themselves. I can't do anything for other people if they can't do anything for themselves. It's along these lines that concepts such as those of 'cognition' and 're-cognition', of 'sympathy' and 'sympathising', should be re-examined.

Cognition is only of value if it leads to the recognition of a common project – to the reflex of identity. To realise radical imagination requires a varied knowledge, but this knowledge is nothing without the style with which it is handled. As the first years of the SI have known, the worst crises within a coherent revolutionary group are caused by those closest by their knowledge and furthest away by their lived experience and by the importance they place upon it. Likewise, 'partisans'. They both identify themselves with the group and get in its way. They understand everything except what is really at stake. They demand knowledge because they are incapable of demanding themselves.

By seizing myself, I break other people's hold over me. Thus I let them see themselves in me. No one can evolve freely without spreading freedom in the world.

"I want to be myself. I want to walk without impediment. I want to affirm myself alone in my freedom. May everyone do likewise. Don't worry any more about the fate of the revolution – it will be safer in the hands of everyone than in the hands of political parties." So said Coeurderoy. I agree one hundred per cent. Nothing authorises me to speak in the name of other people. I am only my own delegate. Yet at the same time I can't help thinking that my life isn't solely my own concern but that I serve the interests of thousands of other people by living the way I live, and by struggling to live more intensely and more freely. My friends and I are one, and we know it. Each of us is acting for each other by acting for himself. Honesty is our only hope.

THE PROJECT OF COMMUNICATION

Love offers the purest glimpse of true communication that any of us have had. But, as communication in general tends to break down more and more, the existence of love becomes increasingly precarious. It is threatened on every side. Everything tends to reduce lovers to objects. Real meetings are replaced by mechanical sex: by the posturing of countless playboys and bunnies. Really being in love means really wanting to live in a different world.

Although the three passions underlying the threefold project of self-realisation, communication and participation are of equal importance, they have not been repressed to an equal extent. While creativity and play have been blighted by prohibitions and by every sort of distortion, love, without escaping from repression, still remains relatively the most free experience. The most democratic, all in all.

Love offers the model of perfect communication: the orgasm, the total fusion of two separate beings. It is a glimpse of a transformed universe. Its intensity, its here-and-nowness, its physical exaltation, its emotional fluidity, its grateful acceptance of the value of change – everything indicates that love will prove the key factor in recreating the world. Our emotionally-dead survival cries out for multi-dimensional passions. Lovemaking sums up and distils both the desire for, and the reality of, such a way of life. The universe lovers build of dreams and one another's bodies is a transparent universe, lovers want to be at home everywhere.

Love has been able to stay free more successfully than the other passions. Creativity and play have always 'been granted' an official representation, a spectacular acknowledgement which did its best to cut them off at their source. Love has always been clandestine – 'being alone together'. It turned out to be protected by the bourgeois concept of private life; banished from the day, reserved for work and consumption, and driven into the darkest corners of the night; lit by the moon. Thus it partly escapes the major mopping-up of daily activities. The same cannot be said for communication, and it is precisely the ashes of false (daily) communication that choke the spark of sexual passion. And today consumer society is extending falsification further and further... into the reaches of the night.

People who talk about 'communication' when there are only things and their mechanical relations are working on the side of the process of reification that they pretend to attack. 'Understanding', 'friendship', 'being happy together' – so much bullshit. All I can see is exploiters and exploited, rulers and ruled, actors and spectators. And all of them flailed like chaff by Power.

Things aren't necessarily expressionless. Anything can become human if someone infuses it with their own subjectivity. But in a world ruled by privative appropriation, the only function of the object is to justify its proprietor. If my subjectivity overflows, if my eyes make the landscape their own, it can only be ideally, without material or legal consequences. In the perspective of power, people and things aren't there for my enjoyment, but to serve a master; nothing really is, everything functions as part of an order of possessions.

There can't be any real communication in a world where almost everything one does is ruled by fetishes. The space between people and things isn't empty: it's packed with alienating mediations. And as power becomes increasingly abstract, its own signals become so numerous, so chaotic, as to demand systematic interpretation on the part of a body of scribes, semanticians and mythologists. Brought up to see only objects around him, the proprietor needs objective and objectified servants. Only subjective truth, as historically it becomes objective, can withstand this sort of thing. One must start with immediate experience itself if one wants to attack the most advanced points to which repression has penetrated.

The main pleasure of the middle class seems to have been degrading pleasure in all its forms. It wasn't enough to imprison people's freedom to fall in love in the squalid ownership of marriage (interlarded, of course, with the occasional one-night stand). It wasn't enough to set things up so that dishonesty and jealousy were bound to follow. The great thing was to sabotage people on the few occasions they really did *meet*.

Love's despair doesn't come from sexual frustration. It comes from suddenly losing contact with the person in your arms; of both of you suddenly seeing one another as an object. Swedish social democracy, as hygienic as ever, has already got its own horrible caricature of free love out on the market: one-night stands dealt out like a deck of cards.

How sickening these endless lies one says and hears. How much one wants to be straight with someone. Sex really does seem to be our only break. Sometimes I think that nothing else is as real, nothing else is as human, as the feel of a woman's body, the softness of her skin, the warmth and wetness of her cunt. Even if there were nothing else at all, this alone would be enough for ever.

But even during really magical moments, the inert mass of objects can suddenly become magnetic. The passivity of a lover suddenly unravels the bonds which were being woven, the dialogue is interrupted before it really began. Love's dialectic freezes. Two statues are left lying side by side. Two objects.

Although love is always born of subjectivity – a girl is beautiful because I love her – my desire cannot stop itself objectifying what it wants. Desire always makes an object of the loved person. But if I let my desire transform the loved person into an object, have I not condemned myself to conflict with this object and, through force of habit, to become detached from it?

What can ensure perfect communication between lovers? The union of these opposites:

— the more I detach myself from the object of my desire and the more objective strength I give to my desire, the more carefree my desire becomes towards its object
— the more I detach myself from my desire insofar as it is an object and the more objective strength I give to the object of my desire, the more my desire finds its *raison d'être* in the loved person.

Socially, this playing with one's attitudes can be expressed by changing partners at the same time as one is attached more or less permanently to a 'pivotal' partner. All these meetings would be the communication of a single purpose experienced in common. I have always wanted to be able to say: "I know you don't love me because you only love yourself. I am just the same. So love me."

Love can only be based on radical subjectivity. The time is up for all self-sacrificial forms of love. To love only oneself through other people, to be loved by others through the love they owe themselves. This is what the passion of love teaches; these are the only conditions of authentic communication.

And love is also an adventure; an attempt to break free of dishonesty. To approach a woman in any spectacular, exhibitionist way is to condemn oneself to a reified relationship from the very first. The choice is between spectacular seduction – that of the playboy – and the seduction exercised by something that is qualitatively different – the person who is seductive because he isn't trying to seduce.

De Sade analyses two possible attitudes. On the one hand, the libertines of the *120 Days of Sodom* who can only really enjoy themselves by torturing to death the object they have seduced (and what more fitting homage to a thing than to make it suffer?); or, on the other, the libertines of the *Philosophy in the Boudoir,* warm and playful, who do all they can to increase one another's pleasure. The former are the feudal-type lords, vibrant with hatred and revolt; the latter, the masters without slaves, discovering in one another only the reflection of their own pleasure.

Today, seduction tends to become increasingly sadistic. Sadism is inability to forgive the desired person for being an object. Truly seductive people, on the contrary, contain the fullness of desire in themselves; they refuse to play a part and owe their seductiveness to this refusal. In de Sade this would be Dolmance, Eugénie or Madame de Saint-Ange. This plenitude can only exist for the desired person if they can recognise their own will to live in the person who desires them. Real seduction seduces only by its honesty. And not everyone is worth seducing. This is what the *Beguines* of Schweidnitz and their companions (thirteenth century) meant by saying that resistance to sexual advances was the sign of a crass spirit. The Brethren of the Free Spirit expressed the same idea: "Anyone who knows the God inhabiting him carries his own Heaven in himself. By the same token, ignorance of one's own divinity really is a mortal sin. This is the meaning of the Hell which one carries with oneself in earthly life."

Hell is the emptiness left by separation, the anguish of lovers lying side by side without being together. Non-communication is always like the collapse of a revolutionary movement. The will to death is installed where the will to life has disappeared.

Love must be freed from its myths, from its images, from its spectacular categories; its authenticity must be strengthened and its spontaneity renewed. There is no other way of fighting its reification and its recuperation in the spectacle. Love can't stand either isolation or fragmentation; it is bound to overflow into the will to transform the whole of human activity, into the necessity of building a world where lovers feel themselves to be free everywhere.

The birth and the dissolution of the moment of love are bound to be the dialectic of memory and desire. At first desire and the possibility of its reciprocation strengthen one another. In the *moment* of love itself, memory and desire coincide. The moment of love is the space-time of authentic, lived experience, a present containing both the past and the future. At the *stage of breaking up*, memory prolongs the impassioned moment but desire gradually ebbs away.

The present disintegrates, memory turns nostalgically towards past happiness, while desire foresees the unhappiness to come. In dissolution the separation is real. The failure of the recent past cannot be forgotten and desire gradually melts away.

In love, as in every attempt to communicate, the problem is avoiding the stage of breaking up. One could suggest:

— developing the moment of love as far as one can, in as many directions as possible; in other words, refusing to dissociate it from either creativity or play, raising it from the state of a moment to that of the real construction of a situation;
— promoting collective experiments in individual realisation; thus of multiplying the possibilities of sexual attraction by bringing together a great variety of possible partners;
— permanently strengthening the pleasure-principle, which is the life-blood of every attempt to realise oneself, to communicate or to participate. Pleasure is the principle of unification. Love is desire for unity in a common *moment*; friendship, desire for unity in a common *project*.

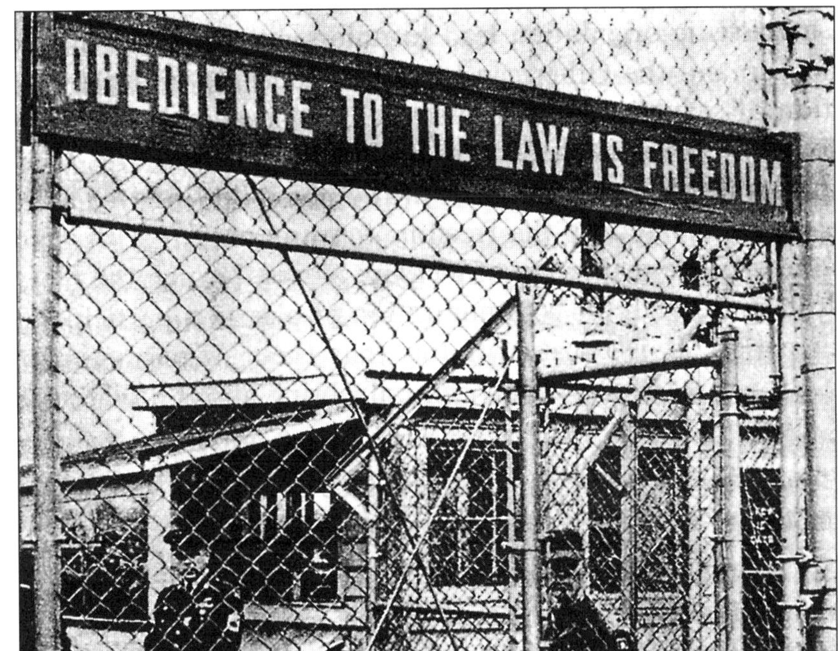

THE EROTIC OR THE DIALECTIC OF PLEASURE

There is no pleasure which is not seeking its own coherence. Its interruption, its lack of satisfaction, causes a disturbance analogous to Reichian 'stasis'. Repression keeps human beings in a state of permanent crisis. Thus the function of pleasure, and of the anxiety born of its absence, is essentially a social function. The erotic is the development of the passions as they become unitary, a game of unity and variety, without which revolutionary coherence cannot exist. ('Boredom is always counter-revolutionary', SI no. 3.)

Wilhelm Reich attributes the majority of neurotic behaviour to disturbances of the orgasm, to what he called "orgiastic impotence". He maintains that anxiety is created by inability to experience a complete orgasm, by a sexual discharge which fails to liquidate all the excitement, all the foreplay, leading up to it. The accumulated and unspent energy becomes free-floating and is converted into anxiety. Anxiety in its turn still further impedes future orgiastic potency.

But the problem of tensions and their liquidation doesn't just exist on the level of sexuality. It characterises all human relationships. And Reich, although he sensed that this was so, fails to emphasise strongly enough that the present social crisis is also a crisis of an orgiastic nature. If "the source of neurotic energy lies in the disparity between the accumulation and the discharge of sexual energy", it seems to be that the source of energy of our neuroses is also to be found in the disparity between the accumulation and the discharge of the energy called up by human relationships. Total enjoyment is still possible in the moment of love, but as soon as one tries to prolong this moment, to extend it into social life itself, one cannot avoid what Reich called "stasis". The world of the dissatisfactory and the unconsummated is a world of permanent crisis. What would a society without neurosis be like? An endless banquet. Pleasure is the only guide.

"Everything is feminine in what one loves", wrote La Mettrie, "the empire of love recognises no other frontiers that those of pleasure". But pleasure itself doesn't recognise any frontiers. If it isn't growing, it is beginning to disappear. Repetition kills it; it can't adapt itself to the fragmentary. The principle of pleasure cannot be separated from the totality.

The erotic is pleasure seeking its coherence. It's the development of passions becoming communicative, interdependent, unitary. The problem is recreating in social life that state of total enjoyment known in the moment of love. Conditions allowing a game with unity and variety, that is to say, free and transparent participation in particular achievements.

Freud defined the goal of Eros as unification or the search for union. But when he maintains that fear of being separated and expelled from the group comes from an underlying fear of castration, his proposition should be inverted. Fear of castration comes from the fear of being excluded, not the other way round. This anxiety becomes more marked as the isolation of individuals in an illusory community becomes more and more difficult to ignore.

Even while it seeks unification, Eros is essentially narcissistic and in love with itself. It wants a world to love as much as it loves itself. Norman Brown, in *Life against Death*, points out the contradiction. How, he asks, can a narcissistic orientation lead to union with beings in the world? "In love, the abstract antimony of the Ego and the Other can be transcended if we return to the concrete reality of pleasure, to a definition of sexuality as being essentially a pleasurable activity of the body, and if we see love as the relationship between the Ego and the sources of pleasure." One could be more exact: the source of pleasure lies less in the body than in the possibility of free activity in the world. The concrete reality of pleasure is based on the freedom to unite oneself with anyone who allows one to become united with oneself. The realisation of pleasure passes through the pleasure of realisation, the pleasure of communication through the communication of pleasure, participation in pleasure through the pleasure of participation. It is because of this that the narcissism turned towards the outside world, the narcissism Brown is talking about, can only bring about a wholesale demolition of social structures.

The more intense pleasure becomes, the more it demands the whole world. "Lovers seek greater and greater pleasure", said Breton. This is a revolutionary demand.

Western civilisation is a civilisation of work, and, Diogenes observed: "Love is the occupation of the unoccupied." With the gradual disappearance of forced labour, love takes on a greater and greater importance. It has become the major resource to develop. And it poses a direct threat to every kind of authority. Because the erotic is unitary, it is also acceptance of change. Freedom knows no propaganda more effective than people calmly enjoying themselves. Which is why pleasure, for the most part, is forced to be clandestine, love locked away in a bedroom, creativity confined to the back stairs of culture, and alcohol and drugs cower under the shadow of the outstretched arm of the law...

The morality of survival has condemned both the diversity of pleasures and their union-in-variety in order to promote obsessive repetition. But if pleasure-anxiety is satisfied with the repetitive, true pleasure can only exist in terms of diversity-within-unity. Clearly the simplest model of the erotic is the pivotal couple. Two people live their experiences as honestly and freely as possible. This radiant complicity has all the charm of incest. Their wealth of common experiences can only lead to a brother and sister relationship. Great loves have always had something incestuous about them; one should deduce that love between brothers and sisters was privileged from the very first, and that it should be worked on in every possible manner. It's high time to break this, the most ancient and ugliest of all taboos; and to break it once and for all. The process could be described as sororisation. A wife and a sister, whose friends are also my wives and sisters.

In the erotic there is no perversion apart from the negation of pleasure: its distortion into pleasure anxiety. What matters the spring so long as the water is pure? As the Chinese say: immobile in one another, pleasure bears us.

And, finally, the search for pleasure is the best safeguard of play. It defends real participation, it protects it against self-sacrifice, coercion and dishonesty. The actual degree of intensity pleasure reaches marks subjectivity's grasp on the world. Thus, flirtatiousness is playing with desire as it is born; desire, playing with passion as it is born. And playing with passion finds its coherence in poetry, whose essentially revolutionary nature can never be over-emphasised.

Does this mean that the search for pleasure is incompatible with pain? On the contrary, it's a question of re-inventing pain. Pleasure-anxiety is neither pleasure nor pain; it's just scratching yourself and letting the itch get worse and worse. What is real pain? A set-back in the game of desire or passion; a positive pain crying out with a corresponding degree of passion for another pleasure to construct. A delay in full participation.

THE PROJECT OF PARTICIPATION

A society based on organised survival can only tolerate false, spectacular forms of play. But given the crisis of the spectacle, playfulness, distorted in every imaginable way, is being reborn everywhere. From now on it has the features of social upheaval and, beyond its negativity, the foundations of a society of real participation can be detected. To play means to refuse leaders, to refuse self-sacrifice, to refuse roles, to embrace every form of self-realisation and to be utterly, painfully, honest with all one's friends. Tactics are the polemical stage of the game. Individual creativity needs an organisation concentrating and strengthening it. Tactics entail a certain kind of hedonistic foresight. The point of every fragmentary action must be the total destruction of the enemy. Industrial societies have to evolve their own specific forms of guerrilla warfare. Subversion is the only possible revolutionary use of the spiritual and material values distributed by consumer society: supersession's ultimate deterrent.

Economic necessity and play don't mix. Financial transactions are deadly serious: you don't fool around with money. The elements of play contained within feudal economy were gradually squeezed out by the rationality of money exchanges. Playing with exchange means to barter products without worrying too much about strictly standardised equivalents. But from the moment that capitalism forced its commercial relationships on the world, fantasy was forbidden; and the dictatorship of commodities today shows clearly that it intends to enforce these relationships everywhere, at every level of life.

The pastoral relationships of country life in the high Middle Ages tempered the purely economic necessities of feudalism with a sort of freedom; play often took the upper hand even in menial tasks, in the dispensing of justice, in the settling of debts. By throwing the whole of everyday life on the battlefield of production and consumption, capitalism crushes the urge to play while at the same time trying to harness it as a source of profit. So, over the last few decades, we have seen the attraction of the unknown turned into mass tourism, adventure turned into scientific expeditions and the great game of war turned into strategic operations. Taste for change now rests content with a change of taste...

Contemporary society has banned all real play. It has been turned into something only children do. And today, children themselves are getting more and more pacifying gadget-type toys rammed down their throats. The adult is only allowed falsified and recuperated games: competitions, TV sport, elections, gambling... Yet, at the same time, it's obvious that this kind of rubbish can never satisfy anything as strong as people's desire to play – especially today when game-playing could flourish as never before in history.

The sacred knows how to cope with the profane and deconsecrated game: witness the irreverent and obscene carvings in cathedrals. Without concealing them, the Church embraced cynical laughter and biting fantasy and nihilistic scorn. Under its mantle, the demonaic game was safe. Bourgeois power, on the contrary, puts play in quarantine, isolates it in a special ward, as if it wanted to stop it infecting other human activities. Art is this privileged and despised area set apart from commerce. And it will stay that way until economic imperialism refits it in its turn as a spiritual supermarket. Then, hunted down everywhere, play will burst out everywhere.

It was, in fact, from art that play broke free. The eruption was called Dada. "The dadaist events awoke the primitive-irrational play instinct which had been held down in the audience", said Hugo Ball. Pranks and jokes, and Art dragged down in its fall the whole edifice which the Spirit of Seriousness had built to the greater glory of the bourgeoisie. So that, today, the expression on the face of someone playing is the expression on the face of a rebel. Henceforward, the total game and the revolution of everyday life are one.

The desire to play has returned to destroy the hierarchical society that banished it. At the same time it is setting up a new type of society, one based on real participation. It is impossible to foresee the details of such a society – a society in which play is completely unrestricted – but one could expect to see the following characteristics:

— rejection of all leaders and all hierarchies
— rejection of self-sacrifice
— rejection of roles
— freedom of genuine self-realisation
— utter honesty.

Every game has two preconditions: the rules of playing and playing with the rules. Watch children play. They know the rules of the game, they can remember them perfectly well, but they never stop breaking them, they never stop dreaming up new ways of breaking them. But for them, cheating doesn't have the same connotations as it does for adults. Cheating is part of the game, they play at cheating, accomplices even in their arguments. What they are really doing is spurring themselves on to create new games. And, sometimes, they are successful: a new game is found and unfolds. They revitalise their playfulness without interrupting its flow.

The game dies as soon as an authority crystallises, becomes institutionalised and clothed in a magical aura. Even so, playfulness, however lighthearted, never loses a certain spirit of organisation and its required discipline. If a play leader proves necessary, his power is never wielded at the expense of the autonomous power of each individual. Rather it is the focus of each individual will, the collective counterpart of each particular desire. So the project of participation demands a coherent organisation allowing the decisions of each individual to be the decisions of everyone concerned. Obviously, small, intimate groups, micro-societies, offer the best conditions for such experiments. Within them the game can be the sole ruler of the intricacies of communal life, harmonising individual whims, desires and passions. Especially so since this game will reflect the insurrectionary game played by the group as a whole, forced upon them by their intention to live outside the law.

The urge to play is incompatible with self-sacrifice. You can lose, pay the penalty, submit to the rules, spend an unpleasant quarter of an hour, that's the logic of the game, not the logic of a Cause, not the logic of self-sacrifice. Once the idea of sacrifice appears, the game becomes sacred and its rules become rites. For those who play the rules, along with the ways of playing with them, are an integral part of the game. In the realm of the sacred, on the contrary, rituals cannot be played with, they can only be broken, can only be transgressed (not to forget that pissing on the altar is still a way of paying homage to the Church). Only play can deconsecrate, open up the possibilities of total freedom. This is the principle of subversion, the freedom to change the sense of everything which serves Power; the freedom, for example, to turn the cathedral of Chartres into a funfair, into a labyrinth, into a shooting-range, into a dream landscape...

On 28 Spetember 1964 it will be exactly one hundred years since we started the Situationist International. It's really beginning to get going now!"

Can any pleasure we are allowed to taste be compared with the indescribable joy of casting aside every form of restraint and breaking every conceivable law?"

Situationist tract for the centenary of the International Working Men's Association (1964)

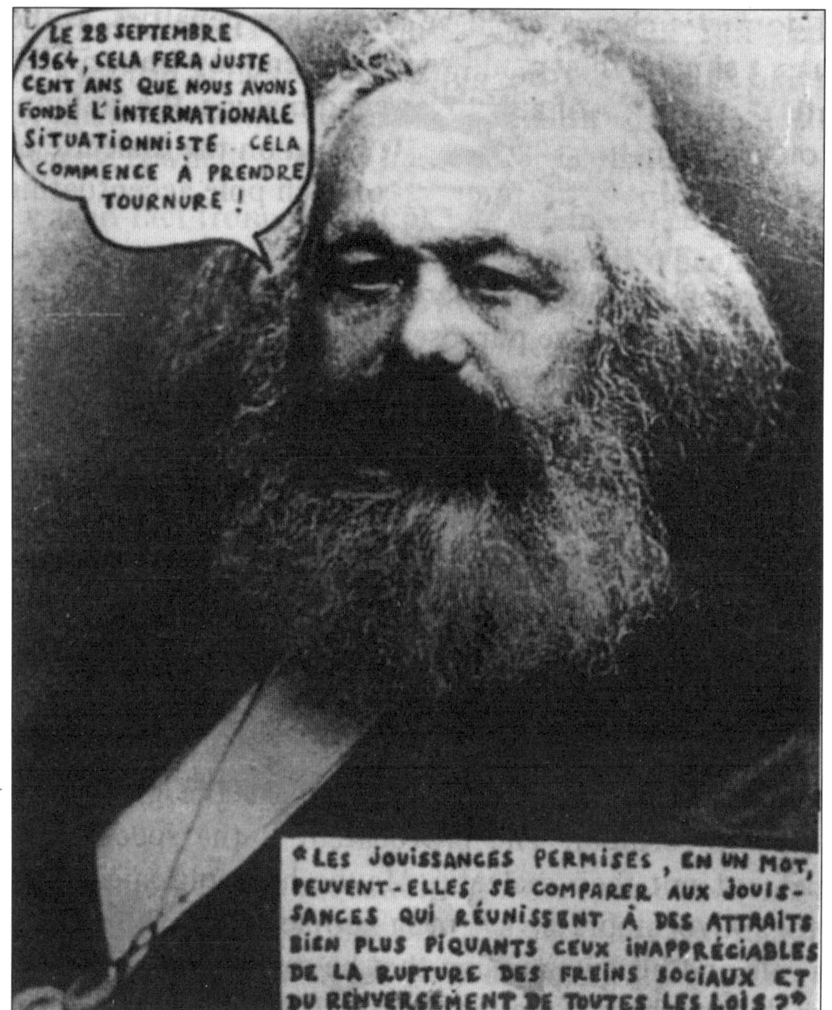

In a group revolving around play, manual and domestic chores could be allotted as penalties, as the price one pays for losing a point in a game. Or, more simply, they could be used to employ unoccupied time, as a sort of active rest; assuming, as a contrast, the value of a stimulant and making the resumption of play more exciting. The construction of such situations can only be based on the dialectic of presence and absence, richness and poverty, pleasure and pain, the intensity of each pole accentuating the intensity of the other.

In any case, any technique utilised in an atmosphere of sacrifice and coercion loses much of its cutting edge. Its actual effectiveness is mixed up with a purely repressive purpose, and to repress creativity is to reduce the productivity of the machine repressing it. Work can only be non-alienating and productive if you enjoy doing it.

The role one plays must be the role one plays with. The spectacular role demands complete conviction; a ludic role, on the contrary, demands a certain distancing. One has to watch oneself over one's own shoulder, in much the same sort of way that professional actors like to swop jokes *sotto voce* in between two dramatic tirades. Spectacular organisation is completely out of its depth with this sort of thing. The Marx brothers have shown what a role can become if you play with it. The only pity is that the Marx brothers were stuck with the cinema. What would happen if a game with roles started in real life?

When someone begins to play a permanent role, a serious role, he either wrecks the game or it wrecks him. Consider the unhappy case of the provocateur. The provocateur is the specialist in collective games. He can grasp their techniques but not their dialectic. Maybe he could succeed in steering the group towards offensive action – for provocateurs always push people to attack here and now – if only he wasn't so involved in his own role and his own mission that he can never understand their need to defend themselves. Sooner or later, this incoherence in his attitude towards offensive and defensive action will betray the provocateur, and lead him to his untimely end. And who makes the best provocateur? The play leader who has become the boss.

Only desire to play can lead to a community whose interests are identical with those of the individual. The traitor, unlike the provocateur, appears quite spontaneously in revolutionary groups. When does he appear? Whenever the spirit of play has died in a group, and with it, inevitably, the possibility of real involvement. The traitor is one who cannot express himself through the sort of participation he is offered and decides to 'play' against this participation: not to correct but to destroy it. The traitor is an illness of old age of revolutionary groups. Selling out on play is an act of treachery that justifies all others.

Tactics. Tactics are the polemical stage of the game. They provide the necessary continuity between poetry as it is born (play) and the organisation of spontaneity (poetry). Of an essentially technical nature, they prevent spontaneity burning itself out in the general confusion. We know how cruelly absent tactics have been from most popular uprisings. And we also know just how offhand historians can be about spontaneous revolutions. No serious study, no methodical analysis, nothing approaching the level of Clausewitz's book on war. Revolutionaries have ignored Makhno's battles almost as thoroughly as bourgeois generals have studied Napoleon's.

A few observations, in the absence of a more detailed analysis.

An efficiently hierarchical army can win a war, but not a revolution; an undisciplined mob can win neither. The problem then is how to organise without creating a hierarchy; in other words, how to make sure that the leader of the game doesn't become just 'the Leader'. The only safeguard against authority and rigidity setting in is a playful attitude. Creativity plus a machine gun is an unstoppable combination. Villa and Makhno's troops routed the most experienced professional soldiers of their day. But once playfulness begins to repeat itself, the battle is lost. The revolution fails so that its leader can be infallible. Why was Villa defeated at Celaya? Because he fell back on old tactical and strategic games, instead of making up new ones. Technically, Villa was carried away by memories of Ciudad Juarez, where his men had fallen on the enemy from the rear by silently cutting their way through the walls of house after house. He failed to see the importance of the military advances brought about by the 1914-18 war, machine-gun nests, mortars, trenches, etc. In political terms, he failed to see the importance of gaining the support of the industrial proletariat. It's no coincidence that Obregon's victorious army included both workers' militias and German military advisers.

The strength of revolutionary armies lies solely in their creativity. Frequently, the first days of an insurrection are a walkover simply because nobody paid the slightest attention to the rules by which the enemy played the game: because they invented a new game and because everyone took part in its elaboration. But if this creativity flags, if it becomes repetitive, if the revolutionary army becomes a regular army, then you can see blind devotion and hysteria try in vain to make up for the military weakness. Infatuation with past victories breeds terrible defeats. The magic of the Cause and the Leader replaces the conscious unity of the will to live and the will to conquer. In 1525, having held the princes at bay for two years, 40,000 peasants whose tactics had given way to religious fanaticism, were hacked to pieces at Frankenhaussen; the feudal army only lost three men. In 1964, at Stanleyville, hundreds of Mulelists, convinced they were invincible, allowed themselves to be massacred by throwing themselves on to a bridge defended by two machine-guns. Yet these were the same men who had previously captured trucks and arms consignments from the ANC by pitting the road with elephant traps.

Hierarchical organisation and its counterpart, indiscipline and incoherence, are equally inefficient. In a traditional war, the inefficiency of one side overcomes the inefficiency of the other through purely technical superiority; in a revolutionary war, the tactical poetry of the rebels steals from the enemy both their weapons and the time in which to use them, thus robbing them of their only possible superiority. But if the guerrillas begin to repeat themselves, the enemy can learn the rules of their game; at which point the guerrillas can if not destroy at least badly damage a popular creativity which has already hobbled itself.

If troops are to refuse to kow-tow to leaders, how can the discipline necessary for warfare be maintained? How can disintegration be avoided? Revolutionary armies tend to oscillate between the Scylla of devotion to a Cause and the Charybdis of untimely pleasure-seeking.

Stirring pleas, in the name of freedom, for restraint and renunciation, lay the foundations of future slavery. But, equally, premature rejoicing and the quest for small pleasures are always followed closely by the mailed fist and the bloody weeks of 'restoring order'. Discipline and cohesion can only come from the pleasure principle. The search for the greatest possible pleasure must always run the risk of pain: this is the secret of its strength. Where did the old troopers of the *ancien régime* find the strength to besiege a town, be repulsed ten times and still attack ten times more? In their passionate expectation of festivity – in this case, it must be admitted, largely looting and rape – of pleasure all the sweeter for having been attained so slowly. The best tactics go hand-in-hand with anticipation of future pleasure. The will to live, brutal and unrestrained, is the fighter's deadliest secret weapon. A weapon which should be used against anyone who endangers it: a soldier has every reason to shoot his officers in the back. For the same reasons, revolutionary armies will be stronger if they make each man a resourceful and independent tactician; someone who takes his pleasure seriously.

In the coming struggles, the desire to live life to the full will replace pillage as a motive. Tactics will merge with the science of pleasure – for the search for pleasure is already pleasure itself. Lessons in these tactics are given free every day. Anyone who is ready to learn, from his everyday experience, what undermines his independence and what makes him stronger, will gradually earn his colours as a tactician.

However, no tactician is isolated. The will to destroy this sick world calls for a federation of the tacticians of everyday life. It's just such a federation the SI intends to equip technically without delay. Strategy is collectively building the launching-pad of the revolution on the tactics of individual everyday life.

The ambiguous concept of 'humanity' sometimes causes spontaneous revolutions to falter. All too often the desire to make man the heart of a revolutionary programme has been invaded by a paralysing humanism. How many times have revolutionaries spared the lives of their own future firing-squad; how many times have they accepted a truce that meant no more to their enemies than the opportunity of gathering reinforcements? The ideology of humanity is a fine weapon for counter-revolution, one which can justify the most sickening atrocities (the Belgian paras in Stanleyville).

There can be no negotiation with the enemies of freedom, there's no quarter which can be extended to man's oppressors. The annihilation of counter-revolutionaries is the only 'humanitarian' act which can prevent the ultimate inhumanity of an integrally-bureaucratised humanism.

Lastly: power must be *totally* destroyed by means of *fragmentary acts*. The struggle for pure economic emancipation has made survival possible for everyone by making anything beyond survival impossible. But the traditional workers' movement was clearly struggling for more than that: for a total change in people's way of life. In any case, the wish to change the whole world at one go is a magical wish, which is why it can so easily degenerate into the crudest reformism. Apocalypticism and demands for gradual reform end up by merging in the marriage of reconciled differences. It isn't surprising that pseudo-revolutionary parties always end up by pretending that compromises are the same as tactics.

The revolution cannot be won either by accumulating minor victories or by an all-out frontal assault. This is the path on which the SI is set: calculated harassment on every front – cultural, political, economic and social. Concentrating on everyday life will ensure the unity of the combat.

Subversion. In its broadest sense, subversion is an all-embracing *re-entry into play*. It is the act by which play grasps and reunites beings and things which were frozen solid in a shattered hierarchic array.

One evening, as night fell, my friends and I wandered into the *Palais de Justice* in Brussels. The building is a monstrosity, crushing the poor quarters beneath it and guarding, like a sentry, the fashionable Avenue Louise – out of which, some day, we will make a breathtakingly beautiful bombsite. As we wandered through the labyrinth of corridors, staircases and suite after suite of rooms, we discussed what could be done to make the place habitable. For a time we occupied the enemies' territory; through the power of our imagination we transformed the thieves' den into a fantastic funfair, into a sunny pleasure dome, where the most amazing adventures would, for the first time, be really lived. In short, subversion is the basic expression of creativity. Day-dreaming subverts the world. People subvert, just as Jourdain did with prose and James Joyce did with *Ulysses*, spontaneously and with considerable reflection.

It was in 1955 that Debord, struck by Lautréamont's systematic use of subversion, first drew attention to the virtually unlimited possibilities of the technique. In 1960, Jorn was to write: "Subversion is a game which can only be played as everything loses its value. Every element of past culture must either be re-invested in reality or be scrapped." Debord, in *Internationale Situationniste* no. 3, developed the concept still further: "The two basic principles of subversion are the loss of importance of each originally independent element (which may even lose its first sense completely), and the organisation of a new significant whole which confers a fresh meaning on each element." Recent history allows one to be still more precise. From now on it's clear that:

— as more and more things rot and fall apart, subversion appears spontaneously. Consumer society plays into the hands of those who want to create new, significant wholes;
— culture is no longer a particularly privileged theatre. The art of subversion can be an integral part of any rebellion against the nature of everyday life;
— since part-truths rule our world, subversion is now the only technique at the service of a total view.

As a revolutionary act, subversion is the most coherent, most popular and the best adapted to revolutionary practice. By a sort of natural evolution – the desire to play – it leads people to become more and more extreme, more and more radical.

Our experience is falling to pieces about our ears, and its disintegration is a direct consequence of the development of consumer society. The phase of devaluation, and thus

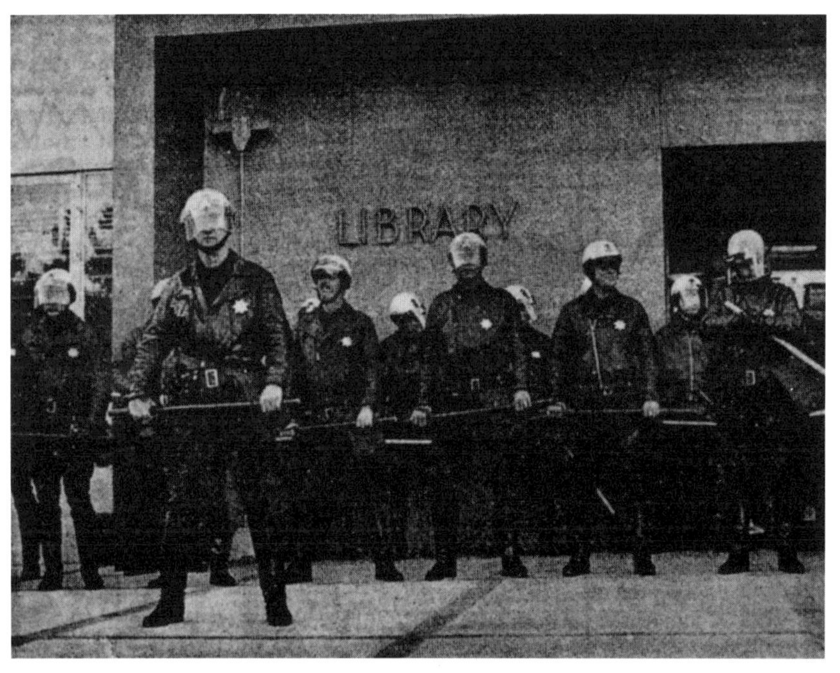

the possibility of subversion, is the work of contemporary history. Subversion has become part of the tactics of supersession; an essentially positive act.

While the abundance of consumer goods is hailed everywhere as a major step forward in evolution, the way these goods are used by society, as we know, invalidates all their positive aspects. Because the *gadget* is primarily a source of profit for capitalism and the socialist bureaucracies, it cannot be used for any other ends. The ideology of consumerism acts like a fault in its manufacture, it sabotages the commodity coated in it; it turns what could be the material equipment of happiness into a new form – of slavery. In this context, subversion broadcasts new ways of using commodities; it invents superior *uses* of goods, uses by which subjectivity can strengthen itself with something that was originally marketed to weaken it. The problems of tactics and strategy revolve around our inability to turn against capitalism the weapons that commercial necessity has forced it to distribute. Methods of subversion should be spread as an 'ABC of the consumer who wishes to stop being so'.

Subversion, which forged its first weapons from art, has now become the art of handling every sort of weapon. Having first appeared amidst the cultural crisis of the years 1910-25, it has gradually spread to every area touched by social decomposition. Despite which, art still offers a field of valid experiment for the techniques of subversion; and there's still much to be learnt from the past. Surrealism failed because it tried to re-invest dadaist anti-values which had not been completely reduced to zero. Any other attempt to build on values which have not been thoroughly purged by a nihilistic crisis will end in the same way: with recuperation. Contemporary cyberneticians have taken their 'combinatory' attitude towards art so far as to believe in the value of any accumulation of disparate elements whatsoever, even if the particular elements *haven't been devalued at all*. Pop art or Jean-Luc Godard, it's the same apologetics of the junk-yard.

There are no limits to creativity. There is no end to subversion.

From *The Revolution of Everyday Life*, Raoul Vaneigem, 1967

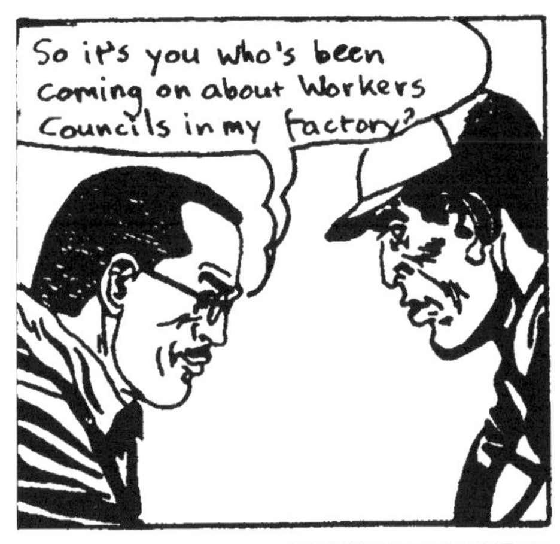

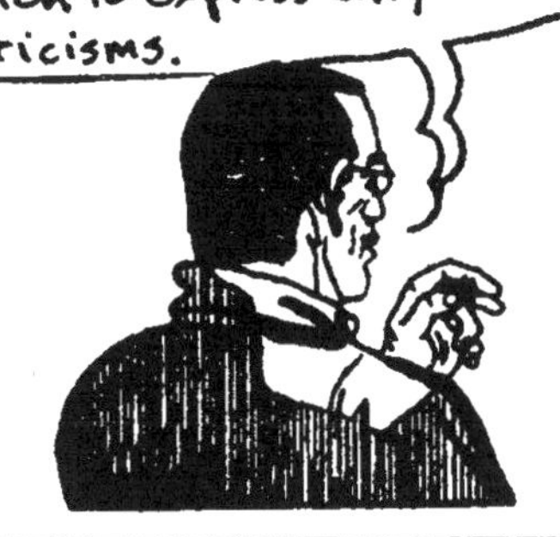

The unions have just shown everyone that they are a mechanism to integrate us into capitalist society!

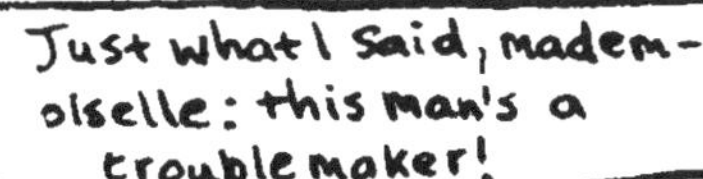

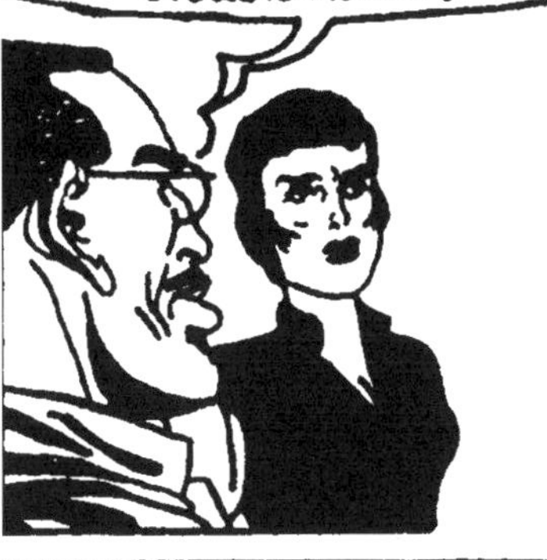

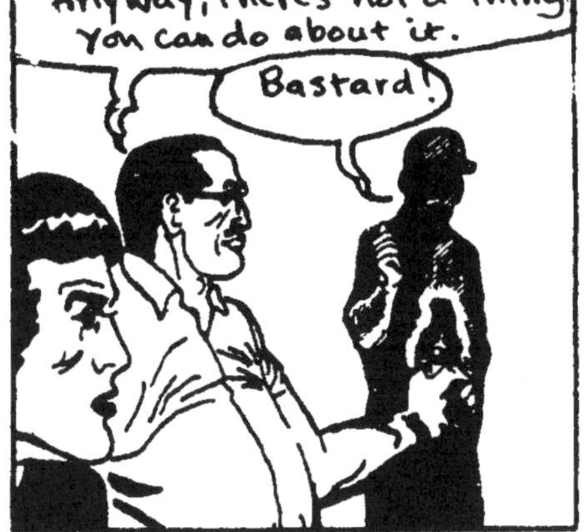

The commodity, whose cop you are, enriches your class while it forces us...

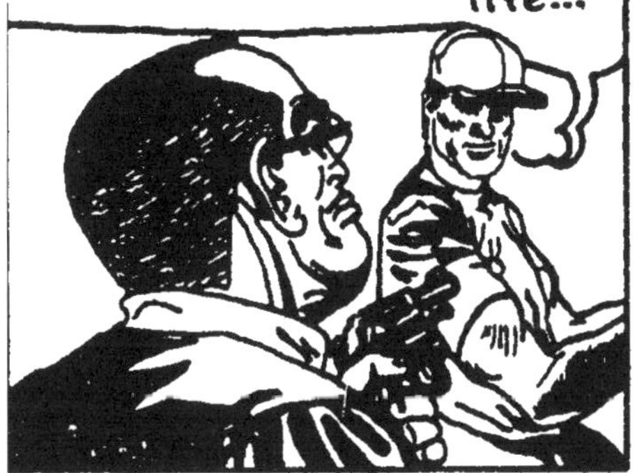

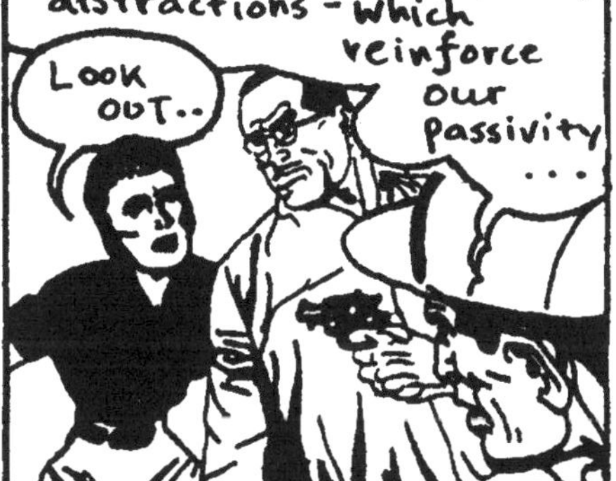

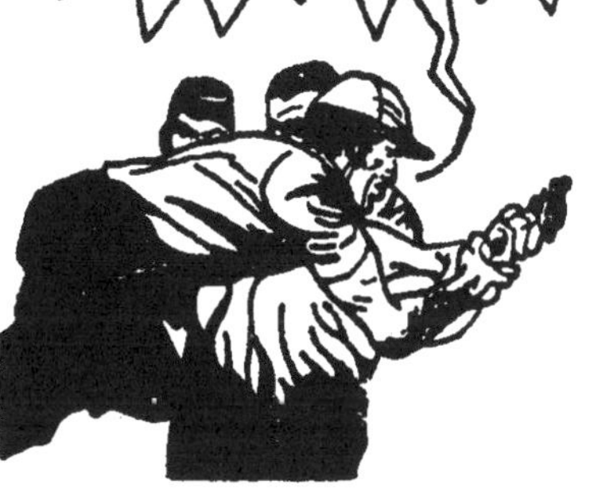

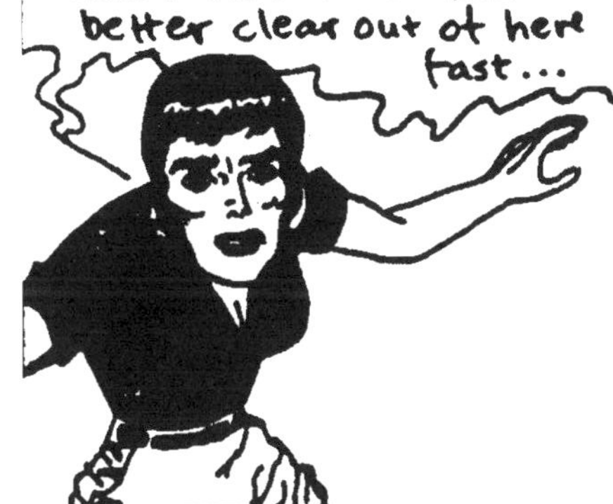

The working class shouldn't hesitate to liquidate anyone who gets in the way of their desire for total freedom.

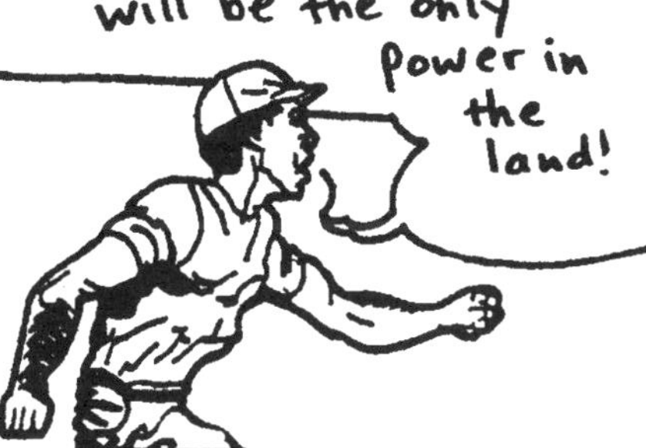

ADDRESS TO ALL WORKERS

What we have done in France now haunts Europe. Soon it will threaten all the ruling classes of the world, from the bureaucrats of Moscow and Peking to the millionaires of Washington and Tokyo. *Just as we have made Paris dance* the international proletariat will take up arms against every capital city of every state, every citadel of every alienation. The occupation of factories and of government buildings throughout the entire country hasn't just stopped the economy – it has called the whole meaning of social life into question. Almost everybody wants to stop living in this way. We are already a revolutionary movement. All we need is widespread *consciousness of what we have already done* and we will be masters of the revolution.

Who will try to save capitalism? The regime can only save itself by the threat of calling in the army (along with the promise of general elections as soon as everyone has gone home). It may even use sudden armed repression straight away. As for the eventual rise to power of 'the left', it will also try to defend the old world by concessions on the one hand and by violence on the other. The so-called Communist Party, the party of Stalinist bureaucrats, which has fought the whole movement from the very first and only began to question de Gaulle's government when it saw that de Gaulle could no longer protect it, would in this event be the chosen safeguard of a Popular Front government. Such a transitional government could only become a 'Kerenskyism' if the Stalinists were to be defeated. Essentially this depends upon the workers: upon their consciousness and upon their ability to organise themselves autonomously. Those who turned down the ridiculous contract agreements offered them (agreements that overjoyed the trades union leaders) have still to discover that while they cannot 'receive' much more within the framework of the existing economy, they can *take everything* if they transform the very bases of the economy on their own behalf. The bosses can hardly pay any more; *but they could* disappear.

The movement today was not 'politicised' by going beyond the unions' penny-pinching demands for increased wages and pensions, and other so-called 'social problems'. The movement is beyond *politics*: it poses the social question in all its nudity. A revolution that has been building up for a hundred years is about to erupt again. It must evolve its own forms. It is already too late for a bureaucratic-revolutionary facelift. When André Barjonet, all fresh from his de-Stalinisation, calls for a single organisation grouping "all the true forces of the revolution – forces whose roots lie in Trotsky, or in Mao, in anarchy or in situationism" we have to remember that neither the Trotskyists nor the Maoists, to say nothing of the pitiful 'Anarchist Federation', have got anything whatsoever to do with the present revolution. The bureaucrats may want to change their minds about what is 'authentically revolutionary'; the authentic revolution, however, doesn't have to change its mind about what is bureaucratic.

Today, with the power they hold and with the parties and unions for what they are, the workers can only throw themselves into a direct takeover of the economy, into a complete reconstruction of the whole of social life. This by means of unitary committees at the base, maintaining their autonomy *vis-à-vis* all political and trade union leadership, protecting themselves by federating locally and nationally. By following this pattern they will become the only real power in the country, the power of the workers' councils. If it does not do this, then because it is 'either revolutionary or it is nothing', the proletariat will become nothing again. It will be back glued to the TV.

What distinguishes the power of the councils? The disappearance of all exterior power; direct and total democracy; strictly mandated delegates subject to immediate recall; the abolition of hierarchy and of all detached specialisation; the permanent creative participation of all ordinary people; international extension and co-ordination. Nothing less will do. *Watch out for recuperators*, however updated they may be – including priests – however much they may talk about self-management, even about workers' councils. They always give themselves away by one thing: they try to save the value of their own intellectual specialisation, thus assuming their role in any future bureaucracy.

What is essential today is what has been essential since the beginning of the working class movement: the autonomy of the working class; the struggle for the abolition of wage labour, of commodity production and of the state; the creation of conscious history; the elimination of all forms of separation, of "everything that exists apart from individuals". The proletarian revolution has spontaneously evolved its own forms in the councils: in St Petersburg in 1905, in Turin in 1920, in Catalonia in 1936, in Budapest in 1956. The continued existence of the previous ruling classes, or the formation of new ones, necessitated each time the suppression of the councils. Now the working class knows its enemies and the way they fight. "The revolutionary organisation had to learn that it could no longer *fight alienated forms*" (*The Society of the Spectacle*). The workers' councils are the only answer. Every other form of revolutionary struggle has ended up with the very opposite of what it was originally looking for.

Leaflet, May 1968

Ettinger describes the refrigeration of human bodies as a "history's greatest promise – and perhaps its greatest problem". Whatever the truth of this may be – one should try to remain sensible – the American scientist advises anyone worried about their future to specify in their will that they want to be frozen and to put money to one side both for their temporary death and for their second life. Their stay in the refrigerated 'dormitories', where the corpses will be stored (an estimated 15 million tons of them in the USA) will, according to Ettinger, cost some two hundred dollars (F1,000) per year.

France-Soir, 17 June 1964

BONN, 26 JUNE

Marshal Tito of Yugoslavia disclosed today that when young he once contemplated emigrating to the United States. The Marshal, who was talking to Yugoslav migrant workers here added: "If I had done so, I would probably be a millionaire today."
"You probably are", one of the migrant workers retorted, but the Yugoslav leader denied the charge. "I have no millions, only millions of Yugoslavs", he said.

SOME THOUGHTS ON GENERAL SELF-MANAGEMENT

Never sacrifice a present good to a future good. Enjoy the moment; don't get into anything which doesn't satisfy your passion right away. Why should you work today for jam tomorrow, since you will be loaded down with it anyway, and in fact in the new order you will only have one problem, namely how to find enough time to get through all the pleasures in store for you?"

Charles Fourier, Some Thoughts on the Coming Social Metamorphosis

1

In their failure, the occupations of May 1968 created a confused popular awareness of the need for change. The universal feeling that a total transformation is just around the corner must now find its practice: the move forward to generalised self-management through the setting up of workers' councils. The point to which consciousness has been brought by revolutionary high spirits must now become the point of departure.

2

Today, history is answering the question which Lloyd George asked the workers and the old world's servants have been echoing ever since: "You want to destroy our social organisation, what are you going to put in its place?" We know the answer now, thanks to the profusion of little Lloyd Georges who advocate the state dictatorship of the proletariat of their choice and then wait for the working class to organise itself in councils so they can dissolve it and elect another one.

3

Each time the proletariat takes the risk of changing the world, it rediscovers the memory of history. The reality of the past possibilities of a society of councils, which has been hidden by the history of the repeated suppression of such a society, is revealed by the possibility of its immediate realisation. This was made clear to all workers in May; Stalinism and its Trotskyist droppings showed that, although they wouldn't have had the energy to crush a vigorous council movement, they were still able to hold up its emergence by sheer dead weight. Nevertheless, the workers' council movement discovered itself as the necessary resultant of two opposing forces: the internal logic of the occupations and the repressive logic of the parties and trade unions. Those who still open their Lenin to find out what is to be done are sticking their heads in a dustbin.

4

A great many people rejected any organisation which was not the direct creation of the proletariat in the process of destroying itself as proletariat, and this rejection was inseparable from the feeling that a daily life without dead time was possible at last. In this sense the idea of workers' councils is the first principle of generalised self-management.

5

May was an essential step in the long revolution: the *individual history* of millions of people, all looking for an authentic life, joining up with the historical movement of the proletariat fighting against the whole *system* of alienation. This spontaneous unity in action, which was the passionate motor of the occupation movement, can only develop its theory and practice in the same *unity*. What was in everyone's heart will soon be in everyone's head. A lot of people who felt that they "couldn't go on living the same old way, not even if things were a bit better" can remember what it was like to really *live* for a while and to believe that great changes were possible. And this memory would become a revolutionary force with the help of one thing: a greater lucidity about the *historical construction of free, individual relationships*, generalised self-management.

6

Only the proletariat can create the project of generalised self-management, by refusing to carry on existing as the proletariat. It carries this project in itself objectively and subjectively. So the first steps will come from the merging together of its historical battles and the struggle for everyday life; and from the awareness that all its demands are obtainable right away, but only if it grants them itself. In this sense the importance of a revolutionary organisation must be measured from now on by its ability to dissolve itself into the reality of the society of workers' councils.

7

Workers' councils constitute a new type of social organisation, one by which the proletariat will put an end to the proletarianisation of all men. Generalised self-management is simply the totality according to which the councils will create a style of life based on permanent liberation, which is at once individual and collective.

8

It is clear from the preceding that the project of generalised self-management must involve as many details as each revolutionary has desires, and as many revolutionaries as there are people dissatisfied with their daily life. Spectacular commodity society produces the contradictions which repress subjectivity, but this also leads to the refusal which frees the positivity of subjectivity; in the same way, a formation of councils, which also arises from the struggle against general oppression, is the basis of the conditions for a general realisation of this subjectivity, without any limits but its own impatience to make history. So generalised self-management means the ability of workers' councils to *realise* historically the imagination.

9

Without generalised self-management, workers' councils lose all significance. We must treat as a future bureaucrat, and therefore as a present enemy, anyone who speaks of workers' councils as economic or social organisms, anyone who doesn't put them at the centre of everyday life.

10

One of Fourier's great merits is that he showed us that we must create in the here-and-now – which means, for us, at the beginning of the general insurrection – the objective conditions for individual liberation. For everyone, the beginning of the revolutionary moment must bring an *immediate increase in the pleasure of living*: a consciously lived beginning of totality.

11

The accelerating rate at which reformism, with its tricontinental bellyache, is leaving ridiculous droppings behind it (all those little piles of Maoists, Trotskyists, Guevarists) shows everyone what the right, especially socialists and Stalinists, have suspected for a long time: partial demands contain in themselves the impossibility of a total change. Rather then fighting one reformism to conceal another, the temptation to turn the old trick inside-out like a bureaucrat's skin has all the marks of the final solution to the problem of recuperation. This implies a strategy which arrives at general upheaval through more and more frequent insurrectionary moments; and tactics involving a qualitative break in which necessarily partial actions each contain, as their necessary and sufficient condition, the liquidation of the commodity world. It is time to begin the *positive sabotage* of spectacular commodity society. As long as our mass tactics are based on the law of immediate pleasure, there will be no need to worry about the consequences.

12

It's easy to write down a few suggestions which the practice of liberated workers will soon show the poverty of: *inaugurating the realm of freeness* at every opportunity – openly during strikes, more or less clandestinely at other times – by giving the products in factories and warehouses away to friends and to revolutionaries, making presents (radio transmitters, toys, weapons, decorations, all kinds of machines), organising giveaways of the merchandise in department stores; *breaking the laws of exchange and beginning the abolition of wage-labour* by collectively appropriating the products of work, collectively using machines for personal and revolutionary purposes; *devaluing money* by generalised payment strikes (rent, taxes, hire-purchase instalments, fares, etc); *encouraging everybody's creativity* by starting up the production and distribution sectors, perhaps intermittently, but *only* under workers' control, and looking upon this as a necessarily hesitant but perfectible exercise; *abolishing hierarchies and the spirit of sacrifice*, by treating bosses (and union bosses) as they deserve, and rejecting militantism; *acting together everywhere against all separations; getting the theory out of every practice, and vice versa* by the production of handouts, posters, songs, etc.

13

The proletariat has already shown that it knows how to answer the oppressive complexity of capitalist and 'socialist' states with the simplicity of organisation managed directly by everyone and for everyone. In our times, the problems of survival are only posed on condition that they can never be solved; on the other hand, the problems of history which is to be lived are stated clearly in the project of workers' councils, at once as positivity and as negativity; in other words, as the basis of a unitary passionate society, and as anti-state.

14

Because they exercise no power separate from the decision of their members, workers' councils cannot tolerate any power other than their own. For this reason, advocating universal demonstrations against the state cannot mean the premature creation of councils which, without absolute power in their own area and separated from generalised self-management, would necessarily be empty of content and ready to mess around with all kinds of ideology. Today, the only forces lucid enough to be able to respond to the history that *is made* with the history that is *ready to be made* will be revolutionary organisations which can develop, in the project of workers' councils, an adequate awareness of who are enemies and who are allies. An important aspect of this struggle has already appeared before our eyes: *dual power*. In factories, offices, streets, houses, barracks, schools, a new reality is materialising: contempt for bosses, whatever name is on their collar. Now this contempt must develop until it reaches its logical conclusion: the concerted initiative of workers must discover that the bosses are not only contemptible but also useless, and what is more can be liquidated without any ill effects.

15

Recent history will soon come to be seen by both revolutionaries and bosses in terms of a single alternative: generalised self-management or insurrectionary chaos; the new society of abundance, or 'things fall apart', terrorism, looting, repression. Dual-power situations already illustrate this choice. Coherence demands that the paralysis and destruction of all forms of government must not be distinct from the construction of councils; if the enemy have any sense at all they will have to adapt to the fact that this new organisation of everyday relationships is all that will be able to stop the spread of what an American police specialist has already called "our nightmare": little rebel commandos bursting out of subway entrances, shooting from the rooftops, using the mobility and the infinite resources of the urban guerrilla to kill policemen, liquidate authority's servants, fan up riots, destroy the economy. But it is not our job to save the bosses against their will. All we have to do is prepare councils and make sure they can defend themselves by all possible means. In a play by Lope de Vega some villagers kill a despotic royal official. When they are hauled before investigating magistrates, all that the villagers will say under examination is the name of the village, Fuentoeovejuna. It is not enough for a collective action to avoid repression (imagine the impotence of the forces of law and order if the bank clerks who occupied their banks had appropriated the funds); it must also and in the same movement, lead towards a greater revolutionary coherence. Workers' councils are *order* in the face of the decomposition of the state, challenged in its form by the rise of regionalism and in its principle by sectoral demands. The police can only answer its questions with lists of their fatalities. Only workers' councils offer a definitive answer. What will put a stop to looting? The organisation of distribution and the end of commodity exchange. What will prevent sabotage and waste? The appropriation of machines by the creativity of the collective. What will put an end to explosions of anger and violence? The abolition of the proletariat by means of the collective construction of everyday life. The only justification for our struggle is the immediate satisfaction of this project: which is whatever satisfies us immediately.

16

Generalised self-management will have only one source of support: the exhilaration of universal freedom. This is quite enough to make us absolutely certain about some preliminary matters, which our revolutionary organisations will have to get straight. Likewise, their practice will already involve the experience of direct democracy. This will allow us to pay more attention to certain slogans. For example, "all power to the general assembly" implies that whatever escapes the direct control of the autonomous assembly will recreate, in mediated forms, all the autonomous varieties of oppression. The whole assembly with all its tendencies must be present through its representatives at the moment when decisions are made. Even if the destruction of the state will prevent a revival of the farce of the Supreme Soviet, we must still make sure that our organisation is so simple that no neo-bureaucracy can possibly arise. But the complexity of communication techniques (which might appear to be a pretext for the survival or return of specialists) is just what makes possible the continuous control of delegates by the base – the confirmation/correction/rejection of their decisions at all levels. So base groups must always have teleprinters, televisions etc: their ubiquity must be *realised*. It would also be a good idea for local, city, regional and international councils to elect (and remain in control of) a *supply section* to look after supplies and production; an *information council* to keep in continuous and close contact with other councils; a *co-ordinating section* whose job would be (as far as the demands of the struggle will let them) to radicalise the Fourierist project, to take responsibility for the satisfaction of the demands of the passions, to give individual desires whatever they need to use, to make the means available for experiments and adventures, to harmonise playful dispositions with the organisation of the jobs that have to be done (cleaning services, looking after kids, education, cooking, etc); and a *self-defence section*. Each section would be responsible to the full assembly; delegates would be revocable and would regularly meet and report to one another, and their positions would rotate vertically and horizontally.

17

The logic of the commodity system, sustained by alienated practice, must be confronted by the social logic of desires and its immediate practice. The first revolutionary steps will have to involve the reduction of hours of work and the widest possible abolition of forced labour. Workers' councils could distinguish between *priority sectors* (food, transport, communications, engineering, building, clothing, electronics, printing, weapons, medicine, comfort, and in general whatever is necessary for the permanent transformation of historical conditions); *conversion sectors*, whose workers consider that they can divert them to revolutionary purposes, and *parasitical sectors*, whose assemblies decide simply to abolish them. Clearly the workers in the eliminated sectors (administration, offices, spectacular and trading businesses will prefer to work a few hours a week at whatever job they like in the priority sector, rather than eight hours a day at their old workplace. The councils will have to experiment with unattractive forms of work, not to conceal its unpleasantness but to make up for it by a playful organisation and to replace work as far as possible with creativity (following the principle of 'work no, fun yes'). As the transformation of the world becomes identified with the construction of life, necessary work will disappear in the pleasure of history-for-itself (for its own sake).

18

To affirm that the councils' organisation of distribution and production will prevent looting and wholesale destruction of machinery and stores, is to continue to define oneself solely in terms of the anti-state. The councils, as the organisation of the new society, will do away with all remaining separations by their *collective politics of desire*. Wage-labour can be ended the moment the councils start functioning – the moment the 'equipment and supplies' section of each council has organised production and distribution along the lines desired by the full assembly. At this point, in homage to the best part of Bolshevik foresight, urinals made of solid gold and silver can be built, and baptised 'lenins'.

19

Generalised self-management entails extension of the councils. Initially, work areas will be taken over by the workers concerned, organised as councils. To get rid of this somewhat corporative structure, the workers will, as soon as possible, throw them open to their friends, to people living in the same area, to those freed by the dissolution of the parasitical sectors, so that they rapidly take the form of local councils, part of the Commune (units of perhaps some eight to ten thousand people?)

20

The internal growth of the councils must be counterbalanced by their external, geographical growth. Maintaining the total radicality of liberated zones will demand continual attention. One cannot, as Fourier did, rely exclusively on the magnetic quality of the first communes, but, at the same time, one cannot afford to underestimate the power to seduce exercised by every attempt at authentic emancipation. The self-defence of the councils could be summed up by the maxim: "armed truth is revolutionary".

21

Generalised self-management will soon evolve its own *code of possibilities*, destined to liquidate repressive legislation and its millenary empire. Perhaps it will appear during the period of dual power, before the present legal system has been totally annihilated. The new rights of man – everyone's right to live as they please, to build their own house, to take part in every assembly, to bear arms, to live as a nomad, to publish whatever they see fit (everyone has his own wall-newspaper), to love without any sort of restriction; the right to meet everyone, the right to the material equipment necessary for the realisation of their desires, the right to creativity, the right to the conquest of nature; the end of time as a commodity, the end of history-in-itself, the realisation of art and the imaginary, etc – await their anti-legislators.

Raoul Vaneigem, IS no. 12, 1969

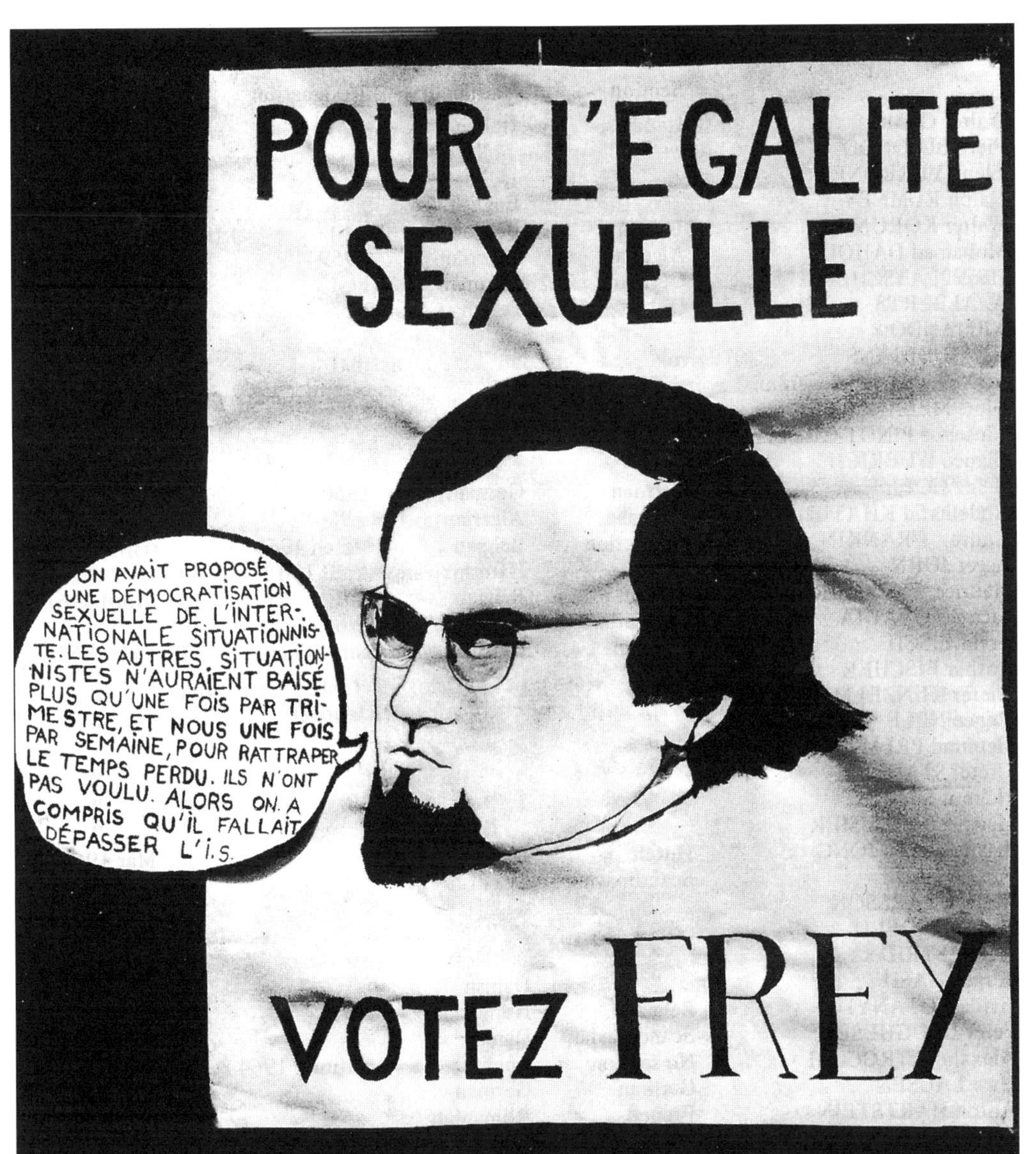

VOTE FREY FOR SEXUAL EQUALITY

We were discussing the sexual democratisation of the IS. The other situationists were to have a fuck every three months and us once a week, to make up for lost time. They didn't agree. That was when I knew the IS had to be transcended.

On the other hand, the economic and social context where an idea of this sort can appear and flourish is clearly defined: the prevailing system which multiplies schisms, separations and inequalities in the development of the whole and therefore *delays* each particular sphere...

L'Unique et sa Propriété

(IS polemic against four excluded situationists, early 1967)

MEMBERS OF THE SITUATIONIST INTERNATIONAL

	Section	*Nationality*	*Resigned*	*Excluded*
Walter OLMO	Italian	Italian		Jan 1958
Piero SIMONDO	Italian	Italian		Jan 1958
Elena VERRONE	Italian	Italian		Jan 1958
Ralph RUMNEY	Italian	English		Mar 1958
Walter KORUN	Belgian	Belgian		Autumn 1958
Mohamed DAHOU	Algerian	Algerian	1959	
Hans PLATSCHEK	German	German		Feb 1959
A ALBERTS	Dutch	Dutch		Spring 1960
ARMANDO	Dutch	Dutch		Spring 1960
Har OUDEJANS	Dutch	Dutch		Spring 1960
CONSTANT (Nieuwenhuis)	Dutch	Dutch	Summer 1960	
Giors MELANOTTE	Italian	Italian		Summer 1960
Guiseppe PINOT-GALLIZIO	Italian	Italian		Summer 1960
Glauco WUERICH	Italian	Italian		Summer 1960
Heinz HOFL	German	German	1960	
Abdelhafid KHATIB	Algerian	Algerian	1960	
André FRANKLIN	No section	Belgian	Mar 1961	
Asger JORN	French	Danish	Apr 1961	
Maurice WYCKAERT	Belgian	Belgian		Apr 1961
Jacques OVADIA	No section	Israeli	1961	
Ervin EISCH	German	German		Feb 1962
Lothar FISCHER	German	German		Feb 1962
Dieter KUNZELMANN	German	German		Feb 1962
Renee NELE	German	German		Feb 1962
Heimrad PREM	German	German		Feb 1962
Gretel STADLER	German	German		Feb 1962
Helmut STURM	German	German		Feb 1962
Hans-Peter ZIMMER	German	German		Feb 1962
Jacqueline DE JONG	Dutch	Dutch		Mar 1962
Ansgar ELDE	Scandinavian	Swedish		Mar 1962
Steffan LARSSON	Scandinavian	Swedish		Mar 1962
Katja LINDELL	Scandinavian	Swedish		Mar 1962
Hardy STRID	Scandinavian	Swedish		Mar 1962
Jorgen NASH	Scandinavian	Danish		Mar 1962
Attila KOTANYI	Belgian	Hungarian		Oct 1963
Peter LAUGHESEN	Scandinavian	Danish		Oct 1963
Alexander TROCCHI	No section	English	Autumn 1964	
Uwe LAUSEN	German	German		Mar 1965
Anton HARTSTEIN	French	Romanian		July 1966
Jan STIJBOSCH	Belgian	Dutch		July 1966
Rudi RENSON	Belgian	Belgian	1966	
Edith FREY	French	French	Jan 1967	
Théo FREY	French	French		Jan 1967
Jean GARNAULT	French	French		Jan 1967
Herbert HOLL	French	French		Jan 1967
Michèle BERNSTEIN	French	French	1967	
Ndjangani LUNGELA	French	Congolese	1967	
Charles RADCLIFFE	English	English	Nov 1967	
Timothy CLARKE	English	English		Dec 1967

	Section	**Nationality**	**Resigned**	**Excluded**
Christopher GRAY	English	English		Dec 1967
Donald NICHOLSON-SMITH	English	English		Dec 1967
Mustapha KHAYATI	French	Tunisian	Sept 1969	
Alain CHEVALIER	French	French		Oct 1969
Robert CHASSE	American	American		Jan 1970
Bruce ELWELL	American	American		Jan 1970
François DE BEAULIEU	French	French	1970	
Patrick CHEVAL	French	French	1970	
Claudio PAVAN	Italian	Italian		Spring 1970
Eduardo ROTHE	Italian	Venezuelan		Spring 1970
Paolo SALVADORI	Italian	Italian		Summer 1970
Raoul VANEIGEM	Belgian	Belgian	Nov 1970	
Jon HORELICK	American	American	*Scission* Dec 1970	
Tony VERLAAN	American	Dutch	*Scission* Dec 1970	
Christian SEBASTIANI	French	French	Dec 1970	
René VIENET	French	French	Feb 1971	
René RIESEL	French	French		Sept 1971
Ivan CHTCHEGLOV	No section	French	Member from afar	
Guy DEBORD	French	French		
Jeppesen Victor MARTIN	Scandinavian	Danish		
Gianfranco SANGUINETTI	Italian	Italian		

There were a total of:

70 individuals
19 resignations
2 scissionists
45 exclusions

Pseudonyms:

Gilles IVAIN for Ivan CHTCHEGLOV
George KILLER for Asger JORN (after his official resignation)

"THOSE WHO MAKE HALF A REVOLUTION ONLY DIG THEIR OWN GRAVES": THE SITUATIONISTS SINCE 1969

by Christopher Gray

Nous vivons en enfants perdus nos aventures incomplètes...

Debord, Hurlements en faveur de Sade

May 1968 and France on the verge of anarchy... An atmosphere of martial law in Paris and hundreds of factories occupied... one hundred and forty American cities in flames after the killing of Martin Luther King... German and English universities occupied... Hippie ghettos directly clashing with the police state... The sudden exhilarating sense of how many people felt the same way... The new world coming into focus... The riots a great dance in the streets...

Today – nothing. The Utopian image has faded from the streets. Just the endless traffic, the blank eyes that pass you by, the nightmarish junk we're all dying for. Everyone seems to have retreated into themselves, into closed occult groups. The revolutionary excitement that fired the sixties is dead, the 'counter-culture' a bad joke. No more aggression, no more laughter, no more dreams. "To talk of life today is like talking of rope in the house of a hanged man."

Yet there were thousands and thousands of people there. What has happened to us all?

The Paris May Days were the end for the SI. On the one hand, the police state pressure on the French left after May made any overt action virtually suicidal. On the other, the SI, because it couldn't think its way beyond the débâcle, finally received the cultural accolade it had always dreaded: it entered 'the heaven of the spectacle' by the scruff of the neck, and that was that. The atmosphere in France after May was one of utter defiance coupled with complete impotence, and 'situationism' was the perfect ideological expression of this frustration. The SI became famous, and its truth stood out in all its bitterness: a brilliant theoretical critique of society without any grasp of the real problems of what to do about it. What is to be done? Reread Korsch and Duchamp, *mon vieux*.

The movement disintegrated. The last copy of the magazine came out in late 1969. The only significant text to emerge in four years is *La Veritable Scission dans l'Internationale* (1972) by Debord and Sanguinetti – a laboured and increasingly desperate attempt to come to grips with French students' attitude of passive and lifeless worship of revolutionary ideas, but remaining silent on the vital issues of organisation and activity which alone could lead them out of their dilemma. The organisation itself broke up amidst bitter tactical wrangling over 1969-70. Khayati and Vienet resigned. Vaneigem fried, predictably enough. The others went their different ways.

At present there are said to be between two and four members of the SI – including poor Chtcheglov in his Central European madhouse. Perhaps one should add there are stories that the SI remained intact and really just disappeared owing to police pressure and is now working on a real underground organisation. Sounds a bit like King Arthur and His Knights, but you never can tell. Certainly it seems unlikely that the last has been heard of either Debord or Vaneigem.

The presence of the SI never made itself properly felt in either England or America. The English and what could well have become the American sections of the SI were excluded just before Christmas 1967. Both groups felt that the perfection and publicising of a theoretical critique was not sufficient: they wanted political subversion and individual 'therapy' to converge in an uninterrupted everyday activity. Some of this they saw, though on a very limited and local scale, the following year: the Americans as *The Motherfuckers* and the English as *King Mob*. Neither group survived that apocalyptic summer of 1968.

Henceforward the dissemination of situationist ideas in both countries was dissociated from the real organisation that alone could have dynamised them. On the one hand this led to obscure post-grad groups sitting over their pile of gestetnered situationist pamphlets, happy as Larry in their totally prefabricated identity. On the other, the more sincere simply went straight up the wall: *The Angry Brigade*, very heavily influenced by situationist ideas (translate *Les Enragés* into English...), destroying themselves at the same time as they took the critique of the spectacle to its most blood-curdlingly spectacular extreme.

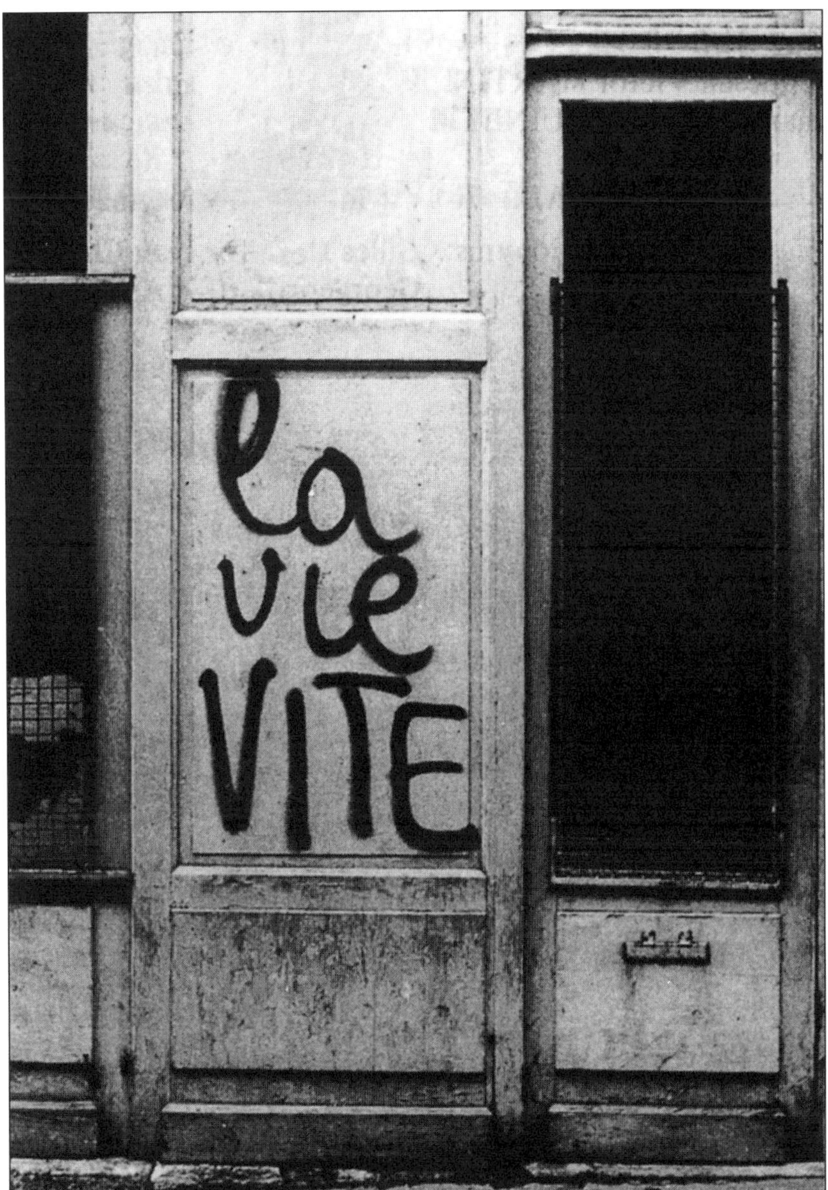

One of the first English members of the SI writes from the States:

Seen from over here, the SI has a lot to answer for: it has spawned a whole stew of 'revolutionary organisations', usually composed of half a dozen moralists of the transparent relationship; these have inevitably foundered after a few months – though not without bequeathing weighty self-criticisms to a breathless posterity. Idiots. Worse: cures. *Yet their traits are undoubtedly linked organically, genetically, to the original SI in its negative aspects: the SI is responsible for its monstrous offspring. Somehow or other, the SI's 'original sin' is tied up with a shift from the sardonic megalomania of iconoclasm to the true megalomania of priesthood. Moving, justifiably, from 'culture' to 'politics' the SI threw the baby out with the bathwater. One day somebody (I forget who) took refuge up a lamp-post, while freaked on acid, from a* dérive*-cum-discussion-of Lukacs with a merry band of situationists. How is it conceivable that this act could be greeted with blank incomprehension (and –* c'est bien la mot *– displeasure) by Debord, drunkard extraordinary? Yet it was so.*

What then remains of the SI? What is still relevant? Above all, I think, its iconoclasm, its *destructiveness*. What the SI did was *to redefine the nature of exploitation and poverty*. Ten years ago people were still demonstrating against the state of affairs in Vietnam – *while remaining completely oblivious to the terrible state they were in themselves*. The SI showed exactly how loneliness and anxiety and aimlessness have replaced the nineteenth century struggle for material survival, though they are still generated by the same class society. They focused on immediate experience – everyday life as the area people most desperately wanted to transform.

Rediscovering poverty cannot be separated from rediscovering what *wealth* really means. The SI rediscovered the vast importance of visionary politics, of the *Utopian tradition* – and included art, in all its positive aspects, in this tradition. People today will never break out of their stasis for the sake of a minor rearrangement. There have been too many already. Only the hope of a total change will inflame anybody. Who the hell is going to exert themselves to get another frozen chicken, another pokey room? But the possibilities of living in one's own cathedral...

What was basically wrong with the SI was that it focused exclusively on an intellectual critique of society. There was no concern whatsoever with either the emotions or the body. The SI thought that you just had to show how the nightmare worked and everyone would wake up. Their quest was for the perfect formula, the magic charm that would disperse the evil spell. This pursuit of the perfect intellectual formula meant inevitably that situationist groups were based on a hierarchy of intellectual ability – and thus on disciples and followers, on fears and exhibitionism, the whole political horror trip. After their initial period, creativity, apart from its intellectual forms, was denied expression and in this lies the basic instability and sterility of their own organisations.

In the last analysis they made the same mistake as all left-wing intellectuals: *they thought that everyone else was plain thick.* The poor workers don't know what's going on, they need someone to tell them. But people in the streets, in the offices and factories know damn well what's going on, even if they can't write essays about all its theoretical ramifications. *The point is that they can't do anything about it.* What needs understanding is the state of paralysis everyone is in. Certainly all conditioning comes from society, but it is anchored in the body and mind of each individual, and this is where it must be dissolved. Ultimately the problem is an *emotional*, not an intellectual one. All the analyses of reification in the world won't cause a neurosis to budge an inch. Certainly a massive propaganda campaign to publicise the possibility of a revolution, of a total transformation of the world, is vitally important – but it will prove totally ineffective if it isn't simultaneous with *the creation of mass therapy.*

Look, after so many, many pages, let's try and be honest, just for a moment. I feel very fucked up myself, and I know it's my responsibility. Yet whenever I go out on the streets my being somehow reels back appalled: these terrible faces, these machines, they are me too, I know; yet somehow that's not my fault. Everyone's life is a switch between changing oneself and changing the world. Surely they must somehow be the same thing and a dynamic balance is possible. I think the SI had this for a while, and later they lost it. I want to find it again – that quickening in oneself and in others, that sudden happiness and beauty. It could connect, could come together. Psychoanalysis and Trotskyists are both silly old men to the child. Real life is elsewhere.